NATIONAL GEOGRAPHIC KiDS
Ultimate Globetrotting
World Atlas

By Sally Isaacs

NATIONAL GEOGRAPHIC
WASHINGTON, D.C.

TABLE OF CONTENTS

This atlas takes you on a journey around the globe. In its colorful maps, amazing pictures, and tons of fun information, you will discover cool things about each of the world's countries. If you plan to visit any of these places, you should always check for alerts published by your government concerning travel to specific countries or locations.

4 How to Use This Atlas
6 How to Use Maps
8 World Map

NORTH AMERICA

10 About the Continent
12 A Regional Overview
14 Canada
16 United States
18 Mexico
20 Belize and Guatemala
22 El Salvador and Honduras
24 Nicaragua
26 Costa Rica
28 Panama
30 Cuba and Jamaica
32 Dominican Republic and Haiti
34 Bahamas
36 Lesser Antilles:
    Antigua and Barbuda,
    Barbados, Dominica,
    Grenada, St. Kitts and Nevis,
    St. Lucia, St. Vincent and
    the Grenadines, Trinidad
    and Tobago

SOUTH AMERICA

38 About the Continent
40 A Regional Overview
42 Colombia and Ecuador
44 Venezuela
46 Guyana and Suriname
48 Brazil
50 Peru
52 Bolivia
54 Chile
56 Argentina
58 Paraguay
60 Uruguay

EUROPE

62 About the Continent
64 A Regional Overview
66 Iceland
68 Denmark
70 Norway
72 Sweden
74 Finland
76 Baltic Countries:
    Estonia, Latvia, Lithuania
78 Germany
80 Austria
82 Czech Republic, Hungary,
    and Slovakia
84 Poland
86 Eastern Europe:
    Belarus, Moldova, Ukraine
88 Portugal
90 Spain and Andorra
92 France and Monaco
94 Ireland
96 United Kingdom
98 Low Countries:
    Belgium, Luxembourg,
    Netherlands
100 Switzerland and Liechtenstein
102 Italy, Malta, San Marino,
    and Vatican City
104 Western Balkan Countries:
    Albania, Bosnia and
    Herzegovina, Croatia,
    Kosovo, Macedonia,
    Montenegro, Serbia,
    Slovenia
106 Eastern Balkan Countries:
    Bulgaria and Romania
108 Greece and Cyprus
110 European Russia

ASIA

112 About the Continent
114 A Regional Overview
116 Asian Russia
118 Caucasus Countries:
    Armenia, Azerbaijan,
    Georgia
120 Turkey
122 Lebanon, Syria, and Jordan
124 Israel
126 Northern Arabian Peninsula:
    Bahrain, Kuwait, Qatar,
    Saudi Arabia, United Arab
    Emirates
128 Southern Arabian Peninsula:
    Oman, Yemen
130 Iraq
132 Iran
134 Afghanistan
136 Pakistan
138 Central Asia:
    Kazakhstan, Kyrgyzstan,
    Tajikistan, Turkmenistan,
    Uzbekistan
140 South Asia:
    India, Maldives, Nepal,
    Sri Lanka
142 Bangladesh and Bhutan
144 China
146 Japan
148 Mongolia
150 North and South Korea
152 Myanmar and Thailand
154 Laos, Vietnam, and Cambodia
156 Brunei, Malaysia, and
    Singapore
158 Timor-Leste and Indonesia
160 Philippines

AFRICA

162 About the Continent
164 A Regional Overview
166 Morocco
168 Algeria and Tunisia
170 Libya
172 Egypt
174 Northern West Africa:
    Cape Verde, Gambia,
    Mauritania, Senegal
176 Central West Africa:
    Côte d'Ivoire (Ivory Coast),
    Guinea, Guinea-Bissau,
    Liberia, Sierra Leone
178 Eastern West Africa:
    Benin, Burkina Faso,
    Ghana, Togo
180 Mali
182 Niger
184 Nigeria
186 Chad
188 Sudan and South Sudan
190 Eritrea and Ethiopia
192 Horn of Africa:
    Djibouti, Somalia
194 Kenya
196 Tanzania
198 Great Lakes Region:
    Burundi, Rwanda, Uganda
200 Central Africa:
    Central African Republic,
    Congo, Democratic
    Republic of the Congo
202 Equatorial Africa:
    Cameroon, Equatorial
    Guinea, Gabon, Sao Tome
    and Principe
204 Angola
206 Zambia and Malawi
208 Mozambique
210 Zimbabwe
212 Botswana and Namibia
214 Southern Africa:
    Lesotho, South Africa,
    Swaziland
216 African Islands:
    Comoros, Madagascar,
    Mauritius, Seychelles

AUSTRALIA AND OCEANIA

218 About the Continent
220 A Regional Overview
222 Australia
224 New Zealand
226 Papua New Guinea
228 Melanesia:
    Fiji, Solomon Islands,
    Vanuatu
230 Micronesia:
    Federated States of
    Micronesia, Kiribati,
    Marshall Islands, Nauru,
    Palau
232 Polynesia:
    French Polynesia,
    Samoa, Tonga, Tuvalu

ANTARCTICA

234 About the Continent
236 A Regional Overview

AROUND THE WORLD FUN

238 Games
244 Glossary
246 Country Data
249 Index
255 Photo Credits
256 Credits

HOW TO USE THIS ATLAS

There are almost 200 countries in the world. Our globetrotter trip starts in Canada, but you can start your adventure in any country you wish. This spread will guide you through the features on each page before you start your own journey. When you're done, buckle up ... and follow Aunt Bertha's tips to experience a trip of a lifetime!

COUNTRY FACTS
For the names of the country's mammal, flower, tree, or bird, look above the country name. The species listed are either official choices or those widely recognized as being iconic or representative of the country.

INTRODUCTION
This brief introduction offers an overview of the country's location, landscape, features, and its people.

ID CARD
Look for the national flag and key facts, figures, and statistics on easy-to-use ID cards. For spreads with more than one country, turn to page 246 to find their ID cards.

MEASUREMENTS
In the text, measurements are given first in U.S. units and then in metric units. Often, these abbreviations are used: ft = feet; mi = miles; m = meters; km = kilometers; F = Fahrenheit; C = Celsius; mph/kph = miles/kilometers per hour.

COUNTRY IMAGE
Iconic images conjure up a real flavor of the country or region.

NATIONAL BIRD: emu

NATIONAL TREE: golden wattle

NATIONAL MAMMAL: red kangaroo

AUSTRALIA
A Land DOWN UNDER

Australia covers an entire continent, and includes the island of Tasmania. Much of the interior is dry desert, mountains, and "bush," but the land is rich in minerals and there are forests, farms, and huge sheep and cattle ranches or "stations." Australia's people come from all over the world, but many of its plants and animals are unique to this giant island.

ID CARD
COUNTRY FACTS

Size: 2,969,906 sq mi (7,692,024 sq km)
Population: 23,106,000
Capital: Canberra
Official language: English
Currency: Australian dollar
Highest point: Mt. Kosciuszko, 7,310 ft (2,215 m)
Life expectancy: 82.0 years

5 **START A LONG TRAIN RIDE**
Perth

The 2,704-mile (4,352-km)-long Indian Pacific passenger train journey from Perth to Sydney takes 65 hours. It runs along coasts and across deserts.

222

DIGITAL TRAVELER!
Australians drive on the left-hand side of the road. Surf the Internet to find other countries that do this.

DIGITAL TRAVELER!
You can discover even more about a country by doing your own investigations and explorations using a digital device and by taking photographs wherever you are.

4

5 COOL THINGS TO DO

These are five places to visit or things to do in the country or region. They will give you a true globetrotter's insight into the location. Follow the pointer from each picture or story to the map to find out exactly where these cool things are. Then plan your journey, save up for your ticket, and get packing!

GLOBETROTTER ATTRACTIONS

Three main landscape features or city highlights are listed and described here.

5 COOL THINGS TO DO HERE

Globetrotter Attractions

1 GO UNDERGROUND
Coober Pedy
Visit opal miners' homes called "dugouts." They are built underground so families can escape outside temperatures of more than 120°F (48.9°C).

2 SEE GREAT WHITE SHARKS
Great Barrier Reef
The 1,429-mile (2,300 km)-long coral reef off the east coast is the world's largest living structure. It is home to several kinds of sharks.

SYDNEY OPERA HOUSE
This is one of the most photographed buildings in the world. It took 30 years to figure out how to build the "sails" on the roof.

ULURU
Rising 1,142 feet (348 m), this huge mass of sandstone is the largest single slab of rock in the world.

AUSTRALIA ZOO
Many of the world's pouched mammals can be seen at this zoo in Beerwah, Queensland. They include kangaroos, possums, bandicoots, and koalas.

3 RIDE THE WAVES
Boomerang Beach
Some of the world's best surfing beaches are along the coast of New South Wales. Like a boomerang, the waves always come back to you!

4 WALK ON GLASS
Melbourne
At the Eureka Tower, you can step into a glass cube almost 1,000 feet (305 m) above street level for a bird's-eye view of the city.

AUSTRALIA & OCEANIA

223

MAP KEY

CITIES

⊛ Country capital

⊛ ⊚ ⊚ Other capitals

●●●• Towns

⬠ Small country or possession

☐ Point of interest

∴ Ruin

WATER FEATURES

Drainage

Intermittent drainage

Canal

Intermittent lake

Dry salt lake

Swamp

Falls or rapids

Dam

BOUNDARIES

Defined

Undefined

Disputed

Offshore line of separation

Disputed area

PHYSICAL FEATURES

+3,348 Elevation in meters

⤬ Pass

Lava and volcanic debris

Sand

Below sea level

Glacier

MAP

To find locations mentioned on the pages, check out the map! Then look for regions, major cities and towns, rivers, mountain ranges, lakes, and islands.

MAP SYMBOLS

Geographical features are shown on the map using a variety of shapes and colors. Use the map key to interpret these symbols. For more information about maps see pages 6 and 7.

HOW TO USE MAPS

Maps tell visual stories about the world, but you have to learn how to read them to understand what they are illustrating. The maps in this book show the shape, size, landscape, and position of continents, regions, and countries. They also show some of the places and features humans have made on Earth—for example cities, canals, and national parks. All maps in this book are shown with North at the top.

PROJECTIONS

To make flat maps, a round image of Earth is cut into sections and spread out. These sections—and the gaps that exist between them—can be different shapes and sizes. The exact way sections are cut and laid flat is known as the map "projection." Projections are usually very close to the actual shape of countries or regions but are not 100 percent accurate.

CONTINENTS

Earth's land area is mainly made up of seven giant landmasses known as continents. People have divided the continents into smaller political units called countries. Australia is a continent and also a single country. Antarctica is a continent with no countries. The five other continents include almost 200 independent countries.

NORTH AMERICA

EUROPE

ASIA

AFRICA

SOUTH AMERICA

AUSTRALIA

ANTARCTICA

SCALE AND DIRECTION

The scale on a map may be shown as a fraction or comparison in words. A bar scale is a line or bar with measurements that compare distances on the map with those in the real world. Maps may include an arrow or compass rose to indicate North. If North is to the top, then East is to the right, West to the left, and South is to the bottom.

Representative Fraction

Verbal Scale

SCALE 1:4,283,000
1 CENTIMETER = 42.8 KILOMETERS OR 1 INCH = 67.6 MILES

0 25 50   100   150   200
KILOMETERS
0 25   50   100   150   200
STATUTE MILES

Scale Bars

0   250   500 MILES
0   250   500 KILOMETERS

Azimuthal Equidistant Projection

Map Projection

N

North Arrow

GRID LINES AND SYMBOLS

The grid lines you see on maps are imaginary. They are lines of longitude and latitude that help locate places. Other lines are used to show boundaries, roads, or rivers and can vary in thickness and color. Points or circles represent the location of places or things. Area symbols use patterns or color to show regions.

● **POINT**
A point symbol, a black dot, indicates a city, such as Kano.

.... **LINE**
Chad's country boundary appears as a dotted line symbol.

▒ **AREA**
Sandy places, such as parts of the Sahara, are shown by a tan, speckled area.

S A H A R A
A F R I C A
N I G E R   C H A D
Niamey
Lake Chad
(Lac Tchad)
BURKINA   MAIDUGURI
FASO   N'Djamena
KANO

LATITUDE AND LONGITUDE

The Equator marks the middle of the world. Lines of latitude indicate distances north or south of the Equator. Lines of longitude indicate distances east or west. They start at the Prime Meridian, which is 0° longitude.

90°N (North Pole)
75°N
60°N
45°N
30°N
15°N
0° (Equator)
15°S

Latitude

Longitude

WORLD MAP

ARCTIC

GREENLAND
(KALAALLIT NUNAAT)
Denmark

RUSSIA

ALASKA
United States

ARCTIC CIRCLE

Nuuk
(Godthåb)

ICELAND

Reykjavík

C A N A D A

Juneau

UNITED
KINGDOM

DUBLIN
IRELAND

LONDON

N O R T H

A M E R I C A

UNITED STATES

Ottawa

Washington

N O R T H

A T L A N T I C

For detail of Europe,
see pages 64–111

MADRID

PORTUGAL
Lisbon   SPAIN

Azores
Portugal

N O R T H

Bermuda Islands
United Kingdom

O C E A N

Madeira Islands
Portugal

RABAT

MOROCCO

P A C I F I C

30°

TROPIC OF CANCER

HAWAII
United States

Honolulu

Canary Islands
Spain

Laayoune   AL

WESTERN
SAHARA
Morocco

O C E A N

Nassau

BAHAMAS

MEXICO

HAVANA CUBA

Kingston

PORT-AU-PRINCE

DOMINICAN REP.

San Juan

San
Juan

Nouakchott

MAURITANIA

BURKINA FA

BELIZE JAMAICA

SANTO DOMINGO

PUERTO RICO
United States

SENEGAL DAKAR

Ouagadougou

MEXICO
CITY Belmopan

HAITI

For detail of the
Lesser Antilles,
see pages 36–37

CAPE VERDE
Praia

GAMBIA BAMAK

GUATEMALA

HONDURAS

Banjul Bissau

GUINEA

GUATEMALA CITY

TEGUCIGALPA

ARUBA Neth.

GUINEA-BISSAU

San Salvador

NICARAGUA

CURAÇAO Neth.

CONAKRY

CÔTE

EL SALVADOR

Managua San José

BONAIRE Neth.

Freetown

D'IVOIRE

COSTA RICA

CARACAS

SIERRA LEONE

MONROVIA

PANAMA

VENEZUELA

Georgetown Paramaribo

LIBERIA

Panama CITY

BOGOTÁ

GUYANA SURINAME

Cayenne

Yamoussoukro ABIDJAN ACC

COLOMBIA

FRENCH GUIANA
France

EQUATOR

QUITO

ECUADOR

GALÁPAGOS ISLANDS
(Archipiélago de Colón)
Ecuador

S O U T H

MARQUESAS
ISLANDS
France

B R A Z I L

KIRIBATI

LINE ISLANDS

LIMA

A M E R I C A

BRASÍLIA

BOLIVIA

AMERICAN
SAMOA
U.S.

COOK ISLANDS
New Zealand

TUAMOTU ARCHIPELAGO

La Paz

Sucre

SAMOA

Apia Pago Pago

FRENCH
POLYNESIA
France

PARAGUAY

S O U T H

S O U T H

TONGA IS. TONGA

SOCIETY ISLANDS

Nuku'alofa

AUSTRAL ISLANDS

A

TROPIC OF CAPRICORN

Asunción

Isla San Félix
Chile

Isla San
Ambrosio

Easter Island
(Isla de Pascua)
Chile

Isla Sala y Gómez
Chile

SANTIAGO

URUGUAY

MONTEVIDEO

P A C I F I C

Juan Fernández
Islands
Chile

BUENOS
AIRES

A T L A N T I C

O C E A N

FALKLAND ISLANDS
(ISLAS MALVINAS)
U.K.

O C E A N

Stanley

ANTARCTIC CIRCLE

A N T A R

COUNTRIES OF THE WORLD

This is a "political" map of the world. It shows
country boundaries, country names, and major
cities. It also shows the world's oceans.

NORTH AMERICA

Wild and WONDROUS

From icy glaciers, lakes, and mountains to deserts, forests, and swamps, North America is a rugged, scenic continent. It is also home to tourist destination cities such as Vancouver, San Francisco, New York, Mexico City, and Acapulco.

Moraine Lake in Banff National Park, Alberta, Canada. The lake is surrounded by boulders and rock debris dumped by glaciers as they move down mountainsides. The lake water is melted ice and snow.

NORTH AMERICA

A Mix of Cultures and Customs in the NEW WORLD

North America has a rich mix of cultures—from the traditions of Native Americans to the customs of immigrants from Europe, Asia, and Africa. It is still sometimes called the "New World" to contrast it with the Old World of Europe, Africa, and Asia. This is because North America was first explored by Europeans as recently as the 1500s.

TIKAL PYRAMIDS
Guatemala

The Maya people built this giant pyramid 1,000 to 2,500 years ago.

BRONCO RIDING
United States

A cowboy rides a bronco, an untrained horse, in a contest called a rodeo. Horses were first brought to North America from Spain in the 1500s.

AUNT BERTHA'S
TRAVEL TIPS

CHOOSE YOUR LANGUAGE
The main languages of North America are European in origin—English, Spanish, and French. Bring your dictionaries!

WATCH YOUR STEP
Traveling east to west you will go back in time, crossing at least 5 of the world's 24 time zones. Be sure to set your watch.

TIME FLIES
Be prepared for a long trip. To fly east to west can take more than 7 hours. Flight time from north to south can be up to 10.5 hours.

THE NORTH

Very few people live in the Arctic region because the climate is so cold. This is the home of native Inuit people.

MID-ZONE

Almost all the big cities of North America are in southern Canada and the United States. They are grouped around the Great Lakes and on the Atlantic and Pacific coasts.

WEST INDIES

Early explorers traveling west from Europe thought they had reached islands lying east of India.

MEXICO

People in Mexico speak Spanish. Spanish is also the predominant language in Central America.

CENTRAL AMERICA

This is a group of small countries that sit between much larger ones in North and South America.

13

5 COOL THINGS TO DO HERE

1 CHEER FOR MUSHERS
Yellowknife

Drivers, called mushers, guide sleds that are powered by 12 dogs each. Visit the Yellowknife Dog Derby, which happens every March, and see who wins.

2 RIDE THE ROCKIES
Kamloops

Take a four-day railroad journey from east to west and view the forests and Rocky Mountains from a railroad observation car.

3 SLIP, SLIDE, AND SKI
Banff National Park

During the SnowDays Festival, try free skiing and snowboarding or enjoy a sleigh ride. In summer, go hiking and horseback riding.

4 EXPLORE "NEW FRANCE"
Québec

With its castle-like hotel, Chateau Frontenac, this is the capital of French-speaking Canada. Be sure to explore the Ramparts, the only remains of a protective city wall in North America.

NATIONAL BIRD:
Canada goose

NATIONAL TREE:
maple

NATIONAL MAMMAL:
beaver

CANADA

The Land of Snow and ICE

Canada is the second-largest country in area in the world, after Russia. At 5,525 miles (8,892 km) from west to east, it stretches nearly a quarter of the way around the globe. This huge country contains some of the world's most spectacular and wildest scenery. In the far north are giant frozen islands of the Arctic Ocean. To the south are the Great Lakes, the largest group of freshwater lakes in the world.

ID CARD
COUNTRY FACTS

Size: 3,855,102 sq mi (9,984,670 sq km)
Population: 35,250,000
Capital: Ottawa
Official languages: English and French
Currency: Canadian dollar
Highest point: Mount Logan, 19,551 ft (5,959 m)
Life expectancy: 81.6 years

Globetrotter Attractions

NIAGARA FALLS
About 3,160 tons (2,867 mt) of water flow over Niagara Falls every second. The falls have the capacity to produce electricity for 1 million homes in Canada and the United States.

CN TOWER
Toronto's 1,815-foot (553-m)-high telecommunications and viewing tower is the tallest structure in North America.

WHISTLER AND BLACKCOMB
These stunning mountains hosted the 2010 Winter Olympics. They are often snowcapped all year long.

5 MEET A MOUNTIE
Ottawa

At the Musical Ride event, the Royal Canadian Mounted Police—the Mounties—show their horseriding skills. Before the event, you can visit the stables.

ARRÊT STOP

DIGITAL TRAVELER!
In eastern Canada, road signs use French and English. On your computer make a two-column chart of English and French travel words for your trip.

15

NATIONAL BIRD:
bald eagle

NATIONAL FLOWER:
rose

NATIONAL TREE:
oak

UNITED STATES

Stretching from the Atlantic to the PACIFIC

1 DRIVE THROUGH A TREE
Leggett

Redwoods are among the world's biggest trees. A tunnel was carved into this one to allow cars to drive through.

The United States stretches across North America and includes Alaska and the Hawaiian islands. The U.S. is the third largest country in the world in population and fourth largest in land area. A drive across the country will take you through small farm towns, bustling cities, and everything in-between. You can find any kind of outdoor fun you want—from sailing off the coast of Maine to hiking in the Rocky Mountains.

Globetrotter Attractions

NEW YORK CITY
From the bright lights of Broadway's theater district to the glorious Statue of Liberty in the harbor, this city of skyscrapers never sleeps.

THE GRAND CANYON
Gaze down from the rim of this one-mile (1,610-m)-deep canyon, ride down on a mule, or raft along the Colorado River.

KENNEDY SPACE CENTER
On the coast of Florida, this space center has been launching astronauts and unmanned rockets into space since 1968.

3 VISIT THE WHITE HOUSE
Washington, D.C.

With 132 rooms and 35 bathrooms, the White House is home to the U.S. President. This historic building also serves as an office for the President and his staff.

ID CARD
COUNTRY FACTS

Size: 3,794,100 sq mi (9,826,675 sq km)
Population: 316,158,000
Capital: Washington, D.C.
Official language: English
Currency: U.S. dollar
Highest point: Mount McKinley (Denali), 20,320 ft (6,194 m)
Life expectancy: 78.6 years

5 COOL THINGS TO DO HERE

2 FIND THE PRESIDENTS
Mount Rushmore

Four presidents' faces are carved into the Black Hills. Try to identify these historic U.S. leaders.

4 RIDE A PADDLE WHEELER
New Orleans

Step aboard and let the boat's giant paddle wheel power you along the Mississippi River, the second longest river in the country.

5 SAIL UNDER A WATERFALL
Niagara Falls

Put on a raincoat and get ready to be misted, and possibly soaked, as the *Maid of the Mist* takes you up close to the continent's most famous waterfalls. These boats have been giving tours of the falls since 1846.

DIGITAL TRAVELER!
Baseball is called "America's National Pastime." Find a list on the Internet of all the teams in Major League Baseball. Which states have more than one team?

17

NATIONAL BIRD:
crested caracara

NATIONAL MAMMAL:
jaguar

NATIONAL FLOWER:
dahlia

MEXICO

From Maya Ruins to Mariachi PARADES

5 COOL THINGS TO DO HERE

Mexico is a large country just south of the United States. Its capital, Mexico City, is one of the world's largest cities in population. You can see signs of Mexico's long history in the ruins of cities left by Maya and Aztec civilizations. Today Mexico's population is a mix of native Indian peoples and the Spanish people who set up a colony there in the 1500s. The beaches on the Pacific Ocean and the Gulf of Mexico are popular vacation destinations.

ID CARD
COUNTRY FACTS

Size: 758,449 sq mi (1,964,375 sq km)
Population: 117,574,000
Capital: Mexico City
Official language: Spanish
Currency: Mexican peso
Highest point: Volcan Pico de Orizaba, 18,406 ft (5,610 m)
Life expectancy: 76.9 years

2 COUNT BUTTERFLIES
Cerro Altamirano

Every year, more than a million Monarch butterflies arrive here to spend the winter. They come from as far away as eastern Canada. Each day at noon you can see swarms of them heading to the river to quench their thirst.

3 CLAP FOR CLIFF DIVERS
Acapulco

Hold your breath as you watch these trained divers plunge 136 feet (41 m) into the Pacific Ocean. They must watch the waves and dive when the water is deepest.

DIGITAL TRAVELER!
Chihuahua dogs came from Chihuahua, Mexico. Search online for photos of these dogs. Look for a variety of sizes, colors, and other features. Which do you think is cutest?

1 SING WITH COWBOYS
Guadalajara

Stop in a restaurant and listen to mariachis singing their favorite tunes. They dress like *charros* (cowboys) but with fancier clothes.

Globetrotter Attractions

PARQUE NATURAL BARRANCA DEL COBRA (COPPER CANYON)

This group of canyons is larger than the Grand Canyon in the U.S.A., and parts of it are deeper. You can hike, drive, or ride a horse through the scenery. Or you can ride a train. The Copper Canyon Railroad travels through cliff walls and over 36 bridges.

CHICHÉN ITZÁ

This was one of the most important Maya cities, built from A.D. 900 to 1200. The ruins of walls, pyramids, and ball courts can be seen today.

THE ARCH

At the tip of the Baja California Peninsula, the Pacific Ocean meets the Sea of Cortez. Here a stunning natural rock formation serves as a window to the blue waters of the ocean.

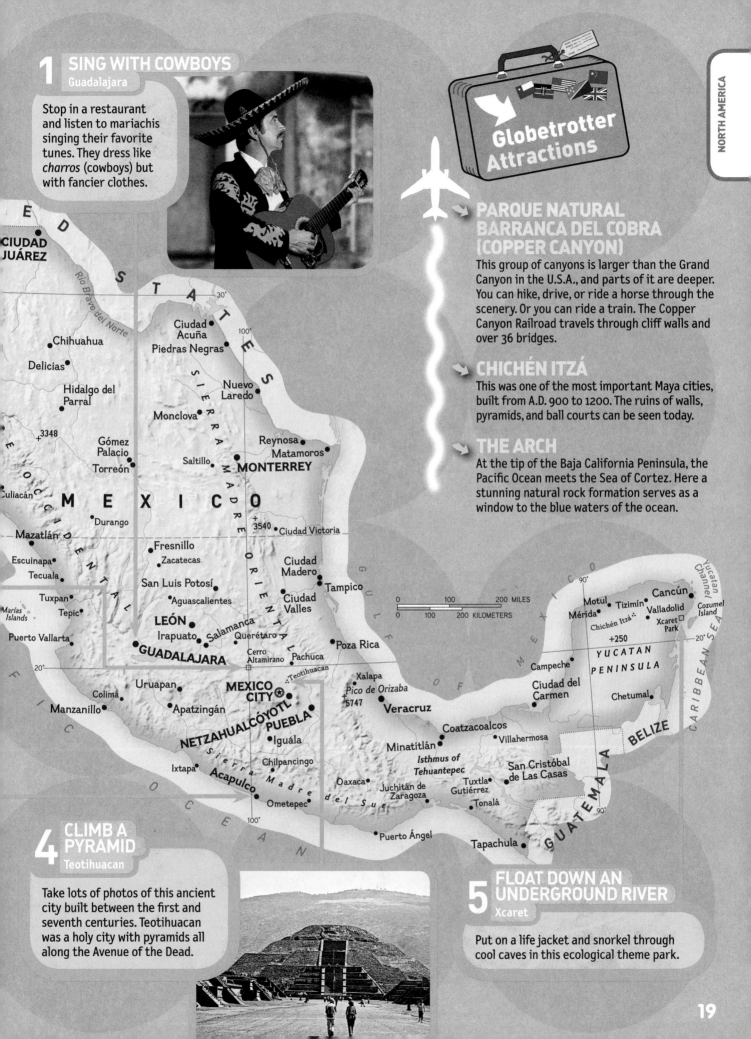

Map labels: CIUDAD JUÁREZ, Rio Bravo del Norte, UNITED STATES, Chihuahua, Delicias, Hidalgo del Parral, +3348, Ciudad Acuña, Piedras Negras, Monclova, Nuevo Laredo, SIERRA MADRE ORIENTAL, Gómez Palacio, Torreón, Saltillo, Reynosa, Matamoros, MONTERREY, Culiacán, MEXICO, Durango, +3540, Ciudad Victoria, Mazatlán, Escuinapa, Tecuala, Fresnillo, Zacatecas, San Luis Potosí, Ciudad Madero, Tampico, Tuxpan, Tepic, Marías Islands, Aguascalientes, Ciudad Valles, Puerto Vallarta, LEÓN, Irapuato, Salamanca, Querétaro, Poza Rica, GUADALAJARA, Cerro Altamirano, Pachuca, GULF OF MEXICO, Uruapan, Colima, Manzanillo, Apatzingán, MEXICO CITY, Teotihuacan, Xalapa, Pico de Orizaba +5747, Veracruz, NETZAHUALCÓYOTL, PUEBLA, Iguála, Chilpancingo, Minatitlán, Coatzacoalcos, Villahermosa, Campeche, YUCATAN PENINSULA, Ciudad del Carmen, Chetumal, CARIBBEAN SEA, Cozumel Island, Cancún, Motul, Tizimín, Valladolid, Mérida, Chichén Itzá, Xcaret Park, +250, Yucatan Channel, Ixtapa, Sierra Madre del Sur, Acapulco, Oaxaca, Juchitán de Zaragoza, Isthmus of Tehuantepec, Tuxtla Gutiérrez, San Cristóbal de Las Casas, Tonalá, GUATEMALA, BELIZE, Ometepec, Puerto Ángel, Tapachula, PACIFIC OCEAN

Scale: 0 100 200 MILES / 0 100 200 KILOMETERS

4 CLIMB A PYRAMID
Teotihuacan

Take lots of photos of this ancient city built between the first and seventh centuries. Teotihuacan was a holy city with pyramids all along the Avenue of the Dead.

5 FLOAT DOWN AN UNDERGROUND RIVER
Xcaret

Put on a life jacket and snorkel through cool caves in this ecological theme park.

BELIZE AND GUATEMALA

Land of Caves, Colors, and COCOA

| BELIZE GUATEMALA | NATIONAL BIRD: keel-billed toucan quetzal | NATIONAL FLOWER: black orchid monja blanca | NATIONAL MAMMAL: Baird's tapir Maya mouse |

Belize is a small country with a flat, swampy, coastal plain and low mountains. It was once home to the ancient Maya people. Guatemala is a larger, more mountainous country. About half its people are descended from the ancient Maya. Many of them also speak native Indian languages.

3 TASTE JUICY FRUIT
Chichicastenango

At the main market, breathe in the smell of flowers and spices, and taste colorful melons and mangoes. Then watch shoppers buy all kinds of goods.

DIGITAL TRAVELER!
From September to January, sea turtles lay their eggs on Guatemala's beaches. Use the Internet to learn what happens when the turtle eggs hatch.

4 RIDE A ROLLER COASTER
Retalhuleu

Choose a roller coaster that's right for you at Xetulul amusement park. Ride the Avalancha, with eight inversions that turn you upside down. If you prefer a calmer coaster, the Choconoy might be a better choice.

5 LEARN TO MAKE CHOCOLATE
Antigua

Tour the cacao plantation, where they pick cacao beans for chocolate. Then step inside the "Chocolate Museum" and learn how to make your own candy.

MEXICO

El Ceibo

Usumacinta

San Mateo Ixtatán
Barillas

Sierra de los Cuchumatanes

Negro

3834 +

Huehuetenango

Volcán Tajumulco +4211

San Marcos

Quetzaltenango

Coatepeque

Ocós

Retalhuleu

Champerico

Pueblo Nuevo Tiquisate

Santa Cruz del Quiché

Chichicastenango

Atlitán Nature Reserve

Lago de Atitlán

Chimaltenango

Volcán de Acatenango

Antigua

3976 +

Mazatenango

Santa Lucía Cotzumalguapa

La Democracia

Escuintla

Sipacate

San José

PACIFIC OC

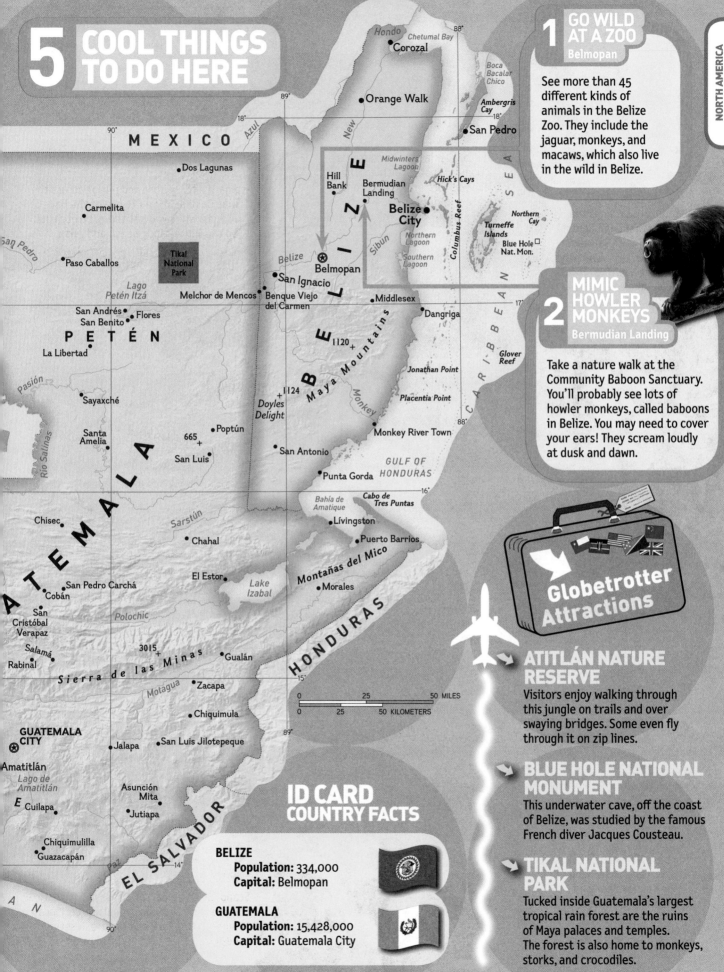

5 COOL THINGS TO DO HERE

1 GO WILD AT A ZOO
Belmopan

See more than 45 different kinds of animals in the Belize Zoo. They include the jaguar, monkeys, and macaws, which also live in the wild in Belize.

2 MIMIC HOWLER MONKEYS
Bermudian Landing

Take a nature walk at the Community Baboon Sanctuary. You'll probably see lots of howler monkeys, called baboons in Belize. You may need to cover your ears! They scream loudly at dusk and dawn.

Globetrotter Attractions

ATITLÁN NATURE RESERVE
Visitors enjoy walking through this jungle on trails and over swaying bridges. Some even fly through it on zip lines.

BLUE HOLE NATIONAL MONUMENT
This underwater cave, off the coast of Belize, was studied by the famous French diver Jacques Cousteau.

TIKAL NATIONAL PARK
Tucked inside Guatemala's largest tropical rain forest are the ruins of Maya palaces and temples. The forest is also home to monkeys, storks, and crocodiles.

ID CARD
COUNTRY FACTS

BELIZE
Population: 334,000
Capital: Belmopan

GUATEMALA
Population: 15,428,000
Capital: Guatemala City

21

5 COOL THINGS TO DO HERE

1 WATCH A SOCCER GAME
San Salvador

Estadio Cuscatlan is the largest stadium in Central America. The El Salvador national soccer team plays here. Soccer is a very popular sport in both El Salvador and Honduras.

2 REEL IN A FISH
Lago de Yojoa

The largest lake in Honduras is a popular spot for fishing. The lake was formed from volcanic craters and lava flow.

3 RIDE A FERRY BOAT
La Ceiba

Board a ferry boat and motor across the blue Caribbean Sea to one of the Bay Islands. When you get there, stretch out on the white sandy beach and relax.

4 EAT MARIA LUISA CAKE
San Miguel

Search the bakeries to find the best Maria Luisa cake. It is a layer cake soaked in orange marmalade and topped with powdered sugar.

5 CHAT WITH MACAWS
Ruinas de Copán

Stand next to a parrot and try to have a conversation—it can repeat words. Macaw Mountain Bird Park and Nature Reserve takes care of rescued tropical birds.

EL SALVADOR HONDURAS	**NATIONAL BIRD:** torogoz scarlet macaw	**NATIONAL FLOWER:** flor de Izote orchid	**NATIONAL MAMMAL:** jaguarundi white-tailed deer

EL SALVADOR AND HONDURAS

The Heart of CENTRAL AMERICA

El Salvador and Honduras are neighbors that have some geographical and cultural similarities. Both countries share Spanish as their official language, and have mountains, beautiful beaches, and coffee plantations. Bananas are another important crop in Honduras. Though El Salvador is smaller in area, it has more people per square mile than Honduras and most other countries on the continent do.

Globetrotter Attractions

CUSUCO NATIONAL PARK

This huge park in Honduras is divided into four different kinds of forests, including "cloud forests" on the mountain slopes and "dwarf forests" with trees no more than 10 feet (3 m) high.

MAYA RUINS AT COPÁN

These ruins in Honduras include a 328-foot (100-m)-wide staircase with more than 1,800 Maya pictures. It is one of the longest known Maya inscriptions. Another stairway has sculptures of jaguars.

PUNTA ROCA

This is one of the most popular beaches in El Salvador. Surfers from all over the world say it is one of the best surfing beaches in the world.

ID CARD COUNTRY FACTS

EL SALVADOR
Population: 6,307,000
Capital: San Salvador

HONDURAS
Population: 8,555,000
Capital: Tegucigalpa

DIGITAL TRAVELER!
What kind of music do they play in Honduras? Search for the answer online. Then download something you like.

23

NATIONAL BIRD:
turquoise-browed motmot

NATIONAL MAMMAL:
puma

NATIONAL FLOWER:
sacuanjoche

NICARAGUA

Land Between Sea and OCEAN

ID CARD
COUNTRY FACTS

Size: 50,336 sq mi (130,370 sq km)
Population: 6,043,000
Capital: Managua
Official language: Spanish
Currency: Gold cordoba
Highest point: Mogoton, 6,913 ft (2,107 m)
Life expectancy: 74.0 years

Nicaragua is a large country with fewer people per square mile than most others in Central America. Most people live by the Pacific Ocean, where Managua, the capital city, is located. The Caribbean Sea region is so swampy that it is called the "Mosquito Coast," but the name originally came from Miskito people who have been living in the region for more than 350 years. Rain forests cover most of this land.

Globetrotter Attractions

CATEDRAL DE LEÓN
The largest cathedral in Central America took more than 100 years to build. It holds the tombs of several famous poets.

BOSAWÁS BIOSPHERE RESERVE
This is one of the largest rain forests in the world with more than 150,000 kinds of insects and at least 100 kinds of birds.

MASAYA VOLCANO
Nicaragua's most active volcano spews gas almost all the time.

5 BOAT OVER TO A VOLCANO
Lake Nicaragua

Sail on the country's largest lake to the Isla del Ometepe and hike up one of its two volcanoes. As you make your way, enjoy some fishing and look out for rare freshwater sharks.

Map labels: Jalapa, Mogotón 6913, Murra, Ocotal, Kilambe 1750, Somoto, Yalagüina, Coco, Pueblo Nuevo, Condega, San Pedro, San Rafael del Norte, Jinoteg, El Tuma, Gulf of Fonseca, Somotillo, Estelí, La Trinidad, El Sauce, Matagalp, Punta Cosigüina, 859, Potosí, Puerto Morazán, La Jicaral, Sébaco, Chinandega, Volcán Momotombo 1280, Corinto, León, Lake Managua, Teuste, Poneloya, San Benito, MANAGUA, Tipitapa, Puerto Sandino, PACIFIC OCEAN, Volcán Masaya, Masaya, Diriamba, Jinotepe, Granac, Masachapa, Casares, San Jorge, Rivas, San Juan del Sur, Salinas Bay

5 COOL THINGS TO DO HERE

1 SHOP AROUND
Masaya

Watch how a craftsperson weaves a rope rug. Many artists sell hammocks, pottery, blankets, and soap. Nicaraguans also go to the main, city-center market to buy meat, vegetables, and live chickens.

2 STROLL ON A BEACH
Bilwi

Walk on the beach at Puerto Cabezas and look at the long wooden dock where ships from the U.S. and elsewhere deliver products and machinery. Nicaragua grows and exports coffee, beef, and sugar.

3 DANCE ROUND A MAYPOLE
Bluefields

Join the Maypole Festival dancers as you pick up a long, colorful ribbon and weave it around the maypole. The festival happens every May.

DIGITAL TRAVELER!
Thousands of vampire bats live in Nicaragua. They survive on the blood of other animals. Surf the Internet to find more fun facts about and pictures of these cool creatures.

4 SEARCH FOR CROCODILES
San Juan del Sur

Hop into a 4 x 4 touring car and drive through a wildlife refuge. Be ready to snap photos of crocodiles, monkeys, and birds.

HONDURAS

Auasbila
Sang Sang
Bocay
Bosawás Biosphere Reserve
+1132
Cordillera Isabelia
+1650
1745
Bonanza
La Constancia
La Rosita
El Salto
Siuna
Kuikuina
Alamikamba
Limbaica
Makantaca
San Pedro del Norte
Río Blanco
Matiguás
Santa Lucía
Boaco
Camoapa
Santo Domingo
La Libertad
Juigalpa
Santo Tomás
El Recreo
Rama
Kama
Acoyapa
Puerto Díaz
Nueva Guinea
+302
Volcán Concepción
+1610
Lake Nicaragua
Isla del Ometepe
Peñas Blancas
Archipiélago de Solentiname
San Carlos
El Castillo de La Concepción
San Juan del Norte

Waspam
Bilwaskarma
Coco
Ulang
Waspuk
Kukalaya
Maniwatla
Bambana
Prinzapolka
Río Grande de Matagalpa
Siquia
Mico
Cordillera Chontaleña
Bahía de Bluefields
Indio
San Juan

Coco
Laguna Bismuna
Morrison Dennis Cays
Muerto Cay
Ninayeri
Dákura
Punta Gorda
Mosquito Cays
Tuapí
The Witties
Bilwi
15°
83°
14°
Laguna Karatá
Karatá
Laguna de Wounta
Prinzapolka
La Barra
13°
Cayos Guerrero
Cayo Tyara
Cayo King
Laguna de Perlas
Cayos Perlas
Laguna de Perlas
Little Corn Island
Great Corn Island
224+
Bluefields
El Bluff
12°
Isla del Venado
Green Point
Mono Point (Monkey Point)
Punta Gorda
Bahía Punta Gorda
83°
11°

CARAGUA

COSTA RICA

NICARAGUA

CARIBBEAN SEA

Mosquito Coast

84°
85°

0   25   50 MILES
0   25   50 KILOMETERS

25

5 COOL THINGS TO DO HERE

1 GET WET AND WARM UP
Fortuna

Relax in the warm water of Tabacon Hot Springs. The water flows in from the Tabacon River, which begins in the Arenal Volcano. The volcano heats the water to 101° F (38° C).

5 WALK IN THE CLOUDS
Monteverde Forest Reserve

Follow hiking trails through the sky-high cloud forests. This reserve was set aside to protect the wildlife, which includes 420 kinds of orchids and 100 kinds of animals including jaguars and ocelots. Be sure to pick a trail that crosses one of the five suspension bridges.

### Map labels

Lake Nicaragua
Salinas Bay
La Cruz
Los Chiles
85°
N I C A R A G U A
Bahía de Santa Elena
11°
86°
Cabo Santa Elena
San Juan
84°
Golfo de Papagayo
Volcán Miravalles 2028
Frío
San Rafael
237+
11°
Liberia
Laguna de Arenal
Fortuna
Altamira
Sardinal
Filadelfia
Cañas
C O S T A
Cabo Velas
Monteverde Forest Reserve
Santa Cruz
Monteverde
Juntas
Quesada
Nicoya
991+
Puerto Jesús
+251
Nicoya Peninsula
10°
Esparza
Alajuela
Heredia
Volcán Irazú +3432
Punta Guiones
Puntarenas
San José
Cartago
Golfo de Nicoya
0 25 50 MILES
0 25 50 KILOMETERS
Cabo Blanco
85°
P A C I F I C
Punta Judas
Parrita
Puerto Quepos
Bahía Manuel Antonio
Dominical
84°
Isla del Caño

4 WATCH A BALLET
San José

When you go to the National Theater, give yourself plenty of time before the performance begins. You will want to walk around the beautiful building. Some say it is the most beautiful building in the country.

ID CARD
COUNTRY FACTS

Size: 19,729 sq mi (51,100 sq km)
Population: 4,713,000
Capital: San José
Official language: Spanish
Currency: Costa Rican colon
Highest point: Cerro Chirripó, 12,530 ft (3,819 m)
Life expectancy: 79.0 years

3 FOLLOW A GHOST CRAB
Manuel Antonio

Try to catch a glimpse of these small but super-fast crabs as they scurry across the beach. They spend most of their time burrowed in the sand waiting for a wave to bring their next meal.

DIGITAL TRAVELER!
Gallo pinto is a favorite breakfast in Costa Rica. Find a recipe and ask a grown-up to help you make it.

NATIONAL BIRD: clay-colored thrush

NATIONAL FLOWER: guaria morada

NATIONAL MAMMAL: white-tailed deer

COSTA RICA
A Jungle PARADISE

The people of Costa Rica call themselves Ticos. When Ticos greet one another, they say, "*Pura vida.*" In Spanish, this means "pure life." The people enjoy their beautiful mountains, forests, and beaches and all the animals and plants that make Costa Rica home. There are many nature reserves and parks to protect the wildlife. Many Ticos work on coffee plantations and cattle ranches, but about one quarter of the people in the country live in and around the busy capital city of San José.

Globetrotter Attractions

MOUNT CHIRRIPÓ
At 12,530 feet (3,819 m), Mount (Cerro) Chirripó is Costa Rica's highest mountain. Hikers who reach the mountaintop can see the Pacific Ocean and the Caribbean Sea.

ARENAL VOLCANO
One day in 1968, there were ten hours of earthquakes followed by the eruption of Arenal Volcano. Now, quite frequently, the volcano explodes with a fiery glow and flowing lava.

TORTUGUERO NATIONAL PARK
This large park is on Costa Rica's Caribbean coast. Its name *Tortuguero*, Spanish for "turtle catcher," is very fitting since hawksbill sea turtles and green sea turtles build their nests in the park's black sand.

2 SEE SLOTHS
Penshurst

Visit the Sloth Sanctuary where people study, protect, and teach others about Costa Rica's two kinds of sloths: two-toed and three-toed sloths.

**Map labels:**

Barra del Colorado
Tortuguero
Guápiles
Parismina
Matina
Bahía de Moín
Puerto Limón
Turrialba
Penshurst
Pandora
Punta Cahuita
Bribrí
Suretka
Cerro Chirripó 3819
San Isidro
Cordillera de Talamanca
Volcán
Cerro Kámuk 3554
Buenos Aires
Ciudad Cortés
Potrero Grande
Palmar Sur
Coronado Bay
Osa Peninsula
657
Punta Llorona
Puerto Jiménez
Dulce Gulf
Golfito
La Cuesta
Cabo Matapalo
Punta Banco
Península Burica
Burica Point
CARIBBEAN SEA
PANAMA
OCEAN
83°
10°
9°
8°

NATIONAL BIRD:
harpy eagle

NATIONAL FLOWER:
holy ghost orchid

NATIONAL MAMMAL:
ocelot

PANAMA
Linking Two CONTINENTS

5 LOOK FOR LEATHERBACKS
Bastimentos

These huge turtles swim in the Caribbean Sea. The females lay hundreds of eggs on the beach every two or three years. Do not disturb the nests and babies.

Panama is often called the "Crossroads of the World." It connects North and South America. The Atlantic Ocean is on one side of the country, and the Pacific is on the other. Every year, thousands of ships sail through the Panama Canal. There is busy city activity around the canal. The rest of the country has quieter towns.

ID CARD
COUNTRY FACTS

Size: 29,119 sq mi (75,420 sq km)
Population: 3,850,000
Capital: Panama City
Official language: Spanish
Currency: balboa
Highest point: Volcán Barú, 11,400 ft (3,475 m)
Life expectancy: 77.0 years

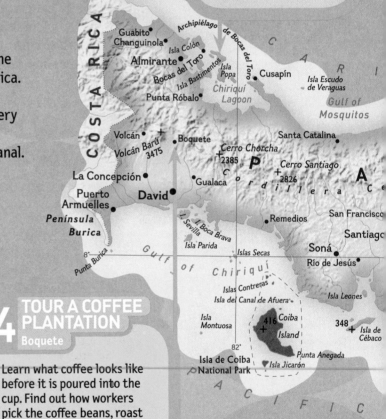

4 TOUR A COFFEE PLANTATION
Boquete

Learn what coffee looks like before it is poured into the cup. Find out how workers pick the coffee beans, roast them, grind them, and ship the coffee all over the world.

DIGITAL TRAVELER!
How did people travel from Europe to California and other places in the western hemisphere before the Panama Canal provided a shortcut? Find a map of the world online and map the journey to find out.

5 COOL THINGS TO DO HERE

Globetrotter Attractions

1 CRUISE THROUGH THE CANAL
Panama Canal

Board a cruise ship and travel on the famous waterway that links two oceans. Learn how ships go through a series of gates that lift them to a higher water level. Before the canal was completed in 1914, ships had to travel about 7,800 miles (12,552 km) more than they do today to go from ocean to ocean.

AMADOR CAUSEWAY
This road starts at the Panama Canal (Panama City) and leads to four islands. There is a beautiful path for walking, jogging, and watching ships coming into the canal. The causeway is made from rock that was dug up when the canal was built.

METROPOLITAN PARK
The only Central American protected area located within a major city (Panama City) is home to many species of plants and animals.

COIBA NATIONAL PARK
The park has 38 islands and is known for its jungle wildlife. It is also famous for a prison that held dangerous criminals until 2004.

0   25   50 MILES
0   25   50 KILOMETERS

2 WATCH WHALES
Archipiélago de las Perlas

Look for humpback whales that migrate to this region each year to give birth.

3 JOIN A CARNIVAL
Panama City

During the four days of Carnival, enjoy nonstop dancing in the streets. Take some photos of the beautiful costumes. Stay up late for the fireworks!

	NATIONAL BIRD:	NATIONAL FLOWER:	NATIONAL MAMMAL:
CUBA	tocororo	white mariposa	Cuban yellow bat
JAMAICA	doctor-bird	lignum vitae	Jamaican coney

CUBA AND JAMAICA

Islands of EXCITEMENT

Cuba and Jamaica are island countries that both have a mix of Caribbean and African cultures. Cuba also has Spanish roots, and almost all Cubans speak Spanish. In Havana, Cuba's capital, classic cars like the one above serve as taxis to take tourists to see the city's beautiful old buildings. Jamaica was once a British colony and English is the main language there.

Globetrotter Attractions

5 EXPLORE A FORT
Havana

Walk around the Castillo de la Real Fuerza, Havana's oldest fort. The castle was built to protect against pirates, though it was too far inside the bay to see much action.

DUNN'S RIVER FALLS

This 600-foot (183-m)-high waterfall attracts many tourists. Swim below the falls or hold hands with friends and let a guide lead you down the rocks to the pool area.

BELLAMAR CAVES

A tour of this network of caves goes by underground fountains, rivers, and ancient cave drawings. Calcite crystals make rock sculptures glitter in the dark. The network of caves lies 1.2 miles (1.9 km) underground.

THE MALECON

This is a pedestrian walkway that runs along Havana's waterfront. It is a popular spot for festivals and parades.

DIGITAL TRAVELER!

Since 1948 Jamaican athletes have won more than 65 medals at the Olympic Games. Search the Internet for the names and sports of five of these medal-winning athletes.

5 COOL THINGS TO DO HERE

ID CARD COUNTRY FACTS

CUBA
Population: 11,258,000
Capital: Havana

JAMAICA
Population: 2,712,000
Capital: Kingston

1 RIDE A STEAM TRAIN
Valle de los Ingenios

Spend a day riding a train through the Valley of the Sugar Mills. Visit a mansion on a former sugar plantation. Trains once carried sugarcane to ports for shipping to other countries.

2 TOUR WITH A GOAT
Bayamo

Jump into a carriage to tour Bayamo. The city decided to use horse-drawn carriages to save gas, keep the air clean, and reduce traffic. Small children take goat-drawn carriage rides for fun.

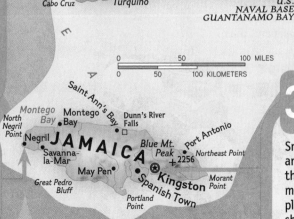

Map labels:
ATLANTIC OCEAN
Nicholas Channel
Archipiélago de Sabana
Old Bahama Channel
Camagüey Archipelago
Cienfuegos
Santa Clara — U
Ciego de Ávila — Morón
Valle de los Ingenios
Trinidad
Sancti Spíritus — B
80°
Gulf of Anna María
Camagüey
Punta Macurijes
San Pedro
Jardines de la Reina
Guayabal
Las Tunas — A
Holguín
75°
Gulf of Guacanayabo
Bahía de Nipe
Punta Guarico
Punta de Maisí
Manzanillo
Bayamo
1231
1175
Guantánamo
Sierra Maestra
2005
Santiago de Cuba
Windward Passage
20°
Cabo Cruz
Pico Turquino
U.S. NAVAL BASE GUANTANAMO BAY
CARIBBEAN SEA

0   50   100 MILES
0   50   100 KILOMETERS

Saint Ann's Bay
Montego Bay
Montego Bay
North Negril Point
Dunn's River Falls
Negril
Port Antonio
JAMAICA
Blue Mt. Peak
2256
Northeast Point
Savanna-la-Mar
May Pen
Kingston
Spanish Town
Morant Point
Great Pedro Bluff
Portland Point
75°

4 RELAX AT THE BEACH
Negril

Build a sand castle, chase a wave, play beach volleyball, or take a walk along the seven miles (11 km) of beautiful beach.

3 DANCE TO REGGAE MUSIC
Kingston

Snap your fingers, smile, and sway your body to the beat of Jamaican music. Reggae singers play guitars, bongos, shakers, cowbells, and other instruments.

5 COOL THINGS TO DO HERE

1 TAKE SNAPSHOTS OF TAP TAPS
Cap-Haïtien

See how many of these brightly painted buses you can photograph. Local people ride these *tap taps* when going on long trips or just traveling around town.

2 FLY A KITEBOARDER
Cabarete Beach

Stand on the sand and watch kite-boarders skim above the waves. Their feet are strapped to boards as they hold the handlebars of their kites.

Tortue Island
St.-Louis du Nord
Anse-à-Foleur
Port-de-Paix
Jean-Rabel
Le Borgne
Limbé
Cap-Haïtien
Fort-Liberté
Manzanillo Bay
Cape Isabela
Luperón
Puerto Plata
Monte Cristi
Imbert
Cabarete
Cape Francés Viejo
Môle St.-Nicolas
Cap-à-Foux
Gros-Morne
Pepillo Salcedo
Abreú
Cabrera
Bombardopolis
Anse-Rouge
Plaisance
Dajabón
Mao
Escoces
Gonaïves
La Citadelle
Grande Rivière du Nord
Sabaneta
Santiago
San Francisco de Macorís
Sánchez
Dessalines
Petite Rivière de l'Artibonite
Moca
DOMINICAN
St.-Marc
Hinche
Lac de Péligre
Cordillera
Pico Duarte 3175
La Vega
Pimentel
REPUBLIC
Gonâve Island
Canal de St.-Marc
HAITI
HISPANIOLA
Bonao
Monte Plata
Anse-à-Galets
Mirebalais
Lascahobas
Central
Grande Cayemite
Canal du Sud
PORT-AU-PRINCE
San Juan
Jérémie
Léogâne
Lago Enriquillo
SANTO DOMINGO
Dame-Marie
Corail
Petit-Goâve
Azua
Baní
San Cristóbal
Anse d'Hainault
Anse-à-Veau
Duvergé
Nizao
Massif de la Hotte 2347
Miragoâne
Jacmel
Marigot
Cabral
Bahía de Ocoa
Cap Carcasse
Aquin
Barahona
Chardonnières
Côtes-de-Fer
Belle-Anse
Port-à-Piment
Bainet
Grand-Gosier
Pedernales
Coteaux
Les Cayes
Port-Salut
Pointe-à-Gravois
Île à Vache
Anse-à-Pitre
Enriquillo
Cape Falso
Oviedo
Beata Island
Cape Beata

0   25   50 MILES
0   25   50 KILOMETERS

5 FACE UP! BE A CHARACTER
Jacmel

Choose a colorful mask at the market. Artists make masks with papier-mâché, a mix of paper, flour, and water. They dry the masks in the sun, then paint them.

4 CHEER FOR A BASEBALL TEAM
Santo Domingo

Sit in the stands of Quisqueya Stadium and cheer for one of the D.R.'s six teams. Many baseball players in the U.S. Major Leagues started playing in this stadium.

DOMINICAN REP. HAITI	NATIONAL BIRD: palmchat Hispaniolan trogon	NATIONAL FLOWER: rose of Bayahibe haitia	NATIONAL MAMMAL: West Indian manatee Caribbean monk seal

DOMINICAN REPUBLIC AND HAITI

Mountains, Marine Life, and Merengue MUSIC

The Dominican Republic (D.R.) and Haiti share the island of Hispaniola. The D.R. makes up more than half the island. Christopher Columbus landed on Hispaniola in 1492 and some historians say he is buried in the Dominican city of Santo Domingo. Both countries were at times colonies of Spain and France. Many Haitians are descendants of African slaves and follow African customs. French is Haiti's official language. In the D.R. most people speak Spanish.

ID CARD COUNTRY FACTS

DOMINICAN REPUBLIC
Population: 10,260,000
Capital: Santo Domingo

HAITI
Population: 10,421,000
Capital: Port-au-Prince

3 SNORKEL IN AN AQUARIUM
Punta Cana

Swim in a real aquarium with nurse sharks and stingrays. The Marinarium will lend you snorkeling gear and guide you through their sea kingdom. If you'd rather stand outside and watch, that is okay, too.

DIGITAL TRAVELER!
The lively merengue dance comes from the Dominican Republic. Go online and find a clip of merengue dancers. See if you can do the steps, too.

### Map labels
Bay
Cabo Cabrón
Cabo Samaná
Samaná
Bahía de Samaná
Cabo San Rafael
Sabana de La Mar
Miches
El Seibo
El Macao
Hato Mayor
San Pedro de Macorís
Higüey
Punta Cana
Cape Engaño
Boca Chica
Cueva de las Maravillas
La Romana
San Rafael del Yuma
Isla Saona

Globetrotter Attractions

CUEVA DE LAS MARAVILLAS
The name means "Cave of Wonders." The Taino Indians drew more than 250 pictures when they lived in this cave in the D.R. long ago. Bats live in the cave now, but they hide during the daytime when people are visiting.

THE CITADELLE
It took 20,000 workers to build this fortress on a mountaintop above Cap-Haïtien, Haiti. In the 1800s, the royal family lived here with 5,000 soldiers. Today the Citadelle still houses 100 cannons and 5,000 cannonballs.

MASSIF DE LA HOTTE
Thirteen endangered frog species live with many other animals in this remote mountain area of Haiti. People are working to preserve this region's plants and animals.

BAHAMAS

Fun in the SUN

NATIONAL BIRD:
Caribbean flamingo

NATIONAL FLOWER:
yellow elder

NATIONAL MAMMAL:
hutia

5 DANCE THE LIMBO
Grand Bahama

Set up some island music and form a line of dancers. Two people will move the limbo pole lower and lower. Bend back and dance under it. See how low you can go!

There are more than 700 islands in the Bahamas. People live on only 30 of them. Many of the people have West African roots and customs: Their ancestors were enslaved and brought here to work on cotton plantations. The country was once a British colony. Nassau, the capital, has many beautiful vacation resorts.

DIGITAL TRAVELER!
Many beaches in the Bahama islands are scattered with seashells of all shapes and sizes. Take photographs of shells, make them into postcards, and send them to your friends.

Globetrotter Attractions

4 GO ON AN AQUAVENTURE
Paradise Island

Explore a huge waterscape park alongside the Atlantis Paradise Hotel. There are swimming pools, high-speed waterslides, and a river ride with rolling rapids and wave surges within a lush, tropical man-made environment.

ANDROS ISLAND
Made up mainly of three large islands, this area is rich in mangrove, tidal swamp, and cave wildlife.

LAKE WINDSOR (LAKE ROSA)
This lake is a protected reserve for flamingos, the national bird. They build their nests in the spring and adult females may each lay one egg a year.

LUCAYAN NATIONAL PARK
This park includes mangrove swamps, tropical beaches, and an underground cave system that is more than 300 miles (480 km) long.

West End

Great Isaac

26° East Isaac

Alice Town • Bimini Islands

Gun Cay

Cat Cays

Ocean Cay

Riding Rocks

Orange Cay

Straits of Florida

Muertos Cays

Deadman's Cays 80°

Dog Rocks

Santaren Channel

24°

Elbow Cays

Cay Sal Bank

Damas Cays

Cay Sal 80°

Anguilla Cays

Nicholas Channel

5 COOL THINGS TO DO HERE

Size: 5,359 sq mi (13,880 sq km)
Population: 350,000
Capital: Nassau
Official language: English
Currency: Bahamian dollar
Highest point: Mount Alvernia, 207 ft (63 m)
Life expectancy: 75.0 years

1 WALK ON THE OCEAN FLOOR
Nassau

Take a boat out to sea where you can walk down a ladder to the ocean floor. One tour provides diving helmets that let you breathe underwater.

2 SWIM WITH STINGRAYS
Blue Lagoon Island

Jump into Stingray City and swim with stingrays, moray eels, and crawfish. If you arrive at mealtime, you can feed the marine animals, too.

3 STAND WHERE OCEAN MEETS SEA
Eleuthera Island

Visit the northern end of Eleuthera Island and stand on the beach. Look into the water and try to see where the churning, dark Atlantic Ocean bumps up to the calm, turquoise Caribbean Sea.

Map labels:
0 25 50 MILES
0 25 50 KILOMETERS

Great Sale Cay
Little Abaco Island
Cooper's Town
Grand Bahama Island
Eight Mile Rock
Great Guana Cay
Man O'War Cay
Hope Town
High Rock
Lucaya
Freeport
Marsh Harbour
Moore's I.
Cherokee Sound
Abaco
Gorda Cay
Crossing Rocks
Tiloo Cay
Northwest Providence Channel
Sandy Point
Island
Great Stirrup Cay
Great Harbour Cay
Southwest Point
Berry Is.
Northeast Providence Channel
Dunmore Town
The Bluff
Bonds Cay
Alice Town
Chub Cay
Whale Cay
Paradise Island
Blue Lagoon Island
Governor's Harbour
Joulter Cays
Nicholls' Town
Nassau
Current
San Andros
Adelaide
Rose I.
Tarpum Bay
Eleuthera Island
New Providence
Deep Creek
Rock Sound
Staniard Creek
Andros Town
Bannerman Town
Flamingo Point
Arthur's Town
Cat Island
Williams I.
Behring Point
Andros Island
Little San Salvador
New Bight
Mount Alvernia
Big Wood Cay
Shroud Cay
Old Bight
206
Port Howe
Middle Bight
Devil's Point
Cockburn Town
Southern Bight
Green Cay
Conception I.
San Salvador (Watling)
Kemps Bay
Great Guana Cay
Cape Santa Maria
Rum Cay
Water Cays
Rolleville
Great Exuma
Stella Maris
Port Nelson
Curley Cut Cays
Cistern Pt.
George-Town
Dolly Cays
TROPIC OF CANCER
Hog Cay
Long Island
Little Exuma
Deadmans Cay
Samana Cay (Atwood)
Water Cay
Clarence Town
Flamingo Cay
Roses
Crooked I.
Man-of-War Cay
Gordon's
Colonel Hill
Northeast Point
Jamaica Cay
Plana Cays (French Cays)
Seal Cay
Long Cay (Fortune I.)
Albert Town
Nurse Cay
Snug Corner
Mayaguana Island
Raccoon Cay
Acklins Island
Abraham's Bay
Duncan Town
The Bight of Acklins
Mayaguana Passage
Ragged I.
Caicos Passage
Cay Verde
Castle Island
Mira Por Vos
Crooked Island Passage
Exuma Sound
Tongue of the Ocean
GREAT BAHAMA BANK
Old Bahama Channel
Little Inagua Island
Great Inagua Island
Lake Rosa
Matthew Town

ATLANTIC OCEAN

LESSER ANTILLES

Cricket, Cannons, and CALYPSO

On a map, this long string of islands looks like the boundary line between the Atlantic Ocean and the Caribbean Sea. Before 1496, the original islanders were the Arawaks, the Caribs, and the Ciboney. By the middle of the 1600s, people from Spain, England, France, and the Netherlands had settled there. They set up trading centers, which also led to pirate raids. Many of the islands are mountainous with beautiful beaches and warm weather.

5 COOL THINGS TO DO HERE

1 HIKE TO A BOILING LAKE
Dominica

Hike through the volcanic debris in Morne Trois Pitons National Park. See steam rise from the world's second-largest actively boiling lake. Scientists say the water is heated by molten lava below the lake. You can see bubbles belching from the center.

2 COUNT CANNONS
Sandy Point Town

Count more than 20 cannons as you walk around Brimstone Hill Fortress National Park. In the 1700s and 1800s, this huge British fort protected present-day St. Kitts and Nevis from invaders. British engineers designed the fort and African slaves built it on the side of a volcanic mountain.

BRITISH VIRGIN ISLANDS United Kingdom

Anegada
Virgin Gorda
St. Thomas
Tortola ● Road Town
St. John

U.S. VIRGIN ISLANDS U.S.
Charlotte Amalie
Christiansted
355 ● St. Croix
Frederiksted ●

PUERTO RICO United States

Sombrero

ANGUILLA
The Valley
United Kingdom
Marigot
Philipsburg–18'

ST. MARTIN (ST. MAARTEN)
France & Netherlands
St.–Barthélemy (St.-Barts) France
Gustavia ●

Saba
Netherlands ● The Bottom
St. Eustatius Netherlands
Oranjestad
Sandy Point Town
1156
SAINT KITTS & NEVIS
Basseterre ● St. Kitts
Charlestown Nevis
Redonda

Brades ● **MONTSERRAT** U.K.
Plymouth (abandoned)

Barbuda
Codrington ●–62
ANTIGUA & BARBUDA
St. John's ● Antigua
402 ● Falmouth

Port-Louis
Grande-Terre
GUADELOUPE France
Basse-Terre
Basse-Terre 1467
Pointe-à-Pitre
La Désirade
204 ● Marie-Galante
Grand-Bourg
Les Saintes

Anegada Passage
Guadeloupe Passage

L E E W A R D   I S L A N D S
C A R I B B

A T L

ATLANTIC OCEAN

DOMINICA
Portsmouth · +1447
Roseau ◉

MARTINIQUE
France
Sainte-Marie
Montagne Pelée +1397
Fort-de- France ◉
Le Lamentin
Pointe d'Enfer

Martinique Passage

St. Lucia Channel

SAINT LUCIA
Castries ◉
14°
950 +
Vieux Fort

St. Vincent Passage

BARBADOS
Speightstown · + 340 ◉
Bridgetown
60°

SAINT VINCENT & THE GRENADINES
Baleine □ 1234 Falls + · Georgetown
Saint Vincent ◉ Kingstown
Bequia · Port Elizabeth
Mustique ◉
Canouan
Union

GRENADA
Carriacou · Hillsborough
+299
12°
840 + *Grenada* · Grenville
Point Salines ◉ St. George's

ANTILLES *LESSER* / *WINDWARD ISLANDS*

Dominica Passage

CARIBBEAN SEA

CARIBBEAN SEA

ARUBA
Neth.
◉ Oranjestad
188 +
Sint Nicolaas

CURAÇAO
Neth.
Willemstad ◉
372 +

BONAIRE
Neth.
Kralendijk
240 +

VENEZUELA
70°   69°   12°

Same scale as main map

See p. 8 for location

Scale:
100 MILES
100 KILOMETERS
50
0

TRINIDAD & TOBAGO
Tobago
Charlotteville ·
Scarborough · +576
Canaan
Galera Point
Toco ·
Blanchisseuse ·
+940
Sangre Grande ·
St. Joseph ·
Arima · *TRINIDAD*
Port of Spain ◉
San Fernando
La Brea · · Guayaguayare
Point Fortin · San
Bonasse · Moruga
Francique
Gulf of Paria
Dragon's Mouths
Serpent's Mouth
62°   10°

VENEZUELA

See p. 8 for location

3 JOIN THE CRICKET CROWD
Bridgetown

Watch the score change as the bowlers and batters play an exciting game. A game can last from one to five days.

4 VISIT PIRATE SCENES
Bequia Island

Visit sites where parts of *Pirates of the Caribbean: The Curse of the Black Pearl* were filmed. Then take a refreshing dip in the nearby Falls of Baleine.

5 LISTEN TO A STEEL BAND
Port of Spain

Enjoy calypso music played on steel drums. These drums are the national instrument of Trinidad and Tobago. They were invented here and originally made from metal containers.

ID CARD
COUNTRY FACTS

BARBADOS
Population: 253,000
Capital: Bridgetown

DOMINICA
Population: 155,000
Capital: Roseau

GRENADA
Population: 112,000
Capital: Saint George's

ST. KITTS & NEVIS
Population: 55,000
Capital: Basseterre

ST. LUCIA
Population: 170,000
Capital: Castries

ST. VINCENT & THE GRENADINES
Population: 108,000
Capital: Kingstown

TRINIDAD & TOBAGO
Population: 1,341,000
Capital: Port of Spain

37

SOUTH AMERICA

Geographical WONDERS

South America is covered with tropical rain forests, mighty rivers, high waterfalls, massive mountains, hot deserts, glaciers, and island chains. It also has big, bustling cities, rural areas, and hilltop villages.

San Rafael Waterfall, Ecuador Park, Ecuador. South America gets more rainfall than any other continent, creating some of the world's longest rivers and highest waterfalls.

SOUTH AMERICA

From Tropical North to Icy Cold SOUTH

The original people of this continent are known as Amerindians. Following the European discovery of the Americas by Christopher Columbus in 1492, Spanish and Portuguese explorers and settlers spread throughout the land. They introduced their languages, cultures, and traditions, which remain to this day.

SOCCER
Brazil

Soccer is a major sport across South America. Brazil, Argentina, and Uruguay have all won the World Cup.

FESTIVAL OF THE SUN
Peru

Amerindians celebrate ancient traditions such as Inti Raymi, the Festival of the Sun, which honors the Incan sun god Inti.

AUNT BERTHA'S
TRAVEL TIPS

LEARN LATIN

Spanish and Portuguese—the two main languages of South America—have origins in Latin, the language of the ancient Romans.

WRAP UP WARM

Parts of South America can be very cold, falling to −14.3 °F (−25.7 °C) in southern Argentina. The coldest temperatures are in July and August, which are winter months in the Southern Hemisphere.

TAKE A BUS

In South America, most people travel long distances across countries by bus or car rather than by train. A bus trip from Rio de Janeiro, Brazil, to Buenos Aires, Argentina, takes about 40 hours.

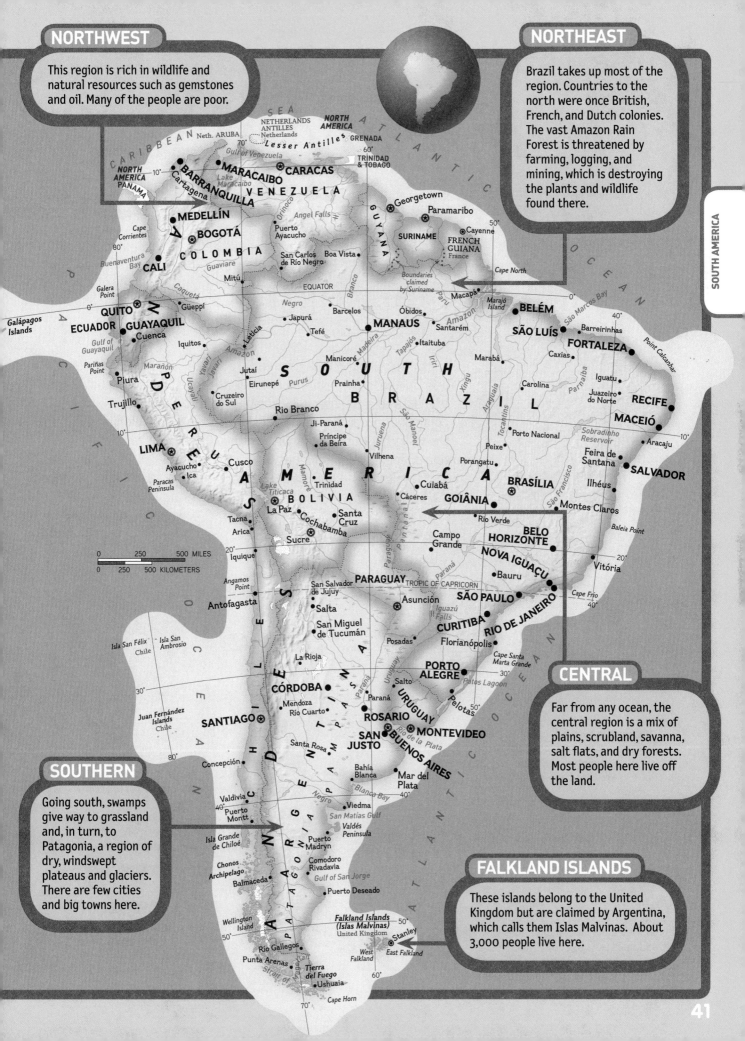

NORTHWEST

This region is rich in wildlife and natural resources such as gemstones and oil. Many of the people are poor.

NORTHEAST

Brazil takes up most of the region. Countries to the north were once British, French, and Dutch colonies. The vast Amazon Rain Forest is threatened by farming, logging, and mining, which is destroying the plants and wildlife found there.

CENTRAL

Far from any ocean, the central region is a mix of plains, scrubland, savanna, salt flats, and dry forests. Most people here live off the land.

SOUTHERN

Going south, swamps give way to grassland and, in turn, to Patagonia, a region of dry, windswept plateaus and glaciers. There are few cities and big towns here.

FALKLAND ISLANDS

These islands belong to the United Kingdom but are claimed by Argentina, which calls them Islas Malvinas. About 3,000 people live here.

41

	NATIONAL BIRD:	NATIONAL FLOWER:	NATIONAL MAMMAL:
COLOMBIA	Andean condor	Columbian orchid	Andean squirrel
ECUADOR	Andean condor	rose	Galápagos fur seal

COLOMBIA AND ECUADOR

Ancient Ruins and Unique ANIMALS

t's hot in lowland Ecuador, for you are on the Equator. To cool off, head inland to the Andes Mountains, or take a boat to the Galápagos Islands, where you may meet the blue-footed booby. Ecuador and Colombia, once a single country, split in 1830. Most Colombians live in the valleys of the Andes Mountains, and Colombia is famous for growing coffee. The capital cities of both countries—Quito (Ecuador) and Bogotá (Colombia)—are more than 8,000 feet (2,438 m) above sea level.

ID CARD COUNTRY FACTS

COLOMBIA
Population: 48,028,000
Capital: Bogotá

ECUADOR
Population: 15,789,000
Capital: Quito

Globetrotter Attractions

MEDELLÍN
This Colombian city has beautiful museums, breathtaking cable-car rides to nearby mountaintops, and the biggest flower parade in the world.

NAPO RIVER
Riverboat cruises take tourists through the Amazon Rain Forest of Ecuador. Everyone hopes to take a picture of a river dolphin, piranha, or giant frog.

INCA RUINS OF INGAPIRCA
The ancient Canari and Inca peoples showed amazing building skills with rocks and mortar. These ruins include the Temple of the Sun where, at the right time of year and day, sunlight beams through the exact center of a doorway.

5 PHOTOGRAPH GIANT TORTOISES
Galápagos Islands

Take this rare opportunity to see the world's largest tortoise. The biggest one ever recorded was five feet (1.5 m) long and weighed 550 pounds (249 kg). They can live more than 100 years.

DIGITAL TRAVELER!
Sugarcane grows in Colombia. Go online and find out how sugarcane becomes the sugar we put into the sweets we eat.

1 JUMP INTO A MUD POOL
Santa Catalina

Climb stairs that lead to the top of Tortumo Volcano and then jump in. It's okay, you'll land in a shallow pool of mud. Relax!

5 COOL THINGS TO DO HERE

2 BLINK AT THE BLING
Bogotá

Walk through the Gold Museum and see shiny objects made by native artists who lived here before the Europeans arrived.

SOUTH AMERICA

3 STAND ON THE EQUATOR
San Antonio

Straddle the yellow line at the Middle of the World Monument. This line represents the Equator, the imaginary line that separates the northern and southern hemispheres. Modern GPS devices show that the real equator is about 800 feet (244 m) north of the monument.

4 TOUR A BANANA PLANTATION
Guayaquil

Learn how bananas grow from tiny reddish flowers into the fruit we eat. Ecuador exports more bananas than any other country.

GALÁPAGOS ISLANDS
(Archipiélago de Colón) Ecuador

PACIFIC OCEAN

Isla Fernandina (Narborough)
Isla San Salvador (Santiago, James)
Isla Isabela (Albemarle)
Isla Santa Cruz (Chaves, Indefatigable)
Puerto Ayora
Isla San Cristóbal (Chatham)
Isla Santa María (Floreana, Charles)
Isla Española (Hood)

0   50 MI
0   50 KM

92°   90°

See p. 8 for location

CARIBBEAN SEA

BARRANQUILLA
Punta Gallinas
Guadjira Peninsula
Gulf of Venezuela
Cabo de la Aguja
Ríohacha
Uribia
Maicao
Puerto Colombia
Santa Marta
Santa Catalina
Ciénaga
Valledupar
Cartagena
Soledad
Sabanalarga
Turbaco
Arjona
Calamar
Carmen de Bolívar
Plato
Bosconia
Santa Cruz del Islote
Tolú
Corozal
Lorica
Magangué
Mompós
El Banco
Sincelejo
San Marcos
Ayapel
Montería
Cúcuta
Turbo
Caucasia
Ocaña
Mutatá
Puerto Wilches
Pamplona
Juradó
Valdivia
Bucaramanga
Cabo Marzo
Cupica
Cisneros
Puerto Berrío
Barrancabermeja
Arauca
Arauca
Gulf de Cupica
Bello
San Gil
Málaga
Tame
Cravo Norte
Punta Solano
Quibdó
Socorro
Casanare
Ariporo
MEDELLÍN
Vélez
Gulf of Tibugá
Sonsón
Chiquinquirá
Duitama
Cape Corrientes
Nuquí
La Dorada
Sogamoso
San Luis de Palenque
Puerto Carreño
Manizales
Honda
Tunja
Yopal
Santa Rita
Cartago
Pereira
BOGOTÁ
Orocué
Docampadó Bay
Armenia
Ibagué
Villavicencio
Puerto Gaitán
San José de Ocuné
Puero Inírida
Punta Charambirá
Sevilla
Girardot
Puerto López
Buenaventura
Tuluá
Buga
San Martín
Gorgona Island
Palmira
CALI
Neiva
Mapiripán
Cejal
Punta Guascama
Guapí
Campoalegre
San José del Guaviare
Calamar
San Felipe
Popayán
Puerto La Concordia
Timbío
Garzón
San Vincente del Caguán
Miraflores
Tumaco Bay
Patía
San Agustín
Florencia
Mitú
Bahía de Ancón de Sardinas
Tumaco
Barbacoas
Esmeraldas
Diviso
Pasto
Mocoa
Raudal Yupurari (Devils Cataract)
Galera Point
San Lorenzo
Esmeraldas
Tulcán
Ibarra
Ipiales
Puerto Asís
Tres Esquinas
Muisne
Otavalo
San Gabriel
Boca de Cojimíes
San Antonio
Cayambe
EQUATOR
QUITO
Puerto Leguízamo
Cabo Pasado
Chone
Cotopaxi
Sangolquí
Napo
Nuevo Rocafuerte
Bahía de Caráquez
Latacunga
Tena
Manta
Portoviejo
Ambato
Cononaco
Cape San Lorenzo
Chimborazo
La Pedrera
Isla de la Plata
Jipijapa
Guaranda
Riobamba
Milagro
Babahoyo
Macas
Arica
Tarapacá
GUAYAQUIL
Alausí
Ingapirca
Salinas
Azogues
Yaupi
La Libertad
Cuenca
Puná Island
Machala
Gulf of Guayaquil
Pasaje
Saraguro
Tarapacá
Piñas
Loja
Leticia
Macará
Zamora

COLOMBIA
VENEZUELA
ECUADOR
PERU
BRAZIL

PACIFIC OCEAN

Gulf of Uraba
Gulf of Morrosquillo
Magdalena
Cauca
Cesar
Arauca
Meta
Casanare
Tomo
Vichada
Orinoco
Guaviare
Inírida
Guainía
Negro
Vaupés
Caquetá
Yari
Caguán
Putumayo
Napo
Igara Parana
Conambo
Pastaza
Amazon (Amazonas)
Apaporis
Traira

3850
5493
910
5750
5790
5897
6267
860

75°   10°   70°
5°   80°   75°   70°
0°   EQUATOR   0°
5°   75°

0   100   200 MILES
0   100   200 KILOMETERS

5 COOL THINGS TO DO HERE

1 SHOUT AT A BULLFIGHT
Valencia

See the matador face the bull in Valencia's bullring. It is the second largest in Latin America.

2 VISIT A PALACE
Caracas

See Miraflores Palace where the President of Venezuela works. Inside is the Sun Room, decorated with gold donated by Peru.

5 VIEW WILDLFE
Hato el Cedral

Take a tour of this wildlife area where you'll see capybaras, the largest living rodents on Earth. They can be more than 4 feet (122 cm) long and weigh more than 100 pounds (45 kg).

4 RIDE A CABLE CAR
El Ávila National Park

Get a bird's-eye view of Caracas as the cable car climbs the mountain. When you get to the top, you can go skating or play at the playground.

NATIONAL BIRD:
Venezuelan troupial

NATIONAL FLOWER:
flor de mayo orchid

NATIONAL TREE:
araguaney

VENEZUELA

From the Andes to the AMAZON

Venezuela is on the north coast of South America. Columbus landed here in 1498. You'll find broad grasslands called llanos, and mountains as tall as 16,000 feet (4,877 m) high. South America's largest lake, Lake Maracaibo, is really a lagoon open to the ocean. Oil and gas make Venezuela one of South America's richest countries, with busy expressways linking the capital Caracas to other cities. Like many South Americans, Venezuelans are mostly Spanish-speaking.

**Map labels:**
Dragon's Mouths
Macuro
Güiria
TRINIDAD & TOBAGO
Gulf of Paria
Serpent's Mouth
ATLANTIC OCEAN
Tucupita
Barrancas
Boca Grande
rinoco
Curiapo
Upata
Pao
San José de Amacuro
El Callao
Tumeremo
Cuyuni
El Dorado
GUYANA
Angel Falls
Total drop 979 meters (3,212 feet)
La Gran Sabana
Mt. Roraima 2739
Santa Elena
acaraima
10°
60°
60°
5°

ID CARD
COUNTRY FACTS

Size: 352,144 sq mi (912,050 sq km)
Population: 29,679,000
Capital: Caracas
Official language: Spanish
Currency: bolivar
Highest point: Pico Bolivar, 16,427 ft (5,007 m)
Life expectancy: 75.0 years

Globetrotter Attractions

ANGEL FALLS
This is the world's tallest waterfall and is 20 times higher than Niagara Falls. It drops 3,212 feet (979 m) over the edge of Auyantepui Mountain in Canaima National Park.

MOCHIMA NATIONAL PARK
Pods of dolphins frequently swim by the 36 islands that make up this national park. Visitors enjoy swimming and snorkeling in the coral reefs.

PARQUE DEL ESTE
This popular park in the capital, Caracas, has a snake house and an awesome planetarium.

3 BEWARE THE DUNGEON!
La Asunción

Walk around Santa Rosa castle, a fort that protected the city 330 years ago. Inside there is a dungeon where prisoners were kept during the Venezuelan War of Independence from Spain of 1811 to 1823.

DIGITAL TRAVELER!
There is a place in Venezuela called The Serpent's Mouth. Search the Internet to find its location and the best way to travel there.

GUYANA SURINAME	NATIONAL BIRD: hoatzin great kiskadee	NATIONAL FLOWER: *Victoria Regia* lily *Sloanea gracilis*	NATIONAL MAMMAL: jaguar water opposum

GUYANA AND SURINAME

From Colonial Houses to Jungle Cats

Neighbors on the northeast coast of South America, Guyana and Suriname are separated by the Corantijn River. Tropical forest covers much of the land, which rises to grassy highlands and mountains more than 9,000 feet (2,743 m) high in Guyana. Most people live along the low-lying coast. Natural resources include forest lumber, and minerals such as bauxite ore, from which aluminum is made. Expect to hear English and Dutch, because Guyana was once British-ruled, while Suriname was Dutch.

5 COOL THINGS TO DO HERE

1 HAVE A FUN DAY
Georgetown

Celebrate the Hindu holiday of Phagwah, also known as Holi. Watch a parade and join in the colorful activities. Many Guyanese are descendants of people brought from India in the 1800s to work on sugar plantations.

2 BE A SUGAR SCHOLAR!
Mariënburg

Take a tour of an old sugar plantation. In the late 1800s, there were sugar fields and a sugar factory here plus Suriname's first railroad, which was used for sending sugar to markets.

3 DO SOMETHING DUTCH
Paramaribo

Take pictures of Dutch houses in Paramaribo. It became a Dutch colonial town in the 1600s. The Dutch West India Company built their trading business here.

FRENCH GUIANA
Overseas Department of France

5°

Maroni

Lawa

Litani

Boundary claimed by Suriname

Afobaka

Brokopondo
Brownsweg
Brownsberg Nature Park

S U R I N A M E

Van Blommestein Meer

Suriname

Brokopondo

Tapanahoni

Wilhelmina Mountains
+1230

Kayser Gebergte
+861

Coeroeni
Corentyne

Lucie

New

Boundary claimed by Suriname

Corantijn

Coppename

Berbice

G U Y A N A

Apoteri

Essequibo

IWOKRAMA MOUNTAINS

Kwitaro

KANUKU MTS.

Rupununi

Lethem

East Takutu

ACARAI MTS.
+1009

B R A Z I L

60°

55°

Orinduik

Kaieteur Falls

MOUNTAINS

2739 Mt. Roraima

5°

0   50   100 MILES
0   50   100 KILOMETERS

LEARN ABOUT 5 TURTLES
Shell Beach

Ride a boat by Shell Beach, where sea turtles make their nests. Special teams tag the turtles to keep track of them. Be sure not to disturb the nests.

---

4 COUNT CRITTERS
Iwokrama Rain Forest

Take the walkway above the trees to look down on anteaters, otters, and jaguars—the continent's largest cats. There are many insects and more recorded species of fish and bats here than anywhere on Earth.

ID CARD COUNTRY FACTS

GUYANA
Population: 800,000
Capital: Georgetown

SURINAME
Population: 558,000
Capital: Paramaribo

DIGITAL TRAVELER!
People in Suriname celebrate Keti Koti on July 1 each year. Go online to find out what they are celebrating.

Globetrotter Attractions

KAIETEUR FALLS
One of the world's most powerful waterfalls lies in Guyana's rain forest. It is powerful because of its height —741 feet (226 m)—and the amount of water rushing over it.

BROWNSBERG NATURE PARK
Guests who stay in hotels in this Suriname park get to watch howler monkeys swinging through the trees.

CENTRAL MARKET
The large marketplace at Paramaribo's waterfront has its special sights, sounds, and smells. See pyramids of fresh fruit, rows of fish, and blankets loaded with trinkets.

BRAZIL
The Center of SOUTH AMERICA

NATIONAL BIRD:
macaw

NATIONAL TREE:
golden trumpet tree

NATIONAL MAMMAL:
jaguar

South America's biggest country has more people than the rest of the continent combined. Brazil is so big it takes 25 hours to drive from Rio Grande on the coast to the capital Brasília. To explore the Amazon Rain Forest, take a plane and see it from above, or sail up the Amazon River. Visit the coastal cities to see where most Brazilians live, and enjoy Rio de Janeiro's colorful Carnival. Learn some Portuguese, too—it's the main language of Brazil.

5 COOL THINGS TO DO HERE

1 BOUNCE THROUGH A RUBBER MUSEUM
Manaus

Walk through a jungle and learn how workers tapped rubber trees to remove the latex sap. Tour the estate owner's home and learn how rubber made many people rich in the late 1800s. Then take a boat ride to the area where ships picked up rubber to deliver it worldwide.

2 IMAGINE THE FUTURE
Brasília

Stroll past this futuristic cathedral in Brazil's capital. Before 1956, this area looked like a desert. The president invited architects and builders to create a modern city.

3 PLAY BEACH VOLLEYBALL
Recife

Join a friendly game of volleyball next to the Atlantic Ocean. Recife has many miles of beaches. After a few games, buy a refreshing coconut drink and take a stroll on the boardwalk.

48

ID CARD
COUNTRY FACTS

Size: 3,287,612 sq mi (8,514,877 sq km)
Population: 195,527,000
Capital: Brasília
Official language: Portuguese
Currency: real
Highest point: Pico da Neblina, 9,823 ft (2,994 m)
Life expectancy: 74.0 years

Globetrotter Attractions

AMAZON RAIN FOREST
Millions of kinds of plants and insects live here. For years people have been destroying the rain forest for land and lumber, but environmental groups are working to protect it.

PANTANAL
Many rare and endangered animals live in this floodplain, including giant anteaters and giant otters.

SUGARLOAF MOUNTAIN
This mountain in Rio de Janeiro looks like a large granite rocket. A cable car zips tourists up to the top.

4 SIZE UP A STATUE
Rio de Janeiro

Ride a cogwheel train to the top of Corcovado Mountain. Look up and gaze at the 124-foot (38-m) statue of Jesus Christ. Look down for a gorgeous view of the city. The mountaintop is sometimes covered in clouds.

DIGITAL TRAVELER!
Carnival in Rio de Janeiro is one of the world's greatest celebrations, with music, dance, costumes, and parades. Learn about, look at, and listen to Carnival on the Internet.

5 EXPERIENCE SOCCER
São Paulo

Cheer for one of the São Paolo soccer teams. The city has several teams and stadiums. Morumbi Stadium is the largest, with 84,000 seats. The famous soccer player, Pele, played for a São Paolo team.

NATIONAL BIRD:
Andean cock-of-the-rock

NATIONAL TREE:
cinchona

NATIONAL MAMMAL:
vicuna

PERU
A Diverse LANDSCAPE

n Peru, look forward to tasty fish dinners because Pacific Ocean fishing is a major industry here. Yet along the coast is a desert drier than the Sahara. Inland to the east rise the Andes Mountains, and farther inland, beyond the Andes, are tropical rain forests and rivers. Lake Titicaca, which Peru shares with Bolivia, is the highest lake in the world that is navigable by ships.

Globetrotter Attractions

NASCA LINES
About 2,000 years ago, the Nasca people etched drawings in the desert floor. From airplanes, we can see these pictures of whales, monkeys, and other figures.

VOLCÁN MISTI
This cone-shaped peak sits in the Andes Mountains near Arequipa, Peru's second largest city. It last erupted in 1600.

LAKE TITICACA
Five major river systems and many streams flow into this lake. There is a single main outlet, to the south.

2 FLUTTER BY BUTTERFLIES
Iquitos
See how many kinds and colors of butterflies you can find at Pilpintuwasi Butterfly Farm. This blue morpho butterfly looks like a delicate work of art. You may also see an owl butterfly. Its wings have dark circles that resemble the eyes of an owl.

5 COOL THINGS TO DO HERE

1 SHOP NONSTOP
Piura
Check out Piura's shops and try to find the city's most famous things. Look for artists making straw hats, pottery, wooden bowls, silver objects, and colorful clothing. Piura was the first city in Peru that was settled by people from Spain.

DIGITAL TRAVELER!

Look for llamas, alpacas, guanacos, and vicunas. Photograph them or go online to see what they look like. Compare them to animals you see near home.

5 DISCOVER TREASURE
Lima

Be amazed by hundreds of objects in the Gold Museum. Long ago, Peru was rich with gold. The people artistically turned the gold into statues, bracelets, rings, and face masks.

4 FOLLOW THE INCA TRAIL
Machu Picchu

Walk the same trails as the ancient Inca up to Machu Picchu, which was probably a mountain estate for the Inca emperor built around 1450. The Incas abandoned it after the Spanish conquered Peru. Hikers can see ruins of a palace, a cemetery, and sacred sites.

3 FLOAT ON ISLANDS
Puno

Take a boat ride on Lake Titicaca to one of the 44 man-made islands. Meet the Uro Indians, who live on islands made of floating reeds. They live in reed huts and eat fish from the lake.

ID CARD
COUNTRY FACTS

Size: 496,224 sq mi (1,285,216 sq km)
Population: 30,475,000
Capital: Lima
Official languages: Spanish and Quechua
Currency: nuevo sol
Highest point: Nevado Huascarán, 22,205 ft (6,768 m)
Life expectancy: 74.0 years

51

ID CARD
COUNTRY FACTS

Size: 424,164 sq mi (1,098,581 sq km)
Population: 11,020,000
Capital: La Paz
Official languages: Spanish, Quechua, and Aymara
Currency: boliviano
Highest point: Nevado Sajama, 21,463 ft (6,542 m)
Life expectancy: 67.0 years

5 COOL THINGS TO DO HERE

1 HAVE SALTENAS FOR BREAKFAST
La Paz

Buy these tasty pastries from a La Paz street vendor. By noon, many vendors are sold out of the baked dough packets filled with a sweet or spicy chicken or meat mixture. Enjoy them for your breakfast or a snack.

5 SAIL TO A LAKE ISLAND
Isla del Sol

Take a boat to Isla del Sol, an island in Lake Titicaca, where no motorized vehicles are allowed. Hike between villages and wander around the pre-Columbian Inca ruins, such as the Temple of the Sun.

4 THINK INCA
Tiwanacu

Examine the ruins of a pyramid built before the Inca Empire. Walk up to the Gate of the Sun, a doorway cut from a huge stone. Find the half-human, half-bird figures carved into it. The pyramid was probably an observatory and used for special ceremonies.

3 DON'T FORGET YOUR CAMERA
Cochabamba

Take a picture of the huge statue of Jesus Christ that stands on San Pedro Hill. Ride the cable car to the top of the hill for a better look at the statue, which is more than 108 feet (33 m) high. Admire the city of Cochabamba spread below.

2 DANCE AT A CARNIVAL
Oruro

Watch up to 28,000 dancers in elaborate costumes and masks as they perform many types of dances. Listen to the 10,000 musicians who play music for the dancers. The Carnaval de Oruro always begins with the devil dance. Other performances reflect the traditions of groups that now make Bolivia their home: Amerindians, Africans, and Spanish.

NATIONAL BIRD: Andean condor

NATIONAL MAMMAL: alpaca

NATIONAL FLOWER: kantuta

BOLIVIA
Summits, Salt and SUN

Landlocked Bolivia is named for Simon Bolivar, a man who helped liberate much of the continent from Spanish rule in the early 1800s. The high Andes Mountains and the windswept Altiplano plateau are in the west, and in the east is the Oriente, a lowland region of grassland, forests, and rivers. Travel by road is difficult, so horses and llamas often get places cars cannot reach. Farmers in the Valles region, with its fertile valleys, produce much of Bolivia's food, including potatoes, corn, and a local grain called quinoa.

Globetrotter Attractions

LA PAZ
High in the Andes is La Paz, the world's highest capital. The city's center is in a deep canyon but newer buildings are being built up the canyon walls. Lake Titicaca is nearby.

BIOCENTRO GUEMBE
Near the city of Santa Cruz is a natural paradise, with a giant butterfly park, orchid garden, and nature trails. It is surrounded by lush forest.

SALAR DE UYUNI
Uyuni Salt Flat is the world's largest inland area of salt. On the dry and very flat land, salt is gathered into big piles before trucks take it to nearby processing plants.

DIGITAL TRAVELER!
La Paz is a Spanish name. Use an online translator to learn its English meaning. Then translate Isla del Sol.

### Map labels

B R A Z I L

Baures
Mateguá
Magdalena
Puerto Villazón
Lake San Luis
Puerto Saucedo
Serranía Negra
Laguna Concepción
Serranía de Huanchaca
Puerto Frey
Tarvo
Blanco
Negro
San Martín
La Unión
Baía Grande
Ascención
San Javier
San Pedro
Concepción
San Ignacio
San Matías
283+
Candelaria
B O L I V I A
Puerto Grether
General Saavedra
San Rafael
El Cerro
Lake Concepción
Montero
Motacucito
Santa Cruz
+2319
Espinal
Lake Uberaba
Laguna Gaiba
Serranía de Sunsas
Ayacucho
San José de Chiquitos
Serranía de Santiago
Santo Corazón
Samaipata
Taperas
Roboré
Tucavaca
Piraí
Oriente
Cabezas
Fortín Suárez Arana
Pucará
Abapó
Iboperenda
El Carmen
Puerto Suárez
Padilla
Salinas de San José
San Miguel
Lagunillas
Charagua
P A R A G U A Y
Camiri
Azero
Parapeti
Cuevo
Macharetí
Villamontes
Pilcomayo
anandita
Villa Ingavi
A R G E N T I N A

0   50   100 MILES
0   50   100 KILOMETERS

53

CHILE
Deserts, Glaciers, and MOUNTAINS

NATIONAL TREE: monkey-puzzle

NATIONAL FLOWER: copihue

NATIONAL MAMMAL: huemul

1 STARGAZE
Atacama Desert

Look up at the stars in the driest place on Earth. The cloudless skies allow a clear view of the heavens. NASA uses this desert to test instruments because its soil is similar to the soil on Mars.

N o other land is so long, yet so thin, as Chile. It stretches along the west side of South America for about 2,650 miles (4,265 km), but is only about 265 miles (426 km) wide. Chile has some of South America's most magnificent scenery: mountains, volcanoes, glaciers, forests, rocky islands, and rainless desert. Right at the southern tip is Tierra del Fuego, the "land of fire"—a group of islands shared between Chile and Argentina.

ID CARD
COUNTRY FACTS

Size: 291,932 sq mi (756,102 sq km)
Population: 17,557,000
Capital: Santiago
Official language: Spanish
Currency: Chilean peso
Highest point: Nevado Ojos del Salado, 22,615 ft (6,893 m)
Life expectancy: 79.0 years

See p. 8 for location

2 CLIMB PIANO STAIRS
Valparaíso

Wander up stairs painted to look like piano keys. Then climb some of the 42 hills in this port city. Investigate the street art and brightly painted houses that cling to the hills. Ride to the top of a hill on a decorated "incline elevator" car that has been used for more than 100 years. Gaze across the Pacific from atop the hills where ocean breezes cool the night air.

5 TELL TIME WITH FLOWERS
Viña del Mar

Viña del Mar is known as "The Garden City." Check the time on this floral clock in one of its gardens. Then ride to its beautiful beaches in a traditional horse-drawn carriage.

4 SNOWBOARD IN JULY
Malalcahuello–Nalcas National Reserve

Swoop down a snow-covered slope in the Andes in July. Winter here is from June to September.

3 KAYAK TO A GLACIER
Puerto Natales

Glaciers, made of moving ice, change the landscape. Watch out for floating ice as you paddle in a glacial lake.

Globetrotter Attractions

EASTER ISLAND
This island, some 2,300 miles (3,680 km) west of South America, is home to 900 huge statues called *moai*. The moai are only heads and bodies and were carved from volcanic stone but no one is sure when or how.

PATAGONIA
The coast of this southern region of Chile has many fjords—long narrow inlets with steep sides that were carved by the local glaciers.

TORRES DEL PAINE NATIONAL PARK
This beautiful park in the Chilean Andes has mountains, lakes, glaciers, and rivers that you can explore.

DIGITAL TRAVELER!
There is an island off the coast of Chile called Robinson Crusoe Island. Search the Internet to learn how the island got its name.

NATIONAL BIRD:
rufous hornero

NATIONAL FLOWER:
ceibo

NATIONAL MAMMAL:
guanaco

ARGENTINA
Land of Beef and COWBOYS

Argentina is the second largest country in South America. The dramatic landscape includes the Andes Mountains in the west, and the windswept plateaus of Patagonia to the south. You will see Inca ruins, volcanoes, and South America's highest mountain, Aconcagua. Argentina's name comes from *argentum*, Latin for silver, which the Spanish sought during the 1500s but did not find. Instead, the Pampas plains are great for crops and cattle: Argentinians eat more beef than anyone else.

ID CARD
COUNTRY FACTS

Size: 1,073,518 sq mi (2,780,400 sq km)
Population: 41,267,000
Capital: Buenos Aires
Official language: Spanish
Currency: Argentine peso
Highest point: Cerro Aconcagua, 22,831 ft (6,959 m)
Life expectancy: 76.0 years

5 COOL THINGS TO DO HERE

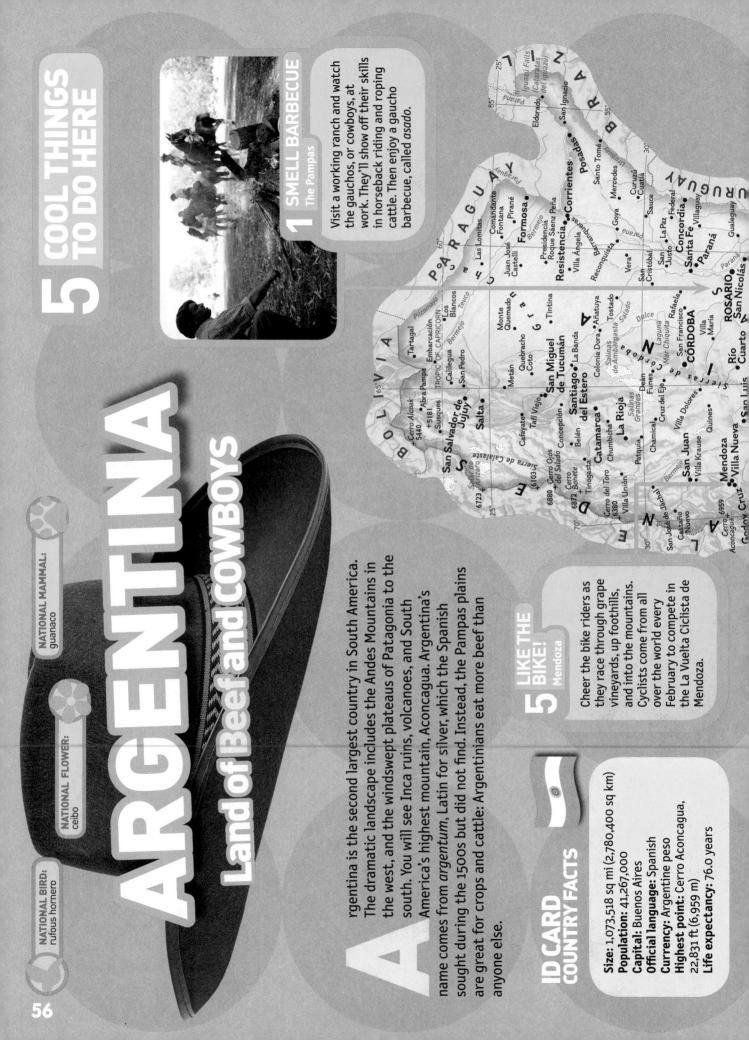

1 SMELL BARBECUE
The Pampas

Visit a working ranch and watch the gauchos, or cowboys, at work. They'll show off their skills in horseback riding and roping cattle. Then enjoy a gaucho barbecue, called *asado*.

5 LIKE THE BIKE!
Mendoza

Cheer the bike riders as they race through grape vineyards, up foothills, and into the mountains. Cyclists come from all over the world every February to compete in the La Vuelta Ciclista de Mendoza.

4 SAMPLE CHOCOLATE
San Carlos de Bariloche

Shop for chocolate in this city's candy stores. Famous for its chocolate, it hosts a Festival of Chocolate every Easter. Drool over the huge Easter egg or the giant chocolate bar that is almost 400 feet (122 m) long.

3 TAKE A TANGO LESSON
Buenos Aires

Dance the tango! This dance began in Buenos Aires more than 100 years ago, then spread to the rest of the world. It has changed over the years and today there are many different tango styles. Sometimes partners do very involved steps to very dramatic music.

2 GET A WHIFF OF SEALS
Mar del Plata

Hold your nose when you visit the colonies of seals or sea lions near this beach resort. The smell is strong, but the animals are fun to watch.

DIGITAL TRAVELER!
When you meet the gauchos, learn why they use lassos. Take a photo of a gaucho with a lasso or go online to see pictures of gauchos.

Globetrotter Attractions

IGUAZÚ FALLS
The horseshoe-shaped waterfall is really 275 separate ones. They are from 200 to 269 feet (61 to 82 m) high.

LOS GLACIARES NATIONAL PARK
In this park, huge masses of moving ice called glaciers drop icebergs into lakes.

TIERRA DEL FUEGO
This archipelago, or group of islands, is at the extreme southern end of South America. Here, summer days have 17 hours of sunlight.

1 LISTEN FOR GROWLS
Defensores del Chaco National Park

Ride through this national park with a guide. Stay inside the vehicle for safety's sake because jaguars and pumas roam the thorn forest. Look out for tapirs and colorful birds.

2 MILK A COW
Filadelfia

Visit a Mennonite dairy farm. Since they arrived in 1927, a group of Christians called Mennonites have kept their European culture, language, and religion. Their successful dairy farms provide more than half of Paraguay's dairy products.

Globetrotter Attractions

→ MUSEO DEL BARRO
The Museum of Clay in Asunción displays art made of clay and mud by pre-Columbian people and modern local artists.

→ YBYCUI NATIONAL PARK
This rain forest is a national park. It is a favorite place for camping and hiking.

→ ITAIPÚ DAM
This hydroelectric dam is on the border of Paraguay and Brazil and provides power to both countries. It took engineers almost 20 years to plan and build it, then move a river. Today, it is called a Wonder of the Modern World.

3 TREK ON THE TRAIN TRACKS
Asunción

Pretend you are riding on the oldest railroad in South America as you visit the Railroad Museum. Wander through restored railroad cars once used for sitting, eating, and sleeping. Check out photos of the trains and railroad tools.

Map labels:

MILES 0 50 100
KILOMETERS 0 50 100

BOLIVIA

Capitán Pablo Lagerenza

Defensores del Chaco National Park

General Eugenio A. Garay

Puerto Bahía Negra

Fortín Madrejón

Fuerte Olimpo

BRAZIL

Fortín Infante Rivarola

Paraguay

Chaco

Puerto La Esperanza

Mariscal Estigarribia

Campo Esperanza

Puerto La Victoria

Apa

Filadelfia

Estancía Rojas Silva

Puerto Pinasco

Fortín Mayor Alberto Gardel

Paraguay

ARGENTINA

Gran Chaco

TROPIC OF CAPRICORN

Fortín Presidente Ayala

Concepción

Horqueta

Belén

Pilcomayo

Fortín General Díaz

Monte Lindo

San Pedro

Rosario

Arroyos y Esteros

Villa Hayes

Asunción

San Lorenzo

Ypacaraí

Itá

Paraguarí

580

Ybycui National Park

Tebicuary

San Juan Bautista

Pilar

Paraguay

Paraná

NATIONAL BIRD:
bare-throated bellbird

NATIONAL FLOWER:
mburucuya

NATIONAL MAMMAL:
Pampas fox

PARAGUAY
A Country of CONTRAST

5 TRY AN ANIMAL MASK
Hernandarias

Discover Paraguay's cultural heritage at the Guaraní Museum. Examine the animal masks worn by the Guaraní people. Learn about their land, life, and language.

Paraguay is near the center of South America, with no sea-coast. Yet ships can travel on the Paraguay River right to the nation's capital, Asunción. The river splits Paraguay into two regions. To the east are ranchland, farms, and forest. To the west lies the hot, barren Chaco lowlands, with scrub and salt marshes. Don't miss the Itaipú Dam on the Paraná River, one of the world's biggest hydroelectric power plants.

ID CARD
COUNTRY FACTS

Size: 157,047 sq mi (406,752 sq km)
Population: 6,798,000
Capital: Asunción
Official languages: Spanish and Guaraní
Currency: guarani
Highest point: Cerro Pero, 2,762 ft (842 m)
Life expectancy: 72.0 years

4 ROCK ON AT RUINS
Trinidad

Wander in the ruins of these buildings that were part of a Christian religious community. Jesuits built them in the 1600s and 1700s to educate the local people. Made of stone, some are elaborately decorated.

DIGITAL TRAVELER!
Yerba mate is the national drink of Paraguay. Search the Internet to find out what yerba mate is and how the Paraguayans prepare it.

Map labels: Pedro Juan Caballero, Ypané, Ypé Jhú, Ygatimí, Paraná, Acaray, Represa de Itaipu, Coronel Oviedo, Hernandarias, Ciudad del Este, Itaipú Dam, Villarrica, Borja, Abaí, Caazapá, Trinidad, Encarnación, ARGENTINA, BRAZIL

NATIONAL BIRD:
southern lapwing

NATIONAL TREE:
árbol de Artigas

NATIONAL MAMMAL:
armadillo

URUGUAY
Fun to EXPLORE

B y South American standards, Uruguay is small and flat—the highest point is only 1,644 feet (513 m). It has a mild climate, and most of the country is grassland, good for ranching and farming. Along the Atlantic Ocean coast are superb beaches, popular with vacationers. Most Uruguayans live along the coastal plain, about a third of them (more than 1 million) in the nation's capital city Montevideo.

MONTEVIDEO PORT
The old buildings in Montevideo's Cuidad Vieja are near an important deep-water port. Shoppers explore its nearby traditional marketplace.

S.O.S. RESCATE DE FAUNA
At this animal rescue center in Piriápolis, volunteers help schoolchildren feed rescued penguins, turtles, and dolphins.

PUNTA DEL ESTE
Visitors flock to the beaches of this city during summer. One side of the peninsula has quiet river beaches, while on the other side the Atlantic Ocean beaches are windier and better for surfing.

5 COOL THINGS TO DO HERE

1 POWER UP
Salto

Take a tour of Salto Grande Dam and see the water-driven turbines that produce 65 percent of Uruguay's electricity.

2 RUN OFF TO A RODEO
Tacuarembó

Visit during Fiesta de la Patria Gaucha. Gauchos, or cowboys, from Uruguay and Argentina compete in rodeo events, and the winners parade through the streets.

B R A Z I L

A R G E N T I N A

Uruguay

Bella Unión

Artigas

Baltasar Brum

Salto

Rivera

Tranqueras

Tacuarembó

420

Cuchilla de Haedo

30°

30°

55°

0   25   50 KILOMETERS

0   25   50 MILES

ID CARD
COUNTRY FACTS

Size: 68,037 sq mi (176,215 sq km)
Population: 3,392,000
Capital: Montevideo
Official language: Spanish
Currency: Uruguayan peso
Highest point: Cerro Catedral, 1,686 ft (514 m)
Life expectancy: 76.0 years

5 WALK ON COBBLESTONES
Colonia del Sacramento

Explore Colonia's historic 17th-century buildings and cobblestone streets. The Portuguese built the oldest buildings, and the Spanish and Uruguayans built the newer ones.

4 HAVE A (SOCCER) BALL
Montevideo

Attend a soccer game at Estadio Centenario. This stadium was built in 1930 for soccer's first World Cup. Uruguay's national soccer team has rarely lost in this stadium.

3 CLIMB ON FINGERS
Playa Brava

Have your picture taken while standing on the giant hand that rises from the sands of Playa Brava. Examine the graffiti that covers it.

DIGITAL TRAVELER!
What kind of food will you eat in Uruguay? Do some online research and pick out some meals you'd like to try.

### Map labels

Mirim Lagoon
Melo
Vergara
Río Grande
Treinta y Tres
Lascano
Laguna Negra
Castillos
La Paloma
ATLANTIC OCEAN
Aiguá
Rocha
Maldonado
Piriápolis
Punta del Este
Minas
San Gregorio
Lake Rincón del Bonete
Paso de los Toros
Durazno
Yi
URUGUAY
Cuchilla
Santa Lucía
San José de Mayo
MONTEVIDEO
Río de la Plata
Colonia del Sacramento
Dolores
Mercedes
Algorta
Paysandú
Uruguay
ARGENTINA
José Batlle y Ordóñez

EUROPE

Mixed and Sweeping LANDSCAPES

Europe's 47 countries range in size from the largest in the world, Russia, to the smallest, Vatican City. This continent is linked to Asia, lies close to Africa, and has a central landmass that is bordered by islands. Europe's Alps Mountains are famous for hiking and winter sports. Its mighty rivers have created important transportation routes, and its sweeping plains provide fertile farmland.

Neuschwanstein Castle in Germany is one of the most popular of the many castles in Europe. Throughout history, European kings, queens, knights, and lords built strongholds or grand houses to secure their territories and house their large families and servants.

EUROPE

Bustling Cities and Serene COUNTRYSIDE

THE NORTH

This area includes Scandinavia (Norway, Sweden, Finland, and Denmark) and the Baltic countries (Estonia, Latvia, and Lithuania).

Europe is home to the 0° meridian—a line on maps from which all time zones are measured. To the left of Greenwich, England—the compass direction west— clocks are set back, to the right (that is east) clocks are set forward. Europe's history includes the Ancient Greek and Roman empires, the Medieval Age of knights, castles, kings, and queens, the Industrial Revolution, and world empires.

Globetrotter Attractions

BIG ISLANDS

Iceland, Ireland, and Britain are islands in northwest Europe.

AUNT BERTHA'S
TRAVEL TIPS

➤ **IT'S ALL FOREIGN**
Every country in Europe has its own language. Changing from one language to another may get your tongue in a twist!

➤ **GETTING AROUND**
Public transportation is BIG in Europe. Experience European life by traveling on its buses, trains, subways, canal boats, ferries, and cable cars.

➤ **TASTY MEALS**
Almost every European country has a favorite dish. Find out in which country you should try fish and chips, paella, croque-monsieur, pizza, bratwurst, smorgasbord, kebabs, borscht, strudel, and Chicken Kiev.

WESTERN EUROPE

The Iberian Peninsula (mainly Portugal and Spain), France, the Alps Mountain countries, and the lowlands of the north make up Western Europe.

### Map labels

ICELAND · Reykjavik · Faxaflói · Húnaflói · Faroe Islands Denmark · Shetland Islands · Orkney Is. · Outer Hebrides · Moray Firth · Ben Nevis 1344 · Glasgow · Edinburgh · Belfast · BRITISH ISLES · IRELAND · DUBLIN · IRISH SEA · UNITED KINGDOM · Great Britain · Manchester · BIRMINGHAM · Cardiff · CELTIC SEA · LONDON · English Channel · Channel Islands · Nantes · Bordeaux · BAY OF BISCAY · Vigo · Oporto · Bilbao · PORTUGAL · Lisbon · Tagus · IBERIAN PENINSULA · Valladolid · MADRID · SPAIN · BARCELONA · ANDORRA · PYRENEES · Toulouse · MARSEILLE · FRANCE · SWITZERLAND · Bern · Lyon · Strasbourg · MUNICH · Massif Central · Loire · Seine · Rhône · LIECHTENSTEIN · AUSTRIA · VIENNA · SLOVENIA · Ljubljana · Zagreb · CROATIA · Po · MILAN · MONACO · SAN MARINO · Corsica · ITALY · VATICAN CITY · ROME · Sardinia · NAPLES · ADRIATIC SEA · Sevilla · Córdoba · Valencia · Balearic Islands · Cádiz · Málaga · Granada · Cartagena · Strait of Gibraltar · GIBRALTAR United Kingdom · MOROCCO · AFRICA · MEDITERRANEAN · TYRRHENIAN SEA · Palermo · Sicily · Catania · MALTA · Valletta · ARCTIC CIRCLE · NORWEGIAN SEA · NORWAY · Oslo · Göteborg · NORTH SEA · Skagerrak · Kattegat · COPENHAGEN · DENMARK · HAMBURG · BERLIN · GERMANY · Elbe · Danube · NETHERLANDS · Amsterdam · BELGIUM · BRUSSELS · LUXEMBOURG · Luxembourg · PARIS · PRAGUE · CZECH REPUBLIC · SCANDINAVIA · ATLANTIC OCEAN

EUROPEAN RUSSIA

The Ural Mountains split Russia between two continents, Europe and Asia. This European section has Europe's longest river, highest mountain, and biggest city.

A commonly accepted division between Europe and Asia – here marked by a green line – is formed by the Ural Mountains, Ural River, Caspian Sea, Caucasus Mountains, and the Black Sea with its outlets, the Bosporus and Dardanelles.

200   400 MILES
200   400 KILOMETERS

CITYSCAPE
Paris

Major cities in Europe, such as Paris, France, are big, modern, traffic-filled, and bustling with people from all over the world speaking many different languages.

LEISURE TIME
Spain

People from across Europe spend their vacations on the coast of the Mediterranean Sea at resorts such as Salou.

EASTERN EUROPE

Once part of the Soviet Union, this region stretches from the Baltic Sea southeast to the Black Sea. All but Hungary and Moldova share Slavic languages, customs, and traditions.

SOUTHEAST EUROPE

The countries of this region are centered on the Balkan Mountains and lie between the Adriatic, Aegean, and Black seas.

### Map labels

NOVAYA ZEMLYA, KARA SEA, BARENTS SEA, Kolguyev Island, Kanin Peninsula, Chesha Bay, WHITE SEA, Dvina Bay, Onega Bay, Nordkapp, Varangerfjorden, Gora Narodnaya 1895, URAL MOUNTAINS

Murmansk, KOLA PENINSULA, Arkhangel'sk, Syktyvkar, Yekaterinburg, Kama Reservoir, Perm', Kirov, UFA, Magnitogorsk

SWEDEN, FINLAND, Österbotten, Västerbotten, GULF OF BOTHNIA, Petrozavodsk, Lake Onega, Lake Ladoga, Helsinki, Gulf of Finland, STOCKHOLM, ST. PETERSBURG, Tallinn, ESTONIA, BALTIC SEA, Gotland, Riga, LATVIA, Rybinsk Reservoir, Yaroslavl', Vladimir, Tver', MOSCOW, Volga, NIZHNIY NOVGOROD, KAZAN', Ul'yanovsk, SAMARA, Orenburg, KAZAKHSTAN

RUSSIA, EUROPEAN RUSSIA

LITHUANIA, Kaliningrad (Russia), Vilnius, MINSK, BELARUS, Smolensk, Tula, Orel, Homyel', Saransk, Penza, Saratov, Balakovo, Tambov, Voronezh, Don, Volgograd Reservoir, Ural

Gdańsk, Poznań, Łódź, WARSAW, POLAND, Kursk, Sumy, KHARKIV, VOLGOGRAD, Astrakhan', Caspian Depression, CASPIAN SEA, Volga

L'viv, UKRAINE, KIEV, Dnieper, DNIPROPETROVS'K, DONETS'K, ROSTOV NA DONU

SLOVAKIA, Bratislava, BUDAPEST, HUNGARY, MOLDOVA, Chişinău, ODESA, CRIMEA, Sea of Azov, Krasnodar, Stavropol', Groznyy

ROMANIA, SERBIA, BELGRADE, BUCHAREST, BALKAN PENINSULA, Danube, Sevastopol', BLACK SEA, Sochi, El'brus 5642, CAUCASUS MOUNTAINS, GEORGIA, AZERBAIJAN, ASIA

BOSNIA HERZEGOVINA, Sarajevo, MONTENEGRO, Podgorica, KOSOVO, Prishtina, SOFIA, BULGARIA, Skopje, MACEDONIA, Tirana, ALBANIA, Salonica, GREECE, Bosporus, Dardanelles, AEGEAN SEA, IONIAN SEA, Athens, Peloponnesus, Sea of Crete, Rhodes, Crete, CYPRUS, Nicosia, TURKEY

ICELAND
Land of Ice and FIRE

5 COOL THINGS TO DO HERE

Hike across Iceland to see snowfields, geysers, glaciers, and waterfalls. Smoking volcanoes sometimes erupt! People bathe in pools heated by hot springs, but it's freezing in winter, and there is little farming because of the poor soil and harsh weather. Most Icelanders work in industry, commerce, tourism, and fishing. Fleets from Iceland fish in the Atlantic Ocean. The capital Reykjavík is a modern city, with links to Iceland's Viking history.

1 GAZE AT A GEYSER
Selfoss

Watch the beautiful Skrokkur geyser erupt every four to eight minutes. A bubble of hot, often boiling, water is forced up from underground. When it becomes steam, stand back as the steam and boiling water can shoot 131 feet (40 m) into the air.

Globetrotter Attractions

EYJAFJALLAJÖKULL VOLCANO
Its eruption in 2010 stopped European air traffic. It is one of 11 active volcanoes in Iceland that have erupted since 1900.

BLUE LAGOON
People visit this spa because the mud and water from a nearby geothermal power plant are warm and rejuvenating.

GOLDEN FALLS
Gullfoss's water looks golden as it makes a steep drop over stone steps and then disappears into a crevice.

ID CARD
COUNTRY FACTS

Size: 39,768 sq mi (103,000 sq km)
Population: 323,000
Capital: Reykjavík
Official language: Icelandic
Currency: Icelandic krona
Highest point: Hvannadalshnúkur, 6,923 ft (2,110 m)
Life expectancy: 82.0 years

Map labels: GREENLAND · Látrar · Straumnes · Hesteyri · Ísafjarðardjúp · Bolungarvík · Hnífsdalur · Suðureyri · Flateyri · Ísafjörður · Súðavík · +957 · Thingeyri · Arnarfjörður · Lambadalsfjall · Patreksfjörður · Sveinseyri · Bíldudalur · Vatneyri · Saurbær · Bjargtangar · Flatey · Breiðafjörður · Grundarfjörður · Stykkishólmur · Hellissandur · Ólafsvík · +1446 · Búðir · Snæfellsjökull · Arnarstapi · Faxaflói · Sandgerði · Hafnir · Reykjanes

DIGITAL TRAVELER!
Iceland is a wonderland of geysers and glaciers. Start a travel journal. Look up the definitions of "geyser" and "glacier" and put them in your journal. Take or find photographs of geysers and glaciers, and use them as illustrations.

2 WATCH WHALES
Húsavík

Climb aboard a ship to go whale watching. More than 23 different types of whales live near Iceland. The best time to see them is from May to September.

3 SAIL BY PUFFINS
Lundey Island

Speed over to Lundey, or Puffin, Island. Spot large colonies of puffins living on the cliffs. Catch a glimpse of their colorful beaks as they fly or swim by.

EUROPE

### Map labels

Horn
STRAIT
22°
925 +
Drangajökull
Nordurfjördur
Kálfshamarsvík
Djúpavík
Gjögur
Arngerdareyri
Hólmavík
Drangsnes
Húnaflói
Saudárkrókur
Skagaströnd
Hóp
Blönduós
Króksfjardarnes
Hvammstangi
Bordeyri
ICELAND
Búdardalur
Arnarvatn
Blanda
Wammsfjördur
affjördur
Eiríksjökull + 1675
+ 1355
Deildartunga
Reykholt
Langjökull
Hvítárvatn
Borgarnes
Hvítá
Thórisjökull +
1340
Bláfell + 1204
+ 1053
Midsandur
Kaldakvísl
orgarfjördur
Akranes
Geysir □ Gullfoss
Thórisvatn
Hvalfjördur
Lundey
Reykjavík
Laugarvatn
Langisjór
ópavogur
Thingvallavatn
eflavík
Hafnarfjördur
Hvítá
818 Laki
Njardvik
Hveragerdi
Selfoss
Thjórsá
+ 1491
Blue Lagoon
Eyrarbakki
Grindavík
Stokkseyri
Hella
Kirkjubæjarklaustur
Thorlákshöfn
Hvolsvöllur
Hlídarendi
Eyjafjallajökull + 1666
Katla
Mýrdalsjökull
Skogafoss
Vestmannaeyjar
Heimaey
Vík
20°
Dyrhólaey
Surtsey
ATLANTIC OCEAN

Grímsey
18°
Rifstangi 16°
ARCTIC CIRCLE
Raufarhöfn
Öxarfjördur
Kópasker
Skinnastadir
Húsavík
Jökulsá á Fjöllum
Dettifoss
Langanes
Skálar
Thórshöfn
Bakkaflói
Bakkafjördur
Skeggjastadir 66°
Vopnafjördur
Vopnafjördur
Héradsflói 14°
Bakkagerdi
Siglufjördur
Haganesvík
Flatey
Skjálfandi
Ólafsfjördur
Hrísey
Dalvík
Grenivík
Hofsós
Hjalteyri
Hólar + 1382
Akureyri
Godafoss
Reykjahlíd
Mývatn
Skútustadir
+ 1222 Bláfell
Laxá
Skjálfandafljót
Skagafjördur
Héradsvötn
Tungnahryggsjökull
Sprengisandur
Trölladyngja + 1460
Odádahraun
Askja
Öskjuvatn
+ 1765
Hofsjökull
Kerlingarfjöll
+ 1477
+ 1540
Tungnafellsjökull
+ 2000
Bárdarbunga
+ Grímsvötn
Vatnajökull
Langisjór
Grænalón
Öræfajökull
Hvannadalshnúkur + 2119
Hof
Fagurhólsmýri
Ingólfshöfdi
Grímsstadir
Smjörfjöll + 1251
Egilsstadir
Lögurinn
Herdubreid + 1682
Snæfell + 1833
Djúpivogur
Vestdalseyri
Seydisfjördur
Neskaupstadur
Eskifjördur
Búdareyri
Gerpir
Búdir
Reydarfjördur
Kirkjuból
Breiddalsvík
Berufjördur
Papey
Hvalnes
Höfn
Lónsvík
Hornafjördur
Stokksnes
14°
64°
18°

NORWEGIAN SEA

4 CLIMB A WATERFALL TRAIL
Skogafoss

Hike this trail from the base to the top of Skogafoss waterfall, one of the highest in Iceland. Once there, you may see a rainbow! Locate even more waterfalls farther along the river.

5 RISE UP AND PIPE DOWN
Reykjavík

Ride the elevator up to the observation deck in the tower of Hallgrimskirkja Church. From there you can see the city of Reykjavík spread below. Listen to the huge pipe organ inside.

5 COOL THINGS TO DO HERE

1 STEP INTO LEGOLAND®
Billund

Explore buildings made of 60 million Lego® bricks. Ride a dragon roller coaster and Lego boats. Swim in Pirate Lagoon or go on an African safari. Watch an exciting 4-D movie with lights, smoke, wind, and even rain.

2 SKIP ACROSS SHIFTING SAND
Skagen

Place one foot in the North Sea and the other in the Baltic Sea. Stay out of the way of the wandering sand dunes for these hills of sand cover anything in their path. Every year they move about 49 feet (15 m).

3 WAKE UP ZOO ANIMALS
Odense

Feed the giraffe before the Odense Zoo opens. Then visit the manatees, zebras, and lions. At the end of the day, help clean the cages before the animals say good night.

4 MARCH BEHIND GUARDS
Copenhagen

Follow the Danish Royal Guard marching through Copenhagen's streets. They're protecting the royal family's winter home, Amalienborg Palace.

NATIONAL BIRD:
mute swan

NATIONAL FLOWER:
daisy

NATIONAL MAMMAL:
lion

DENMARK
Land of FAIRY TALES

Denmark has more than 400 islands, some close together, others way out in the Atlantic Ocean. Even farther west is the vast Arctic island of Greenland, a part of Denmark but self-governing. The largest area of mainland Denmark is Jutland, a peninsula jutting out from Germany. Denmark is famed for farming, fishing, and fairy tales. In Copenhagen, see a mermaid based on a fairy tale by a famous storyteller.

EUROPE

ID CARD
COUNTRY FACTS

Size: 16,638 sq mi (43,094 sq km)
Population: 5,613,000
Capital: Copenhagen
Official language: Danish
Currency: Danish krone
Highest point: Mollehoj/Ejer Bavnehoj, 561 ft (171 m)
Life expectancy: 80.0 years

Hammeren
Christiansø
Sandvig
Allinge
Hasle
Gudhjem
Rønne
162
Svaneke
BORNHOLM
Neksø
Dueodde
14°
I C
S E A

0   25   50 MILES
0   25   50 KILOMETERS

5 BE A VIKING FOR A DAY
Roskilde

Visit the 1,000-year-old Viking ships found in Roskilde Fjord. Learn about the Vikings, their culture, and how they made these ships. Dress in Viking costumes and climb onto the modern copies of a Viking cargo ship and a Viking warship.

Globetrotter Attractions

ROSENBORG CASTLE
Once a royal summer house, this castle in Copenhagen now houses Denmark's crown jewels.

TIVOLI GARDENS
Copenhagen's historic amusement park has something for everyone: exciting rides, music and dance concerts, plays and musicals, and fireworks at night.

FAROE ISLANDS
Halfway between Norway and Iceland, these Danish islands are remote and beautiful. People living there depend on fishing, sheep, and tourists for their livelihoods.

DIGITAL TRAVELER!
A Little Mermaid statue in Denmark celebrates Hans Christian Andersen, the Danish author of the story and other fairy tales. Go online to find out what other stories he wrote.

NATIONAL TREE:
Norway spruce

NATIONAL FLOWER:
saxifrage

NATIONAL MAMMAL:
lemming

NORWAY
Land of the MIDNIGHT SUN

Boats are the best way to explore Norway's long, rugged coast, with its fjords, cliffs, and waterfalls. This land of mountains and forests boasts Europe's largest glacier, but the climate is surprisingly mild until you head north inside the Arctic Circle, where the midsummer sun shines at midnight. You may even see polar bears there! Offshore oil and gas are major sources of income. In Oslo, the capital, Norway's maritime history is honored by statues, monuments, and ship museums.

Globetrotter Attractions

JOSTEDALSBREEN
This glacier is the largest in Europe. The moving mass of ice is about the size of Cape Cod. Hike on the surface of the glacier or raft in its melted waters.

PULPIT ROCK
The top of this rock has a view of Lysefjord and the cruise ships that sail in it.

GEIRANGERFJORD
Cruises and kayaks are a good way to see the waterfalls, mountains, farms, and villages in this protected area.

5 COOL THINGS TO DO HERE

1 LIGHT UP THE NIGHT SKY
Tromsø

Dress warm in this city known as the "Gateway to the Arctic." Try to catch a view of the northern lights—bands of color that dance across the sky. Video the show if you can.

ID CARD
COUNTRY FACTS

Size: 125,020 sq mi (323,802 sq km)
Population: 5,084,000
Capital: Oslo
Official language: Norwegian
Currency: Norwegian krone
Highest point: Galdhøpiggen, 8,100 ft (2,469 m)
Life expectancy: 81.0 years

DIGITAL TRAVELER!
The midnight sun occurs here at the start of the Arctic summer. The sky never gets completely dark at night at this time of year. Use the Internet to find photographs of the midnight sun.

2 GO ISLAND HOPPING
Geiranger

Take a journey on one of the ferry boats that regularly sail far north along the coast. The boats stop at islands and small ports deep within fjords.

3 RIDE A TRAIN
Bergen

Enjoy the scenery of the high plateau between Oslo and Bergen. Take a side trip on the steep Flåm Railway. Watch for tunnels, deep ravines, and beautiful waterfalls along the way.

4 TIME TRAVEL
Oslo

Wander through the historic buildings of the Norse Folk Museum. Experience what farm life was like in the past as you watch people reenact shearing sheep. Then ride in a horse-drawn carriage, or learn folk dancing.

5 SHOUT MUSH!
Ustaoset

Sit in a dogsled behind a team of hardy dogs. When you call "Mush!" the dogs will pull the sled through thick snow.

71

SWEDEN

A Natural WONDERLAND

NATIONAL BIRD:
blackbird

NATIONAL TREE:
birch

NATIONAL MAMMAL:
elk

Similar to its Scandinavian neighbors Norway and Finland, Sweden has forests, lakes, mountains, and more islands than you can see in one trip. Lake Vänern is Europe's third largest lake, and in the far north is Lapland, a winter wonderland where nomads herd reindeer. Sweden's biggest cities, including Malmö and the capital Stockholm, are toward the south of this Scandinavian country that extends north–south more than 950 miles (1,529 km).

DIGITAL TRAVELER!

In delis, cafés, and restaurants, look out for smorgasbord—a table of open-faced sandwiches topped with smoked fish, cheese, or sliced meat. Make a mouth-watering photo collection of all the varieties you see.

1 STAY IN AN ICE HOTEL
Jukkasjärvi

Sleep in a room and on a bed both built of ice. Every winter, artists use river water to create beautiful rooms, amazing statues, and even furniture. Then it all melts away when the temperatures rise in spring.

ID CARD
COUNTRY FACTS

Size: 173,859 sq mi (450,295 sq km)
Population: 9,592,000
Capital: Stockholm
Official language: Swedish
Currency: Swedish krona
Highest point: Kebnekaise, 6,909 ft (2,106 m)
Life expectancy: 82.0 years

5 COOL THINGS TO DO HERE

2 DON'T BREAK IT!
Småland

This region is called the Kingdom of Crystal because handblown glass has been made here since 1742. When you're visiting, watch the hot liquid sand as it's blown into a glass bowl. Then check out local crystalware.

4 CYCLE CITY STREETS
Malmö

Cycle along special paths made so cyclists can travel safely and quickly. This city has worked hard to increase cycle traffic and decrease car travel. Malmö specializes in modern city planning for a better environment.

3 TELL TIME, BIG TIME
Lund

Hear the organ music as it rolls from Lund's cathedral clock that was made in 1424. Twice a day, watch the six wooden figures move together with the music. This unique clock spent almost 90 years in storage before it was restored.

Globetrotter Attractions

FOTEVIKEN VIKING RESERVE

Medieval Viking reenactors show visitors how they do their daily chores at this living museum. They even built a medieval cog ship.

ØRESUND BRIDGE

This almost 10-mile (16-km) ride goes between Sweden and Denmark. It is part bridge, part tunnel, and carries both a road and railroad.

STOCKHOLM ARCHIPELAGO

Ferries regularly go from island to island. See as many of the 30,000 islands as you can!

5 HAVE A (GLASS) BALL
Stockholm

Ride SkyView's glass spheres to the top of this Stockholm arena called the Ericsson Globe. Then view the city from above. Watch a sports event or hear a concert in this, the world's largest spherical building.

5 COOL THINGS TO DO HERE

1 ESCAPE TO A LAKESIDE CABIN
Suonenjoki

Sleep peacefully in a lakeside cabin, but have fun at the town's Strawberry Carnival. Find a lake district town that has a sauna. Enjoy the heat in a steamy, smoky room with friends. When it gets too hot, jump into the lake or roll in the snow.

2 RIDE A REINDEER SLEIGH
Lapland

Ride in a sleigh pulled by a reindeer and glide through the quiet, snowy forest. Watch for more reindeer out in the wild or feeding by the road.

3 GLOW IN THE DARK
Kokkola

Stare up at Tankar Lighthouse. This classic lighthouse, built in 1889, still guides ships along the Kokkola coast. Walk along the island's nature trail and visit its wooden church.

4 STEP INTO A STORYBOOK
Naantali

Admire Finnish children's storybook characters as they come to life. Wander around with them and join in the park's activities. Watch a play, do a craft activity, or walk through the witch's labyrinth.

5 SPEND A DAY WITH A KNIGHT
Savonlinna

Explore Olavinlinna Castle, a fortress built in the late 1500s. Hear the legend about the black ram that saved the castle by scaring away the enemy.

### Map labels

NORWAY
SWEDEN
RUSSIA
LAPLAND
FINLAND

Haltiatunturi +1328
+ Paistunturit 646
Kaamanen
Inari
Ivalo
Enontekiö
Pokka
Sirkka
Muonio
Kittilä
Kolari
Sodankylä
Savukoski
Torvinen
Meltaus
Kemijärvi
Kemijärvi
483 + Maanselkä
ARCTIC CIRCLE
Oulanka N.P.
Rovaniemi
Posio
Tornio
Kuivaniemi
Kuusamo
Taivalkoski
Kemi
Ii
Haukipudas
Pudasjärvi
Hailuoto
Oulu
Liminka
Oulujoki
Hyrynsalmi
Raahe
Paltamo
Pyhäjoki
Paavola
Oulujärvi
Kuhmo
Oulainen
Kajaani
Ylivieska
Ridge
Kokkola (Karleby)
Iisalmi
Nurmes
Nykarleby
Jakobstad (Pietarsaari)
Lapinlahti
Lieksa
Pihtipudas
Pielinen
Vaasa
Kuopio
251
Seinäjoki
Lapua
Outokumpu
Kurikka
Häapamäki
Kaskinen
Suonenjoki
Pieksämäki
Joensuu
Jalasjärvi
Pyhäselkä
Virrat
Varkaus
Näsijärvi
Jyväskylä
Haukivesi
Mäntyluoto
Jämsä
Joutsa
Mikkeli
Savonlinna
Pori
Nokia
Saimaa
Parikkala
Rauma
Tampere
Heinola
Imatra
Uusikaupunki
Hämeenlinna
Lahti
Lappeenranta
Naantali
Forssa
Kouvola
Hamina
Turku (Åbo)
Salo
Porvoo (Borgå)
Kotka
Åland Islands
Espoo (Esbo)
Helsinki (Helsingfors)
(Hanko) Hangö
Gulf of Finland

0   100   200 MILES
0   100   200 KILOMETERS

74

FINLAND

Land of Thousands of LAKES

In this country of many lakes, forests cover 70 percent of the land, and lumber is a major product. The larger lakes, and Finland's main cities, are in the south. In the far north is Lapland, a region shared with Sweden and Norway where, in summer, daylight lasts almost 24 hours. Winters are cold and dark, yet the spring thaw sees the return of migrant birds and forest floors covered in flowers such as lily of the valley.

ID CARD
COUNTRY FACTS

Size: 130,558 sq mi (338,145 sq km)
Population: 5,440,000
Capital: Helsinki
Official language: Finnish
Currency: euro
Highest point: Haltiatunturi, 4,357 ft (1,328 m)
Life expectancy: 81.0 years

Globetrotter Attractions

OULANKA NATIONAL PARK
This park is close to the Arctic Circle and borders a Russian national park. Plants and animals not usually found this far north live here because of the park's fertile soil and mild climate.

FORTRESS OF SUOMENLINNA
This Helsinki historic fort covers three islands. People live behind its thick, strong walls, as they have for hundreds of years.

ÅLAND ISLANDS
People live on 60 of the 6,500 or more islands in this area. Many are just small rocky spots. Here, people have their own government and speak Swedish, not Finnish.

DIGITAL TRAVELER!
The cloudberry is called Finland's Favorite Fruit. Search the Internet and find three facts about the cloudberry. For example, where does it grow? When does it grow? What can you do with it?

	NATIONAL BIRD:	NATIONAL FLOWER:	NATIONAL MAMMAL:
ESTONIA	barnswallow	cornflower	roe deer
LATVIA	white wagtail	oxeye daisy	Latvian horse
LITHUANIA	white stork	rue	wolf

BALTIC COUNTRIES
A Crossroads of CULTURES

Passenger ships sail into Tallinn, Estonia, every day. Tourists can't wait to explore the three Baltic countries of Estonia, Latvia, and Lithuania. They are a crossroads of cultures: German, Polish, Swedish, Danish, and Russian. From cobblestone streets in Tallinn, through the forests of Latvia, to the beaches of the Courland Spit in Lithuania, the sights are as varied as the people, who share a love of music, dance, and song.

5 COOL THINGS TO DO HERE

1 CHUG AND WHISTLE
Ventspils

Ride the old steam train at the Seaside Open-Air Museum in Ventspils, Latvia. Then visit the nearby House of Crafts and 13th-century castle.

2 STALK STORKS
Šiauliai

Search for some of the 13,000 pairs of white storks in Lithuania. These birds, found throughout the Baltic countries, are Lithuania's national bird.

DIGITAL TRAVELER!
Estonia has more than 1,500 islands. Surf the Internet to find the names of the five largest of these islands.

3 SADDLE UP
Kuremäe

Ride across meadows and dunes and through forests on horses rented from local stables. In the stables, you can get friendly with ponies.

EUROPE

4 WALK THE WALL
Tallinn

Wander along the medieval wall around Tallinn, Estonia. Examine the watchtowers and walls of the Old Town area.

Globetrotter Attractions

TALLINN OLD TOWN
Step back in time. Visit Tallinn, Estonia's capital, with its medieval markets and castle-like buildings.

POKAIŅI FOREST
This forest in Latvia is magical with its steep hills, deep valleys, and mysterious stone rivers.

COURLAND SPIT
Trees take the brunt of the winds blowing over these sand dunes that Russia and Lithuania share, stopping them from shifting.

ID CARD COUNTRY FACTS

ESTONIA
Population: 1,283,000
Capital: Tallinn

LATVIA
Population: 2,018,000
Capital: Riga

LITHUANIA
Population: 2,956,000
Capital: Vilnius

5 JOIN THE SHOW
Riga

Sing and dance with tens of thousands of children from all over Latvia as they perform at the Latvian School Youth Song and Dance Festival each year.

GERMANY

Peaks, Rivers, and FORESTS

Much is modern in Germany, the powerhouse of Western Europe's industry and economy. Germany was divided after World War II, when fighting devastated historic cities such as Berlin, Munich, and Hamburg. East and West Germany were reunited in 1990. Remains of the old Germany can still be seen today, with fairy-tale castles beside the Rhine River, and handsome churches and palaces. Nature is unspoiled in the beautiful Black Forest and in the Bavarian Alps.

3 EAT A FRANKFURTER
Frankfurt am Main

Chomp down on a hot dog in the city where they were first made. Buy one with sauerkraut or potato salad, as many are served on a plate, without a bun.

ID CARD
COUNTRY FACTS

Size: 137,846 sq mi (357,022 sq km)
Population: 80,572,000
Capital: Berlin
Official language: German
Currency: euro
Highest point: Zugspitze, 9,721 ft (2,963 m)
Life expectancy: 80.0 years

4 WAKE UP TO SLEEPING BEAUTY
Füssen

Tour the magnificent Neuschwanstein Castle. King Ludwig II planned it as an escape from his stressful duties. It is located in a beautiful mountain setting.

Map of Germany showing cities including Hamburg, Bremen, Hannover, Cologne, Frankfurt am Main, Stuttgart, and surrounding countries Denmark, Netherlands, Belgium, Luxembourg, France, and Switzerland.

5 COOL THINGS TO DO HERE

1 ENTER A LILLIPUTIAN WORLD
Hamburg

Wander through Miniatur Wunderland, the world's largest model train exhibit. See planes land at the model airport and visit many miniature countries.

DIGITAL TRAVELER!
The long, low dog called a dachshund was first bred in Germany in the 1600s. Its name translates in English to "badger dog." Go online to see pictures and find fun facts about these interesting dogs.

2 DRIVE ON AN AUTOBAHN
Würzburg

Ride along these superhighways. The Autobahns form the oldest and fourth longest network of highways in the world. They were started in the 1930s.

5 STRING ALONG WITH ACTORS
Munich

Applaud the marionettes that perform in this historic theater. Watch a fairy tale, opera, or new play. For almost 100 years, these handcarved wooden puppets have been used to act out stories.

Globetrotter Attractions

BAVARIAN ALPS
This section of the Central Alps is along the German–Austrian border. Zugspitze, in Germany, is its highest peak.

BLACK FOREST
Mountain peaks, rivers, and forests fill this region. Tourists walk trails, ski, bike, or enjoy the region's natural spas.

BRANDENBURG GATE
After World War II, this gate in Berlin was a symbol of a divided Germany. It was reopened in 1989 before East Germany and West Germany reunited.

EUROPE

79

AUSTRIA

Mountains and MUSIC

Austria, the heart of an empire from the 1400s to 1900s, is a land of mountains and music. It borders seven countries, including Germany, with whom Austrians share a language. Most of Austria is mountainous, with high pastures, valleys, rivers, and several lakes. Winter sports attract many visitors, while others come to enjoy Salzburg's Mozart festival, and to admire palaces and gardens in Austria's capital city, Vienna.

1 GET A TASTE OF SALT
Hallstatt

Ride a train up a nearby mountain to the world's oldest salt mine. Enter the mountain and see the underground lake. Learn about the "white gold" first mined here 5,000 years ago.

5 ENTER A CRYSTAL WORLD
Innsbruck

Discover 14 underground Chambers of Wonder at Swarovski Crystal Worlds. Watch enormous rooms made of illuminated crystal glass change colors and see crystal animals sparkle.

Map labels: GERMANY, Lake Constance, Bregenz, Lustenau, Dornbirn, Hohenems, Feldkirch, Bludenz, SWITZERLAND, LIECHTENSTEIN, Zugspitze 2963, Innsbruck, Landeck, Hall, Schwaz, Brenner Pass, Wildspitze 3772, Grossvenediger 3674, Hohe Tauern, Hohe Tauern National Park, Glossglockner 3798, ITALY, Kufstein, Eisriesenwelt, Saalfelden, Obervellach, Lienz, Oberdrauburg, Salzburg, Hallein, Inn, ALPS

ID CARD
COUNTRY FACTS

Size: 32,382 sq mi (83,871 sq km)
Population: 8,511,000
Capital: Vienna
Official language: German
Currency: euro
Highest point: Grossglockner, 12,461 ft (3,798 m)
Life expectancy: 81.0 years

5 COOL THINGS TO DO HERE

2 WATCH DANCING HORSES
Vienna

Watch the famed Lipizzaner horses "dance on the air" at Vienna's Spanish Riding School. Attend their morning exercises as they practice their routines to music, or check out a performance. Admire the skill of the riders and horses.

DIGITAL TRAVELER!
The Vienna Boys' Choir is one of the oldest boys' choirs in the world. For nearly 500 years it has been a popular symbol of Austria. Go on the Internet and listen to them sing.

3 TUNE IN TO CLASSICAL MUSIC
Salzburg

Walk through the rooms in two houses: One where Mozart was born and another where he later lived. Learn about Mozart's family and his early music.

EUROPE

Globetrotter Attractions

EISRIESENWELT ICE CAVES
Called the World of the Ice Giants, these ice caves are the largest in the world. Ice formations change every year, but the average temperature remains below zero Fahrenheit (-18°C).

SCHÖNBRUNN PALACE
This huge palace in Vienna was the home of the Habsburg emperors in the 1700s and 1800s. Its magnificent gardens include a large maze and a labyrinth filled with secrets and games.

HOHE TAUERN NATIONAL PARK
This is the largest nature reserve in the Alps and includes the country's highest peak. Discover glaciers, rock faces, lakes, waterfalls, and pastures.

4 HEAR A DRAGON TALE
Klagenfurt

Take a picture of the statue of the Lindwurm, or winged dragon, in the middle of town. Listen to the legend about a few brave men who killed the dragon to protect the local people and then founded Klagenfurt.

	NATIONAL BIRD:	NATIONAL FLOWER:	NATIONAL MAMMAL:
CZECH REPUBLIC	eagle	*Tilia cordata*	lion
HUNGARY	turul	tulip	vizsla dog
SLOVAKIA	great bustard	rose	Eurasian lynx

CZECH REPUBLIC, HUNGARY, AND SLOVAKIA

Lands of Mountains and Mighty RIVERS

C all the Czech Republic "Czechia" and you'll sound local. Czechs and Slovaks in neighboring Slovakia share a Slavic culture, and were one country (Czechoslovakia) until 1993. The Czech capital Prague and Hungary's capital Budapest are two of Central Europe's most historic cities. In Hungary, visit Lake Balaton, the largest lake in the region and a major tourist destination. Much of the region has a continental climate similar to that of the U.S. Midwest.

Globetrotter Attractions

KRKONOŠE MOUNTAINS
This range of mountains is on the border between the Czech Republic and Poland. The range's highest mountain, Mount Snezka, is in the Czech Republic.

KARST CAVES
Belowground, ice caves cover a huge area of the Slovakian region of Slovak Karst. Above-ground, sinkholes, springs, caves, and abysses cover the ground. Careful where you walk!

LAKE BALATON
This lake is known as the "Hungarian Sea." At its many resorts, you can swim, sail, and do other water sports. The surrounding countryside is ideal for cycling and hiking.

DIGITAL TRAVELER!
The capital cities of two of these countries lie on the same major river. What is the name of that river? What two other European capitals also lie on that river? Look at maps and tourist sites on the Internet to find out.

5 COOL THINGS TO DO HERE

1 CHECK THE TIME
Prague

Marvel at the performance put on by the Prague Astronomical Clock. Watch statues move on this 600-year-old clock. Check the day, week, month, and year.

2 EXPLORE LABYRINTHS AND MAZES
Lucen

Walk the ten mazes and labyrinths at Castle Lucen in the Czech Republic. Find your way between trees, lights, or rocks.

3 RAMBLE THROUGH A CASTLE
Spišské Podhradie

Investigate Spis Castle in Slovakia. Although in ruins, this 13th-century castle still commands the region from atop a hill. It is one of the largest castles in Eastern Europe.

5 GO SPLASH IN A SPA
Budapest

Soak in hot, healing waters at spas found throughout Budapest, Hungary. Enjoy the city's baths just as the Roman soldiers did 2,000 years ago.

4 COUNT YOUR CHANGE
Kremnica

Visit the Kremnica Mint to see how coins are made. This high-technology factory in Slovakia has been making coins and medals since 1328. Today, it makes Slovakia's euro coins and remembrance coins for many European countries.

ID CARD COUNTRY FACTS

CZECH REPUBLIC
Population: 10,521,000
Capital: Prague

HUNGARY
Population: 9,892,000
Capital: Budapest

SLOVAKIA
Population: 5,414,000
Capital: Bratislava

5 COOL THINGS TO DO HERE

1 EXPLORE A GIANT CATHEDRAL
Gdańsk

Feel tiny when you stand in St. Mary's Church, the largest historic brick church in the world. Search its many chapels for tombstones and artwork.

2 MEET WITH A KNIGHT
Malbork

Walk across the drawbridge to meet a knight who's the guide for Malbork Castle. Then start your tour through the largest brick castle in the world and see the armor of many knights.

5 BLAST FROM THE PAST
Cracow

Climb to the top of the highest tower of St. Mary's Basilica from where a trumpeter plays an alarm signal every hour. For 600 years, the trumpet has blared from this location as people look up from Cracow's Grand Square 250 feet (76 m) below.

DIGITAL TRAVELER!
The polka is fast-moving music and a dance where the couple moves quickly across the floor. It is popular in Poland. Use the Internet to listen to polka music and to see the dance.

**Map labels:**

BALTIC SEA

Słowiński National Park • Mierzeja Helska • Puck • Rumia • Gulf of Gdańsk • KALININGRAD OBLAST Russia • LITHUANIA

Ustka • Darłowo • Słupsk • Lębork • Wejherowo • Gdynia • Sopot • Gdańsk • Pieniężno • Bartoszyce • Węgorzewo • Suwałki

Sławno • Pruszcz Gdański • EAST RUSSIA • Dobre Miasto • Mrągowo • Ełk • Augustów

Kołobrzeg • Koszalin • Bytów • Kościerzyna • Tczew • Elbląg • Giżycko • Jezioro Śniardwy

Świnoujście • Białogard • POMERANIA • Biały Bór • Starogard Gdański • Malbork • Zalewo • Olsztyn • Pisz • Grajewo

Police • Zalew Szczeciński • Świdwin • 203 • Szczecinek • Chojnice • Kwidzyn • Ostróda • Szczytno • Myszyniec • Sokółka • Białystok

Szczecin • Goleniów • Czaplinek • Złotów • Świecie • Warlubie • Iława • Nidzica • Narew • Łomża • Gródek

Gryfino • Stargard Szczeciński • Wałcz • Jastrowie • Grudziądz • Chełmno • Działdowo • Ostrołęka • Zambrów • Bielsk Podlaski

Chojna • Barlinek • Piła • Nakło nad Notecią • Bydgoszcz • Brodnica • Mława • +171 • Ostrów Mazowiecka • Białowieża Forest

Dębno • Człopa • Wieleń • Chodzież • Toruń • Rypin • Ciechanów • Sierpc • Bug • BELARUS

Gorzów Wielkopolski • Noteć • Wągrowiec • Inowrocław • Lipno • POLAND • Płońsk • Wyszków • Sokołów Podlaski • Siemiatycze

Kostrzyn • Warta • Oborniki • Włocławek • Płock • Legionowo

Międzyrzecz • Pniewy • Poznań • Gniezno • Vistula (Wisła) • Pruszków • WARSAW (WARSZAWA) • Siedlce

Świebodzin • Września • Konin • Izbica • Sochaczew • Piaseczno • Seroczyn • Biała Podlaska

Gubin • Oder (Odra) • Krosno Odrzańskie • Śrem • Koło • Kutno • Łowicz • Łuków

Zielona Góra • Jarocin • Turek • Zgierz • Skierniewice • Grójec • Trojanów • Radzyń Podlaski

Nowa Sól • Żary • Leszno • Krotoszyn • Sieradz • Pabianice • Łódź • Rawa Mazowiecka • Puławy • Lubartów • Włodawa

Żagań • Głogów • Rawicz • Ostrów Wielkopolski • Piotrków Trybunalski • Tomaszów Mazowiecki • Radom • Wieprz • Lublin

Bolesławiec • +188 • Lubin • Trzebnica • Kępno • Bełchatów • Końskie • Skarżysko-Kamienna • Kazimierz Dolny • Świdnik • Chełm

Legnica • Brzeg Dolny • Oleśnica • Wieluń • Radomsko • Góry Świętokrzyskie • Ostrowiec Świętokrzyski • Annopol • Kraśnik • Hrubieszów

Zgorzelec • Wałbrzych • SILESIA • Wrocław • +272 • Warta • Kielce • Sandomierz • Janów Lubelski • Zamość

Jelenia Góra • Świdnica • Oława • Brzeg • Kluczbork • Radomsko • Tarnobrzeg • Stalowa Wola • Biłgoraj • Tomaszów Lubelski

Bielawa • Dzierżoniów • Opole • Lubliniec • Jędrzejów • Mielec • Hrebenne

Kłodzko • Nysa • Kędzierzyn-Koźle • Bytom • Zawiercie • Dąbrowa Górnicza • Dębica • Rzeszów • Jarosław

Prudnik • Gliwice • Zabrze • Katowice • Dąbrowa Górnicza • Cracow (Kraków) • GALICIA • Tarnów • Przemyśl

Rybnik • Tychy • Sosnowiec • Jaworzno • Tarnowska • Skawina • Bochnia • Jasło • Krosno • Sanok

Jastrzębie-Zdrój • Cieszyn • Bielsko-Biała • Andrychów • Nowy Sącz • Gorlice • Dukla • 846 • UKRAINE

Czarny Dunajec • Zakopane • Rysy +2499 • Tatry • CARPATHIAN MOUNTAINS • SLOVAKIA

CZECH REPUBLIC • SUDETEN • GERMANY • Neisse (Nysa Łużycka)

50 100 MILES
50 100 KILOMETERS

POLAND

Between Sea and MOUNTAINS

NATIONAL BIRD: white stork

NATIONAL FLOWER: red poppy

NATIONAL MAMMAL: European bison

Poland has a Baltic Sea coast and long land borders. Between the Vistula River and the Carpathian Mountains are flat plains and farmland. There are both historic and modern cities, as well as factories and coal mines. Old castles and churches are sprinkled across Poland, and you can see wild bison roaming in an ancient forest. Discover Warsaw, the port of Gdańsk, and the beautiful historic city of Cracow.

3 LEARN ABOUT A WARTIME CAMP
Lublin

Learn about Majdanek, a concentration camp the Nazis built during World War II. Read about the experiences of former prisoners and guards.

4 GO RIPPLE-RAFTING
Czarny Dunajec

Raft down the Dunajec River in Pieniny National Park. Drift through a beautiful river gorge and between huge rock cliffs.

Globetrotter Attractions

BIALOWIEZA FOREST

The Bialowieza (Białowieża) in northeastern Poland is the last primeval forest in Europe's lowlands. The trees and wildlife are left to grow and die without people's interference. In the 1950s, the European bison was reintroduced to the forest.

GRAND SQUARE, CRACOW

Cracow has one of the largest city squares in Europe. In the Grand Square, people have gathered to shop and celebrate since the 1200s.

SLOWINSKI SAND DUNES

As these sand dunes in Slowinski (Słowiński) National Park in northern Poland shift in the wind, they uncover fossilized tree stumps.

ID CARD
COUNTRY FACTS

Size: 120,728 sq mi (312,685 sq km)
Population: 38,517,000
Capital: Warsaw
Official language: Polish
Currency: zloty
Highest point: Rysy, 8,199 ft (2,499 m)
Life expectancy: 77.0 years

EASTERN EUROPE
From Mountains to the BLACK SEA

BELARUS	NATIONAL BIRD:	NATIONAL FLOWER:	NATIONAL MAMMAL:
BELARUS	white stork	wild blue flax	European bison
MOLDOVA	black stork	greater pasque	aurochs
UKRAINE	nightingale	viburnum	particolored bat

astern Europe is home to two of the continent's largest countries: Ukraine and Belarus. Until the 1990s they and smaller neighbor Moldova were part of the Soviet Union. Belarus is a land full of forests and plains. Ukraine and Moldova have coasts on the Black Sea, into which the Dnieper River flows. Major cities are Kiev (Ukraine), Minsk (Belarus), and Chişinău (Moldova). Ukraine's plains, called steppes, are fertile croplands.

Globetrotter Attractions

BRASLAU LAKES NATIONAL PARK
More than 30 lakes, big and small, are in this park in northwest Belarus, near its border with Lithuania. Search the lakes and pine forests to see elks, lynx, and bears.

BLACK SEA COAST
The Crimea, in the Ukraine, lies along the Black Sea. It is famous for its resorts where you can bathe in mud pools.

CARPATHIAN MOUNTAINS
The Ukraine shares these low mountains with other countries in the region. Tourists hike and bike by forests, farms, and vast meadows.

5 COOL THINGS TO DO HERE

1 SPOT THE PUCK
Minsk

Visit the two ice hockey arenas in Minsk, Belarus, host to the 2014 World Hockey Championships. Cheer the home team, the Minsk Dynamo.

2 WATCH KNIGHTS COMPETE
Mir Castle

Wander through Mir Castle and its park. Then join the festival of medieval culture and wear a knight's armor. Watch archery contests and listen to medieval music, too.

3 MEET METAL MA
Kiev

Stare up at the 204-foot (62-m)-high titanium metal "Mother of the Fatherland" statue opened in 1981. The statue honors Russia and its allies' victory in World War II.

5 EXAMINE RUSSIA'S NAVAL FLEET
Sevastopol'

Cruise this Ukrainian port and see Russia's Black Sea fleet. Under the Soviet Union the town was closed to visitors, but today tourists can take a harbor tour.

4 ENTER A CAVE MONASTERY
Orhei

Search this cave monastery in wild and remote Moldova. Look down from the cave to follow the paths that lead to other medieval caves.

ID CARD COUNTRY FACTS

BELARUS
Population: 9,463,000
Capital: Minsk

MOLDOVA
Population: 4,114,000
Capital: Chişinău

UKRAINE
Population: 45,513,000
Capital: Kiev

DIGITAL TRAVELER!

In 1991, these countries became independent when the Soviet Union broke apart. Make a set of photographs of statues and memorials that celebrate each country's independence.

PORTUGAL

Cork, Cliffs, and Castles

Portugal is Spain's neighbor on the Iberian Peninsula. Along its border with Spain are old fortresses, but the capital Lisbon is a seaport located along the Tagus River. Reminders of a long history linked to sea-voyaging are present all over this city. Western beaches are favored by surfers riding Atlantic waves, and sun-seekers flock to the Algarve region in the south. Portugal is also famous for cork tree bark, which is harvested to make wine stoppers.

ID CARD
COUNTRY FACTS

Size: 35,556 sq mi (92,090 sq km)
Population: 10,460,000
Capital: Lisbon
Official language: Portuguese
Currency: euro
Highest point: Ponta do Pico (Azores), 7,713 ft (2,351 m)
Life expectancy: 80.0 years

DIGITAL TRAVELER!

Look online for images of two or three Portuguese castles and see if you can re-create them out of craft supplies, or even sand when you're at the beach!

5 COOL THINGS TO DO HERE

1 STOMP GRAPES
Douro Valley

Participate in the grape harvest in this winemaking region. Pick the grapes and then press the juice out of them by stomping on the fruit in huge vats. Learn how this grape juice is made into a world-famous wine.

Map labels: Douro, Brangan. Miranda do Douro, +1320, Vinhais, Macedo de Cavaleiros, Mirandela, Mogadouro, Torre de Moncorvo, Chaves, Murça, Vila Real, Douro, Montemuro +1381, Castro Daire, Pinhel, Almeida, Vilar Formoso, Guarda, Viseu, Serra do Caramulo, Águeda, Aveiro, Ílhavo, Ovar, Esmoriz, São João da Madeira, Pedroso, Gondomar, Douro Valley, Oporto (Porto), Santo Tirso, Fate, Amarante, Guimarães, Braga, Barcelos, Esposende, Póvoa de Varzim, Vila do Conde, Matosinhos, Vila Nova de Gaia, Foz do Rio Vouga, Viana do Castelo, Caminha, Valença, Ponte de Lima, Peneda-Gerês National Park, +1416, +1381, Lima, Minho, Montalegre, Boticas, Tâmega, Foz do Douro

Scale: 0 25 50 MILES, 0 25 50 KILOMETERS, 42°, 8°, N

Globetrotter Attractions

TORRE DE BELEM
Belem Tower is in the middle of the Tagus River in Lisbon. This fortress was built in the early 16th century.

RUÍNAS DE CONIMBRIGA
These ruins are of a Roman town built about A.D. 100. Walk among the well-preserved walls and across the brightly colored mosaic floors.

PENEDA-GERÊS NATIONAL PARK
This park is along Portugal's northern border with Spain. Hikers may find ancient stone tombs or see the wild ponies that live there.

2 STAND AMONG EXPLORERS
Lisbon

Explore the Monument to the Discoveries. It honors the explorers who left from Lisbon harbor 500 years ago to explore Asia and the Americas. Enjoy the scenic view of the harbor from its roof.

3 TEAR OFF A STRIP
Alentejo

Watch as cork, the bark of the cork oak tree, is stripped from the tree trunks. Cork oak trees live for up to 250 years and the cork is harvested every 9 to 12 years.

4 CRUISE BETWEEN CLIFFS
Lagos

Glide across the water on a fishing boat. Weave between rocks, into caves, and along the water at the bottom of rocky cliffs. Then find a quiet beach where you can relax and paddle in the water.

5 BUILD A SAND CASTLE
Pêra

Create a sand sculpture at Fiesa, a huge sand sculpture festival held each spring. Experts spend weeks making enormous sculptures.

EUROPE

SPAIN AND ANDORRA

Beauty, Buildings, and BULLFIGHTS

Landscape and climate in Spain range from the rugged, temperate north to the soft, sandy beaches and sunny Mediterranean weather of the south. There are beautiful cities such as Barcelona, Granada, Toledo, and Madrid with its famous bullfighting ring. Away from the cities, there are traditional and modern farms, as well as tourist hotels and beaches. In the Pyrenees Mountains and landlocked between Spain and France is the tiny country of Andorra.

ID CARD COUNTRY FACTS

SPAIN
Population: 46,647,000
Capital: Madrid

ANDORRA
Population: 74,000
Capital: Andorra la Vella

DIGITAL TRAVELER!
Some famous artists came from Spain, such as Pablo Picasso, Salvador Dalí, and Joan Miró. Search the Internet for some paintings by each artist. Pick your favorites and print them out.

3 TASTE TAPAS
Donostia-San Sebastián

Eat these tasty snacks after a day of sightseeing. Although found all over Spain, tapas in northern Spain are often made with seafood, such as spider crabs or anchovy.

4 DANCE THE FLAMENCO
Madrid

Learn the movements of the flamenco dance set to guitar music and songs that began in Spain. The dance and music express deep emotions and the dance moves are flowing and colorful.

5 COOL THINGS TO DO HERE

1 FOLLOW THE SCALLOP SHELLS
Santiago de Compostela

Hike the Way of St. James, a route in northern Spain that Christian pilgrims have walked for more than 1,000 years. It leads to the tomb of St. James at the cathedral in Santiago de Compostela. Scallop shells are used to mark the route.

2 UNLOCK THE SECRET OF THE SEVEN KEYS
Andorra la Vella

Visit the Casa de la Vall in Andorra la Vella. Built as a home, in 1702 it became Andorra's parliament building. Learn how The Cupboard of the Seven Keys got its name.

EUROPE

5 SEARCH AN UNFINISHED CHURCH
Barcelona

This church has been under construction since 1883. Analyze how Antoni Gaudí, the main architect of La Sagrada Familia Church, used nature and religious symbols in his design.

Globetrotter Attractions

THE PYRENEES
These mountains are famous for hiking and winter skiing. They are home to Andorra.

THE ALHAMBRA
It took the Moors more than 130 years to complete this palace and fortress in Granada, Spain. You can visit it today.

CITY OF ARTS AND SCIENCES
Valencia, Spain, drained a river to build this art and science complex. It houses Europe's largest aquarium, a planetarium, and movie theater that shows 3-D movies.

FRANCE AND MONACO

Cafés, Castles, and Coastal BEAUTY

The landscape of France, Western Europe's largest country, is as varied as its food. It has the snowy Alps and Pyrenees, the rugged Atlantic coast and sunny Riviera, ancient volcanoes, and extensive forests. There are beautiful chateaus and vineyards beside the rivers Rhone, Loire, and Seine. Monaco, the world's second-smallest country, is nestled on the French Riviera. It has an area of less than one square mile (2.6 sq km).

1 REFLECT ON ROYALS
Versailles

Pretend to be King Louis XIV as you walk through his Versailles Palace. Kings and queens lived here for more than 100 years. This Hall of Mirrors served as a magnificent setting for lavish parties.

DIGITAL TRAVELER!
Claude Monet was one of the first Impressionist painters. He was born in Paris and painted French scenes from his home in Giverny. Use the Internet to see examples of his Impressionist art.

ID CARD COUNTRY FACTS

FRANCE
Population: 68,851,000
Capital: Paris

MONACO
Population: 37,000
Capital: Monaco

0   50   100 MILES
0 50 100 KILOMETERS

5 COOL THINGS TO DO HERE

2 TASTE CHEESE
Camembert Village

Visit a cheese shop and try some Camembert, one of more than 300 kinds of cheese made in France. Stop by the onetime home of Marie Harel, the woman who is believed to have created this creamy treat in 1791.

3 GET A BIRD'S-EYE VIEW
Paris

Climb 704 steps, then take an elevator to the top of the Eiffel Tower. On a clear day, you'll have a panoramic view of the city. The tower is 984 feet (300 m) tall. When it was built in 1889, it was the tallest structure in the world.

4 HEAR THE VA, VA, VROOM
Monte Carlo

Grab a place in the stands to watch the annual Formula One Grand Prix race. Race-car drivers from all over the world zip through Monaco's narrow, curvy streets at speeds of more than 100 mph (161 kph).

5 RIDE THROUGH THE MOUNTAINTOPS
Chamonix-Mont Blanc

Travel across the French Alps in cable cars that transport you from peak to peak. Be sure to take a hike at one of the stops. You can travel in these cable cars all the way to Italy!

Same scale as main map

ITALY

Bastia

Monte Cinto 2710

Ajaccio

CORSICA (CORSE) France

1340

See p. 9 for location

Globetrotter Attractions

THE LOUVRE MUSEUM
This museum in Paris is one of the largest and most visited in the world. You can see famous art, such as Leonardo Da Vinci's painting, the "Mona Lisa," and the Greek statue, "Venus de Milo."

THE PRINCE'S PALACE
This grand castle on the cliffs of Monaco has been in Monaco's royal family since 1341.

CHATEAU VILLANDRY
Many awesome castles dot the Loire Valley. This one has spectacular gardens with a labyrinth, or maze.

93

1 SAIL BY SEALS
Donegal Bay

Take a boat ride on the bay. You'll pass quaint villages, the Bluestack Mountains, and Seal Island where about 200 seals live.

2 EXPLORE A CAVE
Doolin

Put on a hard hat and follow your guide as you descend 120 steps underground into Doolin Cave. The cave was carved by a stream that still flows through it. See the longest free-hanging stalactite found in the Northern Hemisphere. It is 23 feet (7 m) in length.

3 SEARCH A CYBER CASTLE
Limerick

Explore King John's castle. Inside, computer touch screens and 3-D models have been installed to show how the castle survived attacks and warfare.

**Map labels:**

UNITED KINGDOM
NORTHERN IRELAND
ULSTER
CONNAUGHT
LEINSTER
MUNSTER
IRELAND

Tory Island, Clonmany, Carndonagh, Inishowen Head, Bloody Foreland, Creeslough, Lough Foyle, Aran Island (Arranmore), Leifear (Lifford), gebarra Bay, Stranorlar, Dawros Head, Glenties, Rossan Point, Ardara, Dunkineely, Malin More, Kilcar, Donegal Bay, Ballyshannon, Grange, Belderg, Sligo Bay, Killala Bay, Sligeach (Sligo), Belmullet, Easky, Swanlinbar, Monaghan, Cora Droma Rúisc, Bangor Erris, Ballina, Ballysadare, Lough Conn, Swinford, Boyle, Carrick on Shannon (Cora Droma Rúisc), Ballyhaise, Nephin 807, An Cabhán (Cavan), Dundalk (Dún Dealgan), Achill Island, Ballycroy, Caisleán an Bharraigh (Castlebar), Mohill, An Longfort (Longford), Ceanannus (Kells), Ardee, Dundalk B., Clare Island, Ballycroy, Westport, Castlerea, Castlepollard, Athboy, An Uaimh (Navan), Newgrange, Drogheda (Droichead Átha), Skerries, Louisburgh, Clew Bay, Claremorris, Ros Comáin (Roscommon), Lough Ree, Castlepollard, Hill of Tara 155, Lambay Island, Killary Harbour, Lough Mask, Ballinrobe, An Muileann gCearr (Mullingar), Boyne, Inishbofin, Inishshark, Clifden, Tuam, Athlone, Kilbeggan, Kilcock, Liffey, DUBLIN (BAILE ÁTH CLIATH), Maam Cross, Mount Bellew, Eyrecourt, GRAND CANAL, Tullamore, Dún Laoghaire (Dunleary), Bray, Roundstone, Lough Corrib, Spiddal, Gaillimh (Galway), Delgany, Gorumna I., Kinvarra, Port Laoise, Nore, Cill Mhantáin (Wicklow), Inishmore, Aran Islands, Galway Bay, Slieve Aughty Mts., Lough Derg, Roscrea 481, Abbeyleix, Carlow, Woodenbridge, Doolin, Ennistymon, Scarriff, Nenagh, Muine Bheag, Wicklow Mts. 607, Gorey, Cliffs of Moher, Ennis, Devilsbit Mt., Thurles, Kilkenny, Bunclody (Bun Clóidi), Cahore Point, Milltown Malbay, Killadysert, Shannon, Cappamore, Cashel, Callan, Barrow, Enniscorthy, Kilkee, Limerick (Luimneach), Tipperary, Clonmel, New Ross, Castlebridge, Loop Head, River Shannon, Kerry Head, Listowel, Ráth Luirc (Charleville), Galty Mts., Port Láirge (Waterford), Wexford, Wexford, Tralee Bay, Abbeyfeale, Newcastle West, Mitchelstown, Suir, Arthurstown, Rosslare Harbour, Castlegregory, Tralee (Trá Lí), Newmarket, Fermoy, Cappoquin, Saltee Islands, Ceann Trá (Ventry), An Daingean (Dingle), Killorglin, Mallow, Youghal, Dingle Bay, Carrantuohill 1041, Blackwater, Valentia Island, Macgillycuddy's Reeks, Ballyvourney, Blarney, Cork (Corcaigh), Kenmare, Macroom, Inishannon, Cork H., Caha Mts., Dunmanway, Oysterhaven, Dursey Island, Glengarriff, Bantry Bay, Rosscarbery, Schull, Castletownshend, Dunmanus Bay, ngwater Bay, Mizen Head, Sherkin Clear I.

0 25 50 MILES
0 25 50 KILOMETERS

NATIONAL BIRD:
lapwing

NATIONAL FLOWER:
shamrock

NATIONAL MAMMAL:
Irish wolfhound

IRELAND
The Emerald ISLE

Globetrotter Attractions

The island of Ireland is shared by the Republic of Ireland and Northern Ireland (part of the United Kingdom). It's known as the Emerald Isle for its lush green pastures. You'll find lakes, called loughs, and mountains dotted with ancient carved stones and prehistoric monuments. There are farms, villages, and Ireland's lively capital city, Dublin. The River Shannon is the longest in the British Isles, at 240 miles (386 km) long.

CLIFFS OF MOHER
Sheer cliffs rise 702 feet (214 m) above the churning ocean. A walking trail attracts thousands of tourists.

ROCK OF CASHEL
With its medieval towers and Gothic cathedral, this is one of Ireland's most famous castles. Kings ruled from here for more than 1,000 years. It is located in Tipperary.

NEWGRANGE
These amazingly built tombs and mounds are older than the Egyptian pyramids. The Newgrange temple mound was built more than 5,000 years ago.

5 DANCE A JIG
Dublin

First you'll hear fiddles and tin whistles playing lively tunes. Then you'll hear the stamping feet. Join in one of the many Irish dances, including step dancing and the jig. Dance events are held throughout the year at halls, pubs, and clubs.

ID CARD
COUNTRY FACTS

Size: 27,132 sq mi (70,273 sq km)
Population: 4,598,000
Capital: Dublin
Official languages: English and Irish
Currency: euro
Highest point: Carrauntoohil, 3,406 ft (1,038 m)
Life expectancy: 81.0 years

4 KISS THE BLARNEY STONE
Blarney

Stretch out on the ground and kiss this famous stone (part of Blarney Castle). If you do, legend says that you will always know the right thing to say and have the power to persuade with words.

DIGITAL TRAVELER!
Be on the lookout for a Claddagh ring. It will show two hands clasped around a heart with a crown above it. Surf the Internet to find out what the symbol means and how it became popular.

95

UNITED KINGDOM

Four Nations, One Country

NATIONAL BIRD:
robin

NATIONAL TREE:
oak

NATIONAL MAMMAL:
bulldog

F our nations make up the United Kingdom: England, Scotland, Wales, and Northern Ireland. Each is represented in the U.K.'s flag and coat-of-arms. The main island, Great Britain, has Scotland's highlands in the north, and more mountains to the west in Wales, while England has lowlands, rolling hills, and a great city, London. Northern Ireland shares a border with Ireland, which is also known as Eire.

Globetrotter Attractions

THE CAIRNGORMS

These eastern Highlands of Scotland are great places for hill walking in summer and skiing in winter.

WHITE CLIFFS OF DOVER

White chalk and black flint give the cliffs their unusual color. They stand at England's closest point to the European mainland.

STONEHENGE

Scientists wonder how in prehistoric times these huge stones near Salisbury, England, were placed in a circle and how some of the huge stones were brought from South Wales, more than 100 miles (160 km) away.

5 COOL THINGS TO DO HERE

5 LISTEN TO BAGPIPES
Edinburgh

See the proud Scottish bagpipe players march by in their plaid kilts at any big event. The sound of bagpipes is like no other instrument. It is the national instrument of Scotland.

4 BE ON YOUR GUARD
London

At 11:00 in the morning, join the crowd to watch one set of guards replace another in front of Buckingham Palace. The Queen of England lives inside the palace. It has 775 rooms and 240 bedrooms.

3 WALK WITH WITCHES
Cornwall

Watch fishing boats come and go through the Cornwall coves, or little inlets. Walk through the narrow village streets. Visit the Witchcraft Museum in Boscastle and the Museum of Smuggling and Fishing in Polperro.

DIGITAL TRAVELER!

Wizards, dragons, monsters, fantasy and mythical characters are popular in the U.K. Do an Internet search to find out about Nessie, Hogwarts, Y Ddraig Goch, Bilbo Baggins, and Puck.

1 VISIT GIANT'S LAND
Giant's Causeway

Stand on the cliffs and check out multi-sided stone pillars that look like giant's boots and a giant's harp. Legends say they were once steps for a giant crossing from Northern Ireland to Scotland.

2 ROOT FOR A RUGBY TEAM
Cardiff

Sit in Millennium Stadium and cheer for a Welsh rugby team as it plays an international match. The stadium is the largest in Wales with 74,500 seats.

ID CARD
COUNTRY FACTS

Size: 94,058 sq mi (243,610 sq km)
Population: 64,092,000
Capital: London
Official language: English
Currency: British pound
Highest point: Ben Nevis, 4,409 ft (1,344 m)
Life expectancy: 82.0 years

EUROPE

97

LOW COUNTRIES

The Heart of EUROPE

	NATIONAL BIRD:	NATIONAL FLOWER:	NATIONAL MAMMAL:
BELGIUM	common kestrel	brome	lion
LUXEMBOURG	goldcrest	rose	lion
NETHERLANDS	common spoonbill	tulip	lion

5 COOL THINGS TO DO HERE

Belgium, the Netherlands, and Luxembourg are known as the Low Countries because they are flat and often below sea level. The Netherlands is famed for flowers, canals, windmills, and farmland. Part of it—known as Holland—is home to Amsterdam with its art museums, and the massive port of Rotterdam. The cities of The Hague (Netherlands), Brussels (Belgium), and Luxembourg (Luxembourg) are the heart of the European Union.

1 CRUISE THE CANALS
Amsterdam

Ride a glass-topped boat through the canals to see some unique sites including Anne Frank's house and the Westerkerk church, with the highest church tower in Amsterdam.

2 STROLL BY WINDMILLS
Zaanstad

Soak up history in the historic village of Zaanse Schans. You'll see windmills, which were once used to power machines that made paint, ground seeds into oil, and sawed lumber.

DIGITAL TRAVELER!
Pierre Marcolini is a world-famous chocolate maker. One of his famous chocolate shops is in Brussels. Use an electronic device to find the location of this shop.

3 SOAR ABOVE THE CITY
Vianden

Sit back and let the chairlift take you 1,476 feet (450 m) above the city. Get a bird's-eye view of city sights and this famous castle where the Counts of Vianden lived 600 years ago.

4 TASTE CHOCOLATE
Brussels

Find out why Belgium is famous for its chocolates. There are excellent chocolate makers in every city. Be sure to try a praline, a chocolate-covered treat with nuts or sweet cream inside.

5 TOUR A TINY COUNTRY
The Hague

Feel like a giant at Madurodam, a miniature model of Holland complete with its canals, buildings, and parks.

Globetrotter Attractions

KEUKENHOF FLOWER GARDEN
More than 7 million tulips, daffodils, and hyacinths fill this garden in Lisse, Netherlands, near Amsterdam, forming what looks like a sea of colors.

GRAND PLACE
The center square in Brussels, Belgium, is surrounded by elegant buildings and statues.

BOCK CASEMATES
This fortress protected Luxembourg against military attacks for many centuries. Its underground passageways had kitchens, horse stables, and sleeping quarters for 1,200 soldiers.

ID CARD COUNTRY FACTS

BELGIUM
Population: 11,164,000
Capital: Brussels

LUXEMBOURG
Population: 543,000
Capital: Luxembourg

NETHERLANDS
Population: 16,798,000
Capital: Amsterdam

Map labels: Venlo, Eindhoven, Valkenswaard, Weert, Roermond, Sittard, Brunssum, Maastricht, Vaals, Eupen, Saint Vith, Houffalize, Vianden, Junglinster, Luxembourg, Arlon, Tintigny, Bastogne, LUXEMBOURG, Bouillon, Neufchâteau, Paliseul, Wellin, Rochefort, Dinant, Philippeville, Châtelet, Charleroi, Gembloux, Namur, Durbuy, Huy, Seraing, Liège, Tongeren, Genk, Bilzen, St. Truiden, Aarschot, Leopoldsburg, Geel, Mol, Turnhout, Essen, Ekeren, Antwerp (Antwerpen), Lier, Mechelen, BRUSSELS (BRUXELLES), Halle, Soignies, Gosselies, Thuin, Ath, Ninove, Aalst, Gent, Temse, Hulst, Terneuzen, Zelzate, Maldegem, Ronse, Kortrijk, Tournai, Torhout, Roeselare, Ieper, Brugge, Blankenberge, Oostende, Knokke-Heist, Adinkerke, BELGIUM, FLANDERS, FRANCE, Meuse, Maas, Schelde, Westerschelde

99

SWITZERLAND AND LIECHTENSTEIN

Fresh Air and Fun in the MOUNTAINS

In Switzerland, road and rail tunnels speed visitors on scenic tours through the Alps. Cattle graze in high pastures, tourists flock to ski slopes and to the Cresta Run ice race track in St. Moritz, and experienced climbers tackle peaks such as the Matterhorn. Enjoy a boat trip on Lake Geneva, and explore the cities of Bern, Lausanne, Zurich, and Geneva. Little Liechtenstein is famous for castles, winter sports, and the production of false teeth and textiles.

5 VISIT FRANKENSTEIN'S TOWN
Lake Geneva

Stand by the lake where the author Mary Shelley dreamed up the famous monster story, *Frankenstein*. You can swim in and go boating on the lake.

4 EAT CHEESE RACLETTE
Gruyères

Share a traditional Swiss *raclette* with your friends. This delicious treat is made with melted cheese and whatever additions you like, such as meats, vegetables, or potatoes. The word raclette comes from the French word meaning "to scrape." After you make the raclette, you must scrape the melted cheese onto your plate.

DIGITAL TRAVELER!
Switzerland is famous for a special kind of singing called yodeling. Surf the Internet to find a recording of a yodeler. After you listen, try it yourself!

Map labels: GE, Rhine (Rhein), FRANCE, Basel, Liestal, Porrentruy, Laufen, Delémont, Olten, Tavannes, Solothurn, Zofingen, La Chaux-de-Fonds, Biel, Bieler See, Le Locle, Lyss, Burgdorf, Neuchâtel, Bern, Fleurier, Lake of Neuchâtel, Estavayer-le-Lac, SWITZ, Brienzersee, Orbe, Yverdon, Thun, Vallorbe, Echallens, Bulle, Spiez, Grindelwal, Thunersee, Morges, Lausanne, Gruyères, Jungfrau 4158, Aletsch Glacier, Nyon, Lake Geneva (Lac Léman), Montreux, Kandersteg, Alps, Rhône, Bernese, Aigle, Bri, Geneva (Genève), Monthey, Sion, Sierre, Visp, Champéry, FRANCE, Martigny, Pennine Alps, Zermatt, Monte Rosa 4634, Matterhorn 4478, ITALY

5 COOL THINGS TO DO HERE

1 SOAR WITH THE EAGLES
Malbun

Ride a chairlift above the treetops where falcons, hawks, and eagles soar. As you walk down the mountain, you'll see the big birds up close.

ID CARD COUNTRY FACTS

SWITZERLAND
Population: 8,078,000
Capital: Bern

LIECHTENSTEIN
Population: 37,000
Capital: Vaduz

Globetrotter Attractions

THE MATTERHORN
The 14,692-foot (4,478-m)-tall mountain peak in the Swiss Alps is capped with snow all year long. It overlooks the town of Zermatt.

ALETSCH GLACIER
The longest glacier in Europe has an area of 66 square miles (171 sq km). The central part is 15 miles (24 km) long and 1 mile (1.6 km) wide.

VADUZ CASTLE
The Prince of Liechtenstein lives here. Parts of the castle were built in the 1100s, and the royal family has lived here since 1938.

3 WATCH A CLOCK COME ALIVE
Bern

See the Zytglogge zodiacal clock and then climb the spiral staircase to see the insides of the instrument. The clock has chimed every hour since 1405.

2 TAKE A TRAIN TO A PEAK
Jungfrau

Climb the Alps to Jungfrau peak on a train that chugs through tunnels and climbs to 13,642 feet (4,158 m)—to the highest train station in Europe.

ITALY, MALTA, SAN MARINO, AND VATICAN CITY

Lands Steeped in HISTORY

I taly is a boot-shaped country with sea on three sides and the Alps and Dolomite mountains to the north. The islands of Sardinia and Sicily are part of Italy. Italy is famous for food, Roman history, and art and architecture. The tiny country of San Marino is nestled in the Apennine Mountains and Vatican City, the world's smallest country, lies within the city of Rome. South across the Mediterranean is Malta, a rocky island of ancient temples and rich military history.

5 COOL THINGS TO DO HERE

1 RIDE A GONDOLA
Venice

Listen to the gondoliers sing as they paddle tourists through the Grand Canal. For centuries, this was the main way people traveled through Venice. The canal, a 2.4-mile (3.9-km)-long water highway, makes a big "S" curve through the city.

2 EXPLORE A LOST CITY
Pompeii

Learn how Mount Vesuvius erupted in the year A.D.79 and buried the city of Pompeii under 60 feet (18 m) of ash. Now that it has been uncovered, visitors can look at the ruins.

3 STAND BY FOR A BLAST
Mount Etna

You can reach the top of Europe's highest and most active volcano by walking, cable car, or a sturdy tour car. Smoke often belches from its craters.

4 ENTER A PREHISTORIC WORLD
Paola

Learn about the ancient underground burial site known as Hal Saflieni Hypogeum. It dates back some 4,600 years. To protect the site, only 50 visitors per hour are allowed inside.

5 MAKE A WISH
Rome

Toss a coin in the Trevi Fountain and make a wish. Then snap a photo of the statues of Neptune's chariot and sea horses.

DIGITAL TRAVELER!
Tourists love to see the Leaning Tower of Pisa in Italy. Search the Internet for a photo of this landmark. Then find out why it is leaning.

Globetrotter Attractions

→ **VATICAN PALACE**
These buildings contain the Pope's apartment, priceless museums, and the Sistine Chapel, which has Michelangelo's Renaissance paintings on its ceiling.

→ **BLUE GROTTO**
Brilliant blue water flows through these caverns on the south coast of the island of Malta.

→ **ROMAN COLOSSEUM**
Nearly 2,000 years ago, Roman gladiators faced off in this sports arena, and crowds cheered them on.

5 COOL THINGS TO DO HERE

1 PICK RASPBERRIES
Brankovina

Taste sweet berries right from the bushes that grow on sunny slopes all over Serbia. Serbia is one of the world's top exporters of raspberries.

2 DUCK UNDER BRIDGES
Ljubljanica River

Cruise under several bridges. One is called Cobblers' Bridge because shoemakers set up their shops there by the river. In the 1200s, the bridge was built of wood. Later it was replaced with iron and concrete for strength.

5 VISIT A MOSQUE
Sarajevo

Enter one of the big mosques in the city to admire the colorful decorations on the walls and inside of the dome. Then listen for the call to prayer given from the minaret.

4 GAZE AT A GOAT HEAD
Krujë

Check out the museum inside this castle. You will learn how the mountaintop castle and its soldiers protected Albania from Ottoman Empire troops in 1450, 1466, and 1467. See a replica of the goat-head-topped helmet worn by the Albanian hero Gjergj Kastrioti Skenderbeu.

WESTERN BALKAN COUNTRIES

A Region of Diverse Beauty

Except for Albania, the countries in the western Balkans were part of former Yugoslavia, which broke up between 1991 and the early 2000s. Serbia has the most people, while Montenegro has fewer than a million citizens. Croatia's sunny Adriatic coast and Roman Empire ruins delight tourists. Throughout Bosnia and Herzegovina, Kosovo, Macedonia, and Slovenia, farmers grow and harvest crops among landscapes of mountains, canyons, forests, and ancient fortresses.

Globetrotter Attractions

OLD BRIDGE OF MOSTAR
The original bridge in Bosnia and Herzegovina was built in 1566 and destroyed by war in 1993. It was rebuilt and reopened in 2004.

RUINS AT BUTRINT
Through history, this has been the site of a Greek colony and city of the Roman Empire. Today visitors to Albania can still see 23 rows of seats of the ancient amphitheater.

DALMATIAN COAST
Croatia's beautiful jagged coast draws people from all over the world for diving, boating, swimming, and enjoying sunny beaches.

3 SHOP IN A BAZAAR
Skopje

Follow the winding cobblestone streets of this immense marketplace. You will pass shops and stalls that sell everything from pastries to jewelry.

ID CARD COUNTRY FACTS

EUROPE

ALBANIA
Population: 2,774,000
Capital: Tirana

BOSNIA AND HERZEGOVINA
Population: 3,834,000
Capital: Sarajevo

CROATIA
Population: 4,253,000
Capital: Zagreb

KOSOVO
Population: 1,824,000
Capital: Prishtina

MACEDONIA
Population: 2,066,000
Capital: Skopje

MONTENEGRO
Population: 623,000
Capital: Podgorica

SERBIA
Population: 7,136,000
Capital: Belgrade

SLOVENIA
Population: 2,060,000
Capital: Ljubljana

DIGITAL TRAVELER!
Choose one of the Western Balkan countries. Then pick a time of year that you would like to travel there. Use your digital device to find out the typical weather at that time of year.

EASTERN BALKAN COUNTRIES

Two Friendly NEIGHBORS

The Danube River winds east between the Transylvanian Alps and the Balkan Mountains, separating Bulgaria and Romania. Both countries have coasts on the Black Sea. Bulgaria welcomes tourists to sunny beaches, and grows roses for perfumes, while Romania has gold mines and oil fields. Transylvania, land of the fabled Dracula, has ancient buildings that are left from the time when Romania was part of the Roman Empire.

5 COOL THINGS TO DO HERE

1 CHECK OUT PAINTED CHURCHES
Bucovina

"Read" Bible stories that were painted on church walls in the 15th and 16th centuries. Long ago, artists painted scenes to tell religious stories to the villagers.

5 VISIT DRACULA'S HOMETOWN
Sighişoara

Stroll through a medieval town and stop by the home of Vlad Dracula, a Transylvanian ruler from 1456 to 1462. He inspired the author Bram Stoker to create in 1897 the Gothic horror vampire character, Count Dracula.

Globetrotter Attractions

BELOGRADCHIK ROCKS
Each stone in this stretch of rock in Bulgaria has a name and legend attached to it. They include the Dinosaur, the Lion, the Bear, and the Stone of Thought.

PALACE OF PARLIAMENT
The capital headquarters in Bucharest is the heaviest building in the world. It has more than 2.5 billion tons (2.27 billion tonnes) of steel, bronze, marble, crystal, and wood.

SEVEN RILA LAKES
These lakes in Bulgaria's Rila National Park are named for their shapes, such as Eye Lake, Kidney Lake, and Fish Lake.

DIGITAL TRAVELER!
The Cyrillic alphabet was developed in Bulgaria in the 10th century. Use the Internet to track down the Bulgarian Cyrillic alphabet. Compare it to the alphabet you use.

4 DISCOVER A BLAST FROM THE PAST
Orsova

Snap a photo of an ancient king, Decebalus, rising from the Danube River. From 1994 to 2004 artists, rock climbers, and construction crews carved the limestone statue with dynamite, air hammers, and pickaxes.

3 EAT YOGHURT, LIVE LONG!
Sofia

At a local café, try true Bulgarian yoghurt made with milk taken from sheep raised on herb-rich pastures, giving it a unique flavor. Bulgarians believe that eating the healthy yoghurt is the reason why the country has the most people living to be more than 100 years old.

2 WATCH A LIGHT SHOW
Veliko Türnovo

As the sun goes down at the Tsarevets Palace complex, spread out a blanket and enjoy the show of laser lights, music, and church bells. The show celebrates key moments in Bulgaria's history.

ID CARD COUNTRY FACTS

BULGARIA
Population: 7,260,000
Capital: Sofia

ROMANIA
Population: 21,269,000
Capital: Bucharest

GREECE AND CYPRUS

Islands in SEAS

	NATIONAL BIRD:	NATIONAL FLOWER:	NATIONAL MAMMAL:
GREECE	little owl	laurel	dolphin
CYPRUS	rock dove	Cyprus cyclamen	Cypriot mouflon sheep

In Greece, ancient and modern buildings are side by side. The ancient Greek civilization arose 2,500 years ago, and spread across the Mediterranean, Ionian, and Aegean seas. Tourists come to admire the Parthenon in Athens, Mt. Olympus, and other historic sites. They also take boat trips around the beautiful Greek islands, including Corfu, Rhodes, and Crete with its Minoan palaces. Farther east is Cyprus, an island with sunny beaches and breathtaking hiking trails.

ID CARD COUNTRY FACTS

CYPRUS
Population: 1,135,000
Capital: Nicosia

GREECE
Population: 11,081,000
Capital: Athens

Globetrotter Attractions

THE HARBOR OF RHODES
Boats pass between two bronze deer perched high above the harbor. It is believed that a huge statue called the Colossus of Rhodes stood over the harbor until an earthquake toppled it in 226 B.C.

THE PARTHENON
With its famous columns, the remains of this temple in Athens have been standing for more than 2,400 years.

TOMBS OF THE KINGS
Near Paphos harbor in Cyprus, this underground burial chamber is more than 2,000 years old.

5 RIDE A GLASS-BOTTOMED BOAT
Corfu

Float by coastal caves and look for beautiful fish and other sea creatures. Some boats have glass bottoms, which can give you a closer look.

5 COOL THINGS TO DO HERE

1 GO FUTURISTIC IN THE PAST
Athens

Peer into the past at the new Acropolis Museum. Displays are built around the ruins of the ancient Acropolis buildings. Go inside to learn about the past in the virtual reality theater, wearing 3-D glasses.

2 RIDE A DONKEY
Oía

To get up to this village, you can take a donkey ride on the narrow, hilly path. Oía is known for white-washed houses and blue-domed churches.

3 FOLLOW BABY TURTLES
Kyrenia

Watch newly hatched turtles creep into the ocean. Mother turtles visit north Cyprus beaches in May to dig holes and hide their eggs. The eggs hatch in July.

See p. 9 for location

4 HIKE THROUGH A GORGE
Samariá

Walk through Samariá Gorge on Crete, Europe's longest gorge. A river carved this route between the mountains thousands of years ago.

DIGITAL TRAVELER!
Can you guess what is in the special Greek dish called spanokopita? Search the Internet for a recipe to learn the ingredients. Decide if it is a food you'd like to try.

5 COOL THINGS TO DO HERE

1 COUNT MAMMOTHS AND MORE
St. Petersburg

Find out how many different kinds of animals you see at the Zoological Museum. There are 5,000 animals on display. See one of the world's few stuffed mammoths along with the skeleton of a blue whale, penguins, and polar bears.

2 KEEP YOUR EYES PEELED FOR ONIONS
Moscow

Take pictures of the swirling domes, squares, and triangles as you walk among the buildings in Red Square. The domes of St. Basil's Cathedral look like colorful flames.

3 CAN IT GET ANY SMALLER?
Kursk

Pull apart the two halves of this doll and find smaller dolls inside. You can find these painted dolls depicting all kinds of characters, from grandmothers to politicians.

4 SKI LIKE A CHAMPION
Sochi

See the ski slopes and skating rinks of the 2014 Olympic Winter Games. The winter sports include bobsleighing, ski jumping, speed skating, and curling.

NATIONAL BIRD:
tundra swan

NATIONAL FLOWER:
chamomile

NATIONAL MAMMAL:
bear

EUROPE

EUROPEAN RUSSIA

In the World's Largest COUNTRY

Russia stretches from Europe across Asia to the Pacific. The Ural Mountains form a natural boundary between Asia and European Russia, which has 80 percent of Russia's people, most of its farms and industries, and the biggest cities—Moscow, St. Petersburg, and Volgograd. Explore the Volga and Don Rivers, and gaze across the Black Sea and the Caspian Sea, a giant lake. Head north to see the polar snows of the Arctic Ocean.

ID CARD
COUNTRY FACTS

Size: 6,601,668 sq mi (17,098,242 sq km)*
Population: 143,493,000*
Capital: Moscow
Official language: Russian
Currency: ruble
Highest point: El'brus, 18,510 ft (5,642 m)*
Life expectancy: 70.0 years*
*These figures are for all of Russia. For Asian Russia, see pp. 116–117.

Globetrotter Attractions

MOSCOW'S KREMLIN
These buildings have been tsars' palaces and Soviet government offices, and are now home for the Russian president.

HERMITAGE MUSEUM
This was the St. Petersburg Winter Palace of Russian Emperor Peter I and Catherine the Great in the early 1700s.

MOTHERLAND STATUE
With her sword raised to remember the Battle of Stalingrad, this 170-foot (52-m)-tall statue in Volgograd was the world's largest when it was built in 1967.

5 SEE BEAUTIFUL BALLET
Moscow

Enjoy the beautiful dancers at the Bolshoi Theater. The world-famous Bolshoi Ballet has been around for more than 200 years.

DIGITAL TRAVELER!
Fabergé eggs are beautiful, jeweled eggs that were made as gifts for Russian royalty from 1885 to 1917. Search the Internet for photographs of Fabergé eggs. Find out where you could see one of the originals in Russia today.

ASIA

Globetrotter GIANT

From the remote, jagged, snowcapped peaks of the Himalaya to the lowest place on Earth, the Dead Sea, Asia is a place of extremes. Spreading almost halfway around the globe, Asia contains enormous rain forests, giant lakes, raging rivers, stunning waterfalls, sprawling deserts, and icy wastelands.

Rice paddy terraces in Chiang Mai, northern Thailand. Rice is the staple grain crop throughout much of eastern Asia.

ASIA

The Most Populated CONTINENT

Asia is a world champion. More people live in Asia than in all the other continents put together. China and India have the two largest populations in the world, each with more than a billion people. Asia has both the most farmers and the most cities with several million inhabitants. Home to more than 40 countries and with a rich diversity of cultures, Asia has a strong influence on world politics and economics.

Globetrotter Attractions

AUNT BERTHA'S
TRAVEL TIPS

WHAT'S ON THE MENU?
Across Asia, rice or noodles are eaten with almost everything. Rice is the grain (seeds) of a cereal plant. Noodles are made from dough shaped and cut into long strips, tubes, shells, or folded shapes.

WHAT TO WEAR?
With climates ranging from freezing cold (polar) to very hot and dry (desert), and from seasonal heavy rain (monsoon) to hot and humid (tropical), you may need to change clothes often.

ON THE MOVE
In addition to cars, trains, and planes, Asia has some unusual forms of transportation: rickshaws, tuc tucs, camels, donkey-drawn carts, elephants, junks, and sampans.

EASTERN MEDITERRANEAN
This region is a bridge between Europe and Asia, and it lies between the Black, Caspian, and Mediterranean Seas.

A commonly accepted division between Europe and Asia — here marked by a green line — is formed by the Ural Mountains, Ural River, Caspian Sea, Caucasus Mountains, and the Black Sea with its outlets, the Bosporus and Dardanelles.

CENTRAL
This region is made up of six countries: the largely Muslim five "stans"—an Iranian word for homelands—and Mongolia, a mainly Buddhist country.

SOUTHWEST
The Arabian Peninsula and countries of the Persian Gulf make up this region. The landscape is mostly deserts and mountains.

INDUSTRY
Japan

Factories in Japan and across the rest of Asia produce most of the world's electronic products including computers, game consoles, smartphones, and televisions.

NORTH

Russia is split into European and Asian parts by the Ural Mountains. Much of the Asian part is made up of Siberia, a portion of which lies north of the Arctic Circle.

GREAT WALL
China

The Great Wall of China was built to stop invasions. Work on the wall first began in 220 B.C. and continued for more than 1,500 years.

EAST

China makes up most of this region, with the Koreas and the islands of Japan along the edge of the Pacific Ocean.

SOUTH

With India at its center, this region is home to three of the world's largest rivers—the Indus, Ganges, and Brahmaputra.

SOUTHEAST

Spreading south from China, along the Malay Peninsula, to the islands of Malaysia, Indonesia, and Timor-Leste, this region links with Australia–Oceania.

115

NATIONAL BIRD:
tundra swan

NATIONAL FLOWER:
chamomile

NATIONAL MAMMAL:
bear

CAVIAR

ASIAN RUSSIA

Rich in Forests, Minerals, and Icy WASTELANDS

By far the biggest part of Russia, Asian Russia stretches from the Ural Mountains east to the volcanic Kamchatka Peninsula and the Bering Sea. It also stretches far north into the Arctic. The world's longest railroad crosses the mineral-rich wilderness of Siberia, the world's biggest plains region. Siberia has conifer forests, or taiga, treeless frozen tundra, long rivers, and lakes. Fish are harvested for caviar (eggs), a favorite delicacy.

ID CARD
COUNTRY FACTS

Size: 6,601,668 sq mi (17,098,242 sq km)*
Population: 143,493,000*
Capital: Moscow
Official language: Russian
Currency: ruble
Highest point: El'brus, 18,510 ft (5,642 m)*
Life expectancy: 70.0 years*
*These figures are for all of Russia. For European Russia, see pp. 110–111.

5 NOMADS R'US
Tyumen'

Wander through a nomad camp at the Archaeological Museum-Reserve on Lake Andreyevskoye. Eat fish soup and dress in the clothes a northern nomad may wear.

**MAP LABELS:**

BARENTS SEA
FRANZ JOSEF LAND (ZEMLYA FRANTSA IOSIFA)
Komsomolets Island
NORTH LAND (SEVERNAYA ZEMLYA)
October Revolution Island
Bol'shevik Island
ARCTIC
NOVAYA ZEMLYA
KARA SEA
Matochkin Shar
Mikhaylova
Ust' Tareya
LAPTE...
Khatanga Gulf
Ust' Olenek
Skla...
Dickson
Layda
Taymyr Peninsula
Khatanga
Yamal Peninsula
Gulf of Ob
Gyda
Gyda Peninsula
Kheta
Boyarka
Zhilinda
Olenek
Novyy Port
Noril'sk
Yessey
Salekhard
Nadym
ARCTIC CIRCLE
Igarka
Chirinda
Udachnyy
Sos'va
Polnovat
Novyy Urengoy
R U S
Turukhansk
Sergino
Ob
Noyabr'sk
Yenisey
Noginsk
Tura
I B E
Severoural'sk
Khanty-Mansiysk
Bakhta
Lower Tunguska
S
Nizhniy Tagil
Surgut
Osinovo
Mutoray
Panolik
Mirny Mine
YEKATERINBURG
Tobol'sk
Kargasok
Severo Yeniseyskiy
Lensk
Miass
Kurgan
Tyumen'
Kolpashevo
Yeniseysk
Vitim
Magnitogorsk
CHELYABINSK
Irtysh
NOVOSIBIRSK
Tomsk
Krasnoyarsk
Ust' Ilimsk
Bratsk
Ust' Kut
Bodaybo
OMSK
Kupino
Achinsk
Nizhneudinsk
Tulun
Severobaykal's
Barnaul
Kemerovo
Zima
Zhigalovo
Lake Baik...
KAZAKHSTAN
Novokuznetsk
Abaza
Abakan
Angarsk
Irkutsk
Ust' Barguzin
Yergaki National Park
Kyzyl
Slyudyanka
Ulan-U...
Zakamensk
Kyakhta
CHINA
MONGOLIA

1 CRUISE ON A LAKE
Irkutsk

Visit the nature reserves of Lake Angara that can only be reached by boat. Stop at an island to see wildlife on the beaches. Admire the forests around the lake.

5 COOL THINGS TO DO HERE

Globetrotter Attractions

LAKE BAIKAL
Lake Baikal, in southeast Siberia, is the world's deepest lake. It holds about one-fifth of Earth's surface fresh water.

YERGAKI NATIONAL PARK
Central Siberia's Yergaki National Park is breathtakingly beautiful. Its lakes, mountains, and forests are unspoiled.

YAKUTIA
Yakutia has the coldest temperatures of anywhere that people live. The ground contains many minerals but is permanently frozen below the surface.

ASIA

2 BLING IT OUT!
Mirnny

Visit the Mirnny Diamond Pit, one of the largest holes, and diamond mines, in the world. Gold is mined here, too. Find jewelry made from local gold and diamonds.

3 TAKE THE LONGEST TRAIN RIDE
Vladivostok

Spend seven nights on one train going from Vladivostok to Moscow. Eat food from the dining car or kiosks at the stations. Make tea in your own cup with hot water from the train car's samovar, or tea urn.

4 SEE RARE ANIMALS
Novosibirsk

Visit the rare liger—half lion and half tiger—at one of Russia's largest zoos. See her babies, called liligers, half liger and half lion.

1 TAKE A WILD RIDE
Tbilisi

Ride the giant Ferris wheel as you look out over the city of Tbilisi and the Caucasus Mountains. Play video games or take the waterslide as you enjoy a day atop Georgia's Mtatsminda Mountain. To get there take a funicular, a cable railroad that goes up the mountain.

DIGITAL TRAVELER!
Apricots, the fruit of a small tree, were cultivated in Armenia more than 2,000 years ago. Search the Internet to find the world's largest producers of apricots. Which ones are neighbors of the Caucasus countries?

2 BEWARE MUD POOLS
Gobustan

Go with a guide to mud volcanoes in Azerbaijan near the Caspian Sea to hear mud pools belch and to watch them bubble and explode.

ABKHAZIA & SOUTH OSSETIA
Soon after Georgia seceded from the U.S.S.R in 1991, separatists in Abkhazia and South Ossetia achieved autonomy by defeating Georgian troops. Russia supports these separatist states—recognizing their independence after its 2008 war with Georgia.

3 BUY A MAGICAL CARPET
Gäncä

Watch weavers in Azerbaijan at their loom as they make a carpet. Many work at home. They create small carpets for prayers or, on a big loom, a room-size rug. Different regions produce different designs, such as shields and diagonals.

4 ENTER A 1,700-YEAR-OLD CHURCH
Echmiadzin

Enter Echmiadzin Cathedral, founded in 303. This ancient church in Armenia has been remodeled over the centuries, but remains the center of the Armenian Christian (Orthodox) religion.

NAGORNO-KARABAKH
This southwestern Azerbaijan region, largely populated by ethnic Armenians, declared independence in 1991. A Russian-brokered cease-fire in 1994 left Karabakh Armenians controlling—but Azerbaijan still claiming—Nagorno-Karabakh

	NATIONAL BIRD:	NATIONAL FLOWER:	NATIONAL MAMMAL:
ARMENIA	eagle	*Althaea armeniaca*	lion
AZERBAIJAN	golden eagle	water fringe	Karabakh horse
GEORGIA	common pheasant	white nettle	Caucasian shepherd dog

CAUCASUS COUNTRIES

Mountains Between Two SEAS

Separating southeast Europe from Asia are the Caucasus Mountains. In the southern Caucasus are Armenia, Azerbaijan, and Georgia, lands that lie between the Black and Caspian seas. Their neighbors are Russia, Turkey, and Iran. The northern Caucasus is a disputed region. Oil-rich Azerbaijan, noted for handmade rugs, borders the Caspian Sea, and Georgia has a sunny Black Sea coast. Armenia has many lakes, the largest being Lake Sevana.

ID CARD COUNTRY FACTS

ARMENIA
Population: 3,048,000
Capital: Yerevan

AZERBAIJAN
Population: 9,418,000
Capital: Baku

GEORGIA
Population: 4,541,000
Capital: Tbilisi

5 CLIMB AN ANCIENT TOWER
Baku

Find the Maiden's Tower in the Walled City in Baku, Azerbaijan. Climb to the top of this ancient eight-story tower. Gaze across the old city and along the coast of the Caspian Sea.

Globetrotter Attractions

LAKE RITSA
Deep forest covers the three mountains that surround this beautiful lake in Abkhazia, Georgia.

ARMENIAN PLATEAU
These highlands in Armenia include mountains, deep river valleys, extinct volcanoes, and giant plateaus formed as flowing lava cooled.

SVANETI
This high, mountainous region of Georgia still has many medieval villages and tower houses.

TURKEY

A Bridge Between Europe and ASIA

5 STAND UNDER AN ANCIENT DOME
Istanbul

Gaze up at the huge dome in Hagia Sophia, a church completed in 537 and once used as a mosque. The dome is held up by half-domes and arches.

T urkish delight is a delicacy in Turkey, a country that is often said to be a bridge between Europe and Asia. The national capital is Ankara, on the high rocky plateau of Anatolia. But the largest city is Istanbul, formerly Constantinople, on the Bosporus Strait. With the Sea of Marmara and the Dardanelles, the Bosporus forms a key waterway linking the Mediterranean and Black seas.

4 STAGE A PLAY FOR A DAY
Ephesus

Climb the steps in this huge amphitheater. The Romans built it so that 25,000 people could watch concerts, plays, political discussions, and gladiator battles.

3 GET SHIPSHAPE
Selimiye

Wander down a road lined with boatyards. Watch the huge wooden boats, called *gulets*, being built using traditional methods. Taste the local figs, almonds, and honey.

5 COOL THINGS TO DO HERE

Globetrotter Attractions

1 RIDE IN A GLASS ELEVATOR
Ankara

Travel on the glass elevator to the top of Atakule, Ankara's highest building. At the tower's top, stand in one place and let the rotating room change the view.

MOUNT ARARAT

This mostly treeless mountain rises above the plains in eastern Turkey, near the border with Iran and Armenia. Many believe Noah's Ark came to rest here.

CAPPADOCIA

Wind and rain shaped the soft rock of this region, located largely in the Nevsehir Province between Yozgat and Niğde. Then people carved tunnels to form underground towns. Some underground buildings are still used today.

PATARA BEACH

Swim at this beach, but don't forget to check out the birds and endangered turtles that nest here, and nearby ancient ruins.

ASIA

DIGITAL TRAVELER!

What is the name of the bridge in Istanbul that links the European and Asian parts of Turkey? Use the Internet to find out.

2 WANDER THROUGH A COTTON CASTLE
Pamukkale

See why this bizarre landscape is called the Cotton Castle. Trickling warm mineral water has left white deposits that form stone waterfalls and forests.

ID CARD
COUNTRY FACTS

Size: 302,535 sq mi (783,562 sq km)
Population: 76,083,000
Capital: Ankara
Official language: Turkish
Currency: Turkish lira
Highest point: Mount Ararat, 16,854 ft (5,137 m)
Life expectancy: 73.0 years

LEBANON	NATIONAL BIRD:	NATIONAL FLOWER:	NATIONAL MAMMAL:
LEBANON	Dunn's lark	starflower	striped hyena
SYRIA	eagle	poppy anemone	Tsolov's hamster
JORDAN	Sinai rosefinch	black iris	Arabian oryx

LEBANON, SYRIA, AND JORDAN

Land Between Seas and DESERTS

S yria is the biggest of these three Middle Eastern states, with deserts, mountains, and dry wadis (valleys), but highways and modern cities, too. Lebanon and Syria have greener Mediterranean Sea coasts. In Jordan, you can wade in the River Jordan and in the salty Dead Sea. There are farm villages, and bustling cities, too, such as Amman, Damascus, and Beirut. In recent times these countries have been troubled by conflicts.

5 COOL THINGS TO DO HERE

1 SEE GIANT WATERWHEELS
Ḥamāh

Marvel at the huge *noria*, or waterwheels, in Syria. These brought water to aqueducts, or artificial water paths, for hundreds of years. The water went to fields in the desert and to the city of Ḥamāh. The biggest waterwheel brought water to the Great Mosque in Ḥamāh.

5 GET A WHIFF OF SOAP
Sidon

Wander through the Sidon Soap Museum in an ancient town in Lebanon. See how handmade olive oil soap has been made for hundreds of years. Smell the sweet soaps drying in the factory.

ROOT AROUND IN ROCKS
2 Petra

Explore the ancient buildings and caves carved into the rocks at Petra, Jordan. Camel caravans stopped here when traveling between the Red Sea and the Dead Sea.

ID CARD COUNTRY FACTS

JORDAN
Population: 7,309,000
Capital: Amman

LEBANON
Population: 4,822,000
Capital: Beirut

SYRIA
Population: 21,898,000
Capital: Damascus

Globetrotter Attractions

PALMYRA
This oasis and ancient city in Syria's desert was on a trade route that linked Persia, India, China, and the Roman Empire.

WADI RUM
Among interesting desert formations, this site in Jordan has evidence that humans have lived here for 12,000 years.

QADISHA VALLEY
For more than 1,000 years, religious holy men have hidden away in the caves and monasteries in this valley in Lebanon.

ASIA

4 EXPLORE A WALLED CITY
Damascus

Visit Syria to see one of the oldest continually inhabited cities in the world. Walk to the ancient gates. Visit the varied ancient religious sites and homes around the city. Careful, though—some of the buildings are not in good repair.

3 SNORKEL CORAL REEFS
Gulf of Aqaba

Watch the coral reef as you drift on this arm of the Red Sea in Jordan. Snorkel or take a glass-bottomed boat or underwater craft to see the sea turtles, dolphins, and multicolored fish.

DIGITAL TRAVELER!
The cedar of Lebanon is a conifer tree that grows in mountain regions of these countries. Search the Internet to find photographs of the tree. Then find out how timber from the tree was used in ancient times.

5 COOL THINGS TO DO HERE

1 CIRCLE AN ANCIENT CITY BY BOAT
Acre

View this ancient city from the sea. See the city walls from boats, just as the Crusaders first saw them. Wander along the winding alleys and through underground passages in the old city of Acre.

2 REPLANT A FOREST
Carmel

Volunteer to help park rangers plant trees to reforest Mount Carmel where a forest fire burned more than 8,000 acres (3,237 ha) of woodland in 2010. Learn how the forest is coming back to life.

3 TAKE A CABLE CAR TO A FORTRESS
Masada

Ride the cable car to the flat top of this steep mountain. Explore the remains of the fortress and learn the story of its heroes. See the desert and the Dead Sea far below.

4 FLOAT WHERE FISH CAN'T SWIM
Dead Sea

Swim in this salty lake on Israel's border with Jordan. The deeper you go, the saltier the water—so salty that no plants or animals can live in the lake. The lake is about 1,300 feet (396 m) below sea level, the lowest body of water on Earth's surface.

5 MEET A KIBBUTZNIK
Hadera

Chat with kibbutzniks who make farming a way of life by sharing everything. In 1927 Polish pioneers began a kibbutz as a lifestyle experiment. Kibbutzniks raise animals, grow crops, and keep bees to make honey.

STATUS OF PALESTINE
In November 2012 the UN General Assembly voted to elevate the diplomatic status of the Palestinian territories to that of a "nonmember observer state." Despite this vote and widespread international support, the West Bank's and Gaza's geographical and political separation, as well as lack of full sovereignty and control over these territories hamper the creation of a formal Palestinian state. Its future and that of some 4 million Palestinians remains subject to Israeli–Palestinian negotiations.

ISRAEL
Desert and Seas in a HOLY LAND

NATIONAL BIRD:
hoopoe

NATIONAL MAMMAL:
Israeli gazelle

NATIONAL FLOWER:
rakefet (cyclamen)

Israel has a Mediterranean coast, borders the Sea of Galilee in the north, and touches the Red Sea (at the Gulf of Aqaba). In the southwest is the Negev desert. Israel shares the Dead Sea with Jordan, but the West Bank of the River Jordan is disputed territory. Jerusalem is a city holy to Jews, Christians, and Muslims as can be seen by their religious symbols in the city: Jewish menorah candleholder, Christian cross, and Muslim star and crescent Moon.

Globetrotter Attractions

JERUSALEM
The ancient city of Jerusalem is the capital of Israel, as well as being important to three religions: Judaism, Christianity, and Islam.

TIMNA PARK
At this lake in the desert, tour the first copper mine and check out ancient rock drawings. Visit incredible rock formations and take a pedal boat out on the lake.

SEA OF GALILEE
This sea, filled by the Jordan River, provides Israel with drinking water and beaches. Visit its many natural, historic, and holy sites.

DIGITAL TRAVELER!
The region of Israel is known as the "Holy Land." The country is home to religious sites of three major religions. Use the Internet to find out who were their spiritual leaders.

ID CARD
COUNTRY FACTS

Size: 8,019 sq mi (20,770 sq km)
Population: 8,054,000
Capital: Jerusalem
Official languages: Hebrew and Arabic
Currency: new Israeli shekel
Highest point: Har Meron, 3,963 ft (1,208 m)
Life expectancy: 82.0 years

NORTHERN ARABIAN PENINSULA

Surrounded by Seas and GULFS

People in the Arabian Peninsula love horses and camels. Their desert land lies between seas and gulfs important for commerce. Oil-rich Saudi Arabia is larger than its neighbors Qatar, Bahrain, Kuwait, and the United Arab Emirates, which is made up of states that border the Persian Gulf sea route. Much of Arabia is barren desert, but oil money and technology have transformed society, with skyscrapers, expressways, and airports in what was once desert.

Globetrotter Attractions

ASIR NATIONAL PARK
Mountains, foggy forests, and even occasional snow are found in this protected area in Saudi Arabia.

RUB' AL KHALI
The largest sand desert in the world, the Rub' al-Khali is in four countries.

PALM ISLANDS
The largest artificial islands in the world, Palm Islands in the United Arab Emirates, are in the shape of palm trees.

5 STARE AT THE WORLD'S TALLEST WATER FOUNTAIN
Jeddah

Search the sky of Jeddah, Saudi Arabia, and you'll find the plume from Jeddah's Fountain. Admire the tallest water fountain in the world. It shoots water more than 1,000 feet (305 m) into the air.

ID CARD COUNTRY FACTS

Saudi Arabia
Population: 30,054,000
Capital: Riyadh

Qatar
Population: 2,169,000
Capital: Doha

Bahrain
Population: 1,131,000
Capital: Manama

Kuwait
Population: 3,459,000
Capital: Kuwait City

United Arab Emirates
Population: 9,346,000
Capital: Abu Dhabi

5 COOL THINGS TO DO HERE

1 CHOOSE A WINNER
Kuwait City

Cheer your favorite camel and robot rider at the camel races in Kuwait. Race alongside the camels in cars with the owners and their remote rider controls.

2 WALK ACROSS A SKY BRIDGE
Riyadh

Zoom on fast elevators to the 99th floor of Kingdom Center. Walk across the bridge at the top. Enjoy the view of the city and desert from this unusual building.

3 RIDE, BOUNCE, BUMP AT A PARK
Adhari

Climb aboard rides at Adhari Park. Ride a flying carousel. Bounce on trampolines or whirl in teacups. Drive bumper cars. Eat food from all over the world before you go bowling or golfing.

4 SLIP DOWN SLIDES
Dubai

Slide down huge waterslides. Surf or ride river rapids in Dubai's water parks. This United Arab Emirates city has much to enjoy!

ASIA

OMAN YEMEN	NATIONAL BIRD: ostrich eagle	NATIONAL FLOWER: frankincense coffea arabica	NATIONAL MAMMAL: Muscat gazelle Arabian leopard

SOUTHERN ARABIAN PENINSULA

Deserts, Wadis, and COASTS

Dates are grown by farmers in Oman and Yemen, at the southern tip of Arabia. For hundreds of years, people here have lived by fishing and trading in the Arabian Sea and Indian Ocean. In the cities, traditional homes stand beside modern buildings. Inland are mountains, dry wadis or valleys, and a hot, sandy desert called (in Arabic) Rub' Al Khalı, meaning "the Empty Quarter."

Globetrotter Attractions

AL JABAL AL AKHDAR
Oman's Green Mountain rises from rocky, dusty land. Agriculture and villages can be seen on its terraces.

SOCOTRA
Many of the plants and animals that live on Yemen's Socotra Islands, such as the dragon's blood trees, do not exist anywhere else on Earth.

DHOFAR SPRINGS
In the Dhofar region of Oman, the 360 springs in and near the mountains are fed by the June to September rains.

5 VISIT A MOUNTAIN VILLAGE
Al Hajjarah

Trek the mountain path to the stone buildings in this Yemeni town. Admire how buildings and mountains blend one into another.

DIGITAL TRAVELER!
Date palms are used for food, shelter, clothing, and fuel. Which countries do you think produce the most date palm fruit? Search the Internet to find out.

5 COOL THINGS TO DO HERE

1 SPY THE LAND
Nizwá

Pass the date palms in Oman's oasis Nizwá on the way to the fort that protected the town for hundreds of years. Locate the huge central tower with such a good view that no sneak attack was possible.

2 CLIMB AN INCENSE BURNER
Maţraḥ

Climb to the top of the giant incense burner in Maţraḥ, Oman's Riyam Park. View the historic harbor where Arab dhows sailed in with trade goods for Maţraḥ's huge souk or marketplace.

3 SEE AN ENDANGERED ANIMAL
Oman

Enjoy Oman's Arabian Oryx Sanctuary. The oryx disappeared in the wild and are slowly being reintroduced. These were brought here from zoos.

4 EXPLORE A DESERT ISLAND
Kamarān Island

Sit on a Red Sea beach on Yemen's Kamarān, or Two Moons, Island. Watch the sky: For two weeks each month, it seems like two moons shine at the same time.

ASIA

### Map labels

IRAN
Strait of Hormuz
Kumzār
Ra's Musandam
PERSIAN GULF
Oman Promontory
Bay'ah
Dībā al Ḩiṣn
Shināṣ
GULF OF OMAN
UNITED ARAB EMIRATES
Jabal Ḩafīt 1166
Ṣuḥār
Ṣa'am
Al Khābūrah
Al Qābil
Maţraḥ
Muscat (Masqaţ)
Dank
TROPIC OF CANCER
Barkā'
Jabal ash Shām 2980
Jabal al Akhdar
Samā'il
Qurayyāt
'Ibrī
Bahlāh
Nizwá
Ibrā'
Qalhāt
Mudayrib
Şūr
Ra's al Ḩadd
Adam
Al Mintirib
As Suwayḩ
Bilād Banī Bū 'Alī
Al Ashkharah
Ra's Jibsh
O M A N
Tur'at Maşīrah
Khalūf
Dawwah
Kalbān
Masira (Jazīrat Maşīrah)
Haymā'
Arabian Oryx Sanctuary
Jiddat al Ḩarāsīs
Duqm
Gulf of Masira
ARABIAN SEA
RUB' AL KHALI (AR RUB' AL KHALĪ)
A R A B I A
Ghubbat Şawqirah
Dawkah
Ash Shişar
Sharbatāt
Şawqirah
Ra's ash Sharbatāt
Sanāw
Shihan
D H O F A R (Z̧UFĀR)
Thamarīt
Ḩāsik
Kuria Muria Islands (Jazā'ir Khurīyā Murīyā)
Thamūd
Ḩabarūt
Salālah
Taqah
Şadḥ
Mirbāţ
Raysūt
Ra's Mirbāţ
Ḩawf
Rakhyūt
Ra's Darbat 'Alī
Damqawt
Al Ghaydah
Ghubbat al Qamar
Nishţūn
Ra's Fartak
Qishn
Say'ūt
Ra's Sharwayn
Ḩarrah
Ḩaşānah
ADEN
INDIAN OCEAN
Qalansīyah
Qāḑub
Ḩadīboh
Rhiy di-Irīsal
Ra's Shū'ab
Socotra (Suquţrá)
'Abd al Kūrī
The Brothers (Al Ikhwān)

0 50 100 MILES
0 50 100 KILOMETERS

ID CARD
COUNTRY FACTS

OMAN
Population: 3,983,000
Capital: Muscat

YEMEN
Population: 25,235,000
Capital: Sanaa

NATIONAL BIRD:
chukar partridge

NATIONAL FLOWER:
rose

NATIONAL MAMMAL:
sand gazelle

IRAQ

Early Civilization Between Two RIVERS

Iraq is mostly flat plains and desert with the Zagros Mountains in the northeast. Traces remain of the ancient civilization of Mesopotamia between the rivers Tigris and Euphrates. Today, oil-rich Iraq still uses the rivers, which join as the Shatt al Arab to flow into the Persian Gulf. Troubled by war since 2003, Iraq's main cities are Baghdad, Mosul in the north, and Basra in the south.

Globetrotter Attractions

MOSUL
Mosul is built along the Tigris River. Across the river from it are the ruins of the ancient city of Nineveh.

NATIONAL PARK OF THE MARSHLAND
Iraq's first national park is a reclaimed marshland. Native reeds, animals, and local people have returned to live there.

MESOPOTAMIA
This region, the fertile valley between the Tigris River and the Euphrates River, is where the first civilization developed.

5 WANDER UNDER A WONDER
Madain

Be amazed that no pillars hold up this brick arch, one of the largest arches in the world. Taq Kisra is all that is left of an ancient palace. Built in the city of Ctesiphon, now Madain, most of the palace was destroyed over the years.

DIGITAL TRAVELER!
The Hanging Gardens of Babylon, one of the Seven Wonders of the Ancient World, were built in Iraq about 2,500 years ago. But where was Babylon? Find out the most likely sites using the Internet.

Sinjār

SYRIA

Euphrates (Al Furāt)

Rāwa

'Ānah

Khutaylah

Al Qā'im

Huşaybah

SYRIAN

JORDAN

Ar Ruṭbah

Ţirbīl

I

Jabal 'Unayzah

941

DESERT

An Nukhayb

SAUDI

5 COOL THINGS TO DO HERE

1 BUY MUSLIN CLOTHING
Mosul

Admire the plain cotton cloth that comes in a variety of weights. Muslin cloth was named for the city, Mosul, where it was first made.

2 SEE A SPIRAL MINARET
Sāmarrā

Locate Sāmarrā's Great Mosque and its spiral minaret. Built more than 1,000 years ago, it has survived many wars.

3 MARVEL AT A MEMORIAL
Baghdad

Honor the Iraqi soldiers who died during the Iran–Iraq War of the 1980s when you visit the al-Shaheed Monument. See this war memorial and its museum built on the bank of the Tigris River.

4 GAZE AT A ZIGGURAT
Ur

Climb the steps on Ur's ziggurat, a 4,000-year-old pyramid-shaped tower made of mud bricks. Imagine what sat on this huge base. No one knows for sure.

ASIA

ID CARD
COUNTRY FACTS

Size: 169,235 sq mi (438,317 sq km)
Population: 35,095,000
Capital: Baghdad
Official languages: Arabic and Kurdish
Currency: New Iraqi dinar
Highest point: Cheeka Dar, 11,847 ft (3,611 m)
Life expectancy: 69.0 years

NATIONAL BIRD:
see-see partridge

NATIONAL TREE:
cypress

NATIONAL MAMMAL:
Persian leopard

IRAN

From Mountains to PLATEAUS

Iran's history dates back to the Persian Empire, and its people speak Farsi, or Persian. Today's Islamic republic has oil fields, modern cities, domed mosques with geometric art, and rural villages of mud-brick houses. Iran has a Caspian Sea coast north of the capital Tehran. Inland are some of the world's most desolate deserts, and mountain ranges that are formidable barriers.

ID CARD
COUNTRY FACTS

Size: 636,372 sq mi (1,648,195 sq km)
Population: 76,521,000
Capital: Tehran
Official language: Persian
Currency: Iranian rial
Highest point: Kuh-e Damavand, 18,406 ft (5,610 m)
Life expectancy: 73.0 years

DIGITAL TRAVELER!
Mosques (Islamic houses of worship) in Iran have tiles and carvings with beautiful repeating geometric patterns. Search the Internet to find a variety of geometric patterns and then invent your own on paper or your computer.

5 GO UP TALL TOWERS
Tehran

Take the trip to the top of the Azandi Tower, built in 1971 to celebrate the Persian Empire. Then look in the distance for the newer Milad Tower, the world's sixth tallest tower.

4 DISCOVER A WATER CAVE
Ali-Sadr

Tour one of the largest caves in the world by boat! Ride along the rivers and walk across an underground island.

ARMENIA
AZERBAIJAN
TURKEY
Mākū
Nāzīk
Ja'farābād
Germī
Khoy
Kaleybar
Ahar
Salmās
Marand
TABRĪZ
Ardabīl
Sarāb
Lake Urmia
(Daryācheh-ye
Orūmīyeh)
Mīāneh
Marāgheh
Mīāndoāb
Mahābād
Nīk Pey
Takāb
Zanjān
Saqqez
Dīvāndarreh
Bījār
Marivan
Sanandaj
Ali-Sadr Cave
Hamadān
Sonqor
Tūyserkān
Kermānshāh
Malāyer
Eslāmābād
Borūjerd
IRAQ
Khorramābād
Dezfūl
AHVĀZ
Ābādān
KUWAIT

5 COOL THINGS TO DO HERE

Globetrotter Attractions

1 SHOP IN A BAZAAR
Tabrīz

Shop at the Tabrīz Historic Bazaar. It began as a trade center along the Silk Road from China. Today, merchants still sell rugs and spices there.

MOUNT DAMAVAND

This inactive volcano is the highest peak in Iran and the highest volcano in Asia. Its top is often covered in snow and visible for miles.

DASHT-E KAVĪR

Almost no one lives in the Kavīr Desert. This great salt desert has a salt crust and seldom gets rain, but it does have salt marshes that act like quicksand!

GOLESTAN NATIONAL PARK

Located in the mountains, this protected area includes rivers and waterfalls and has many rare birds and mammals.

ASIA

2 WATCH CARPETS BEING MADE
Mashhad

Inspect the Persian carpets made in this city. Carpets have been woven here for hundreds of years. Many are dark red or blue-black with a medallion in the center.

3 EXPLORE A 2,500-YEAR-OLD PALACE
Persepolis

Wander through the ruins of this palace complex. Find the carved pictures, statues, remaining columns, throne hall, and even the king's bath.

133

5 COOL THINGS TO DO HERE

1 EXPLORE A FORT
Herat

Explore the restored ancient fortress overlooking Herat. Wander the winding ramps and huge rooms of this fort, built on the Silk Road from China. Examine the museum's ancient items.

2 GO ON A PICNIC
Kandahar

Eat on the green terraces around the Baba Wali Shrine in Kandahar. Walk the steps and wander in the pomegranate gardens around this famous shrine located on the banks of the Arghandab River.

3 PICTURE THE PAST
Bamian

Investigate the Bamian caves. Find the remains of recently destroyed ancient carved statues of Buddha. Admire the murals on the cave walls, some of the world's first oil paintings.

TAJIKISTAN

UZBEKISTAN

TURKMENISTAN

IRAN

AFGHANISTAN

PAKISTAN

CHINA

HINDU KUSH

Shir Khan · Chah-e Ab · Feyzabad · Sarhadd · Baza'i Gonbad
Tash Gozar · Aqcheh · Balkh · Kondoz · Baharak · Chakaran
Andkhvoy · Taloqan · Farkhar · Zibak
Sheberghan · **Mazar-e Sharif** · Kholm · Khanabad · Eshkamesh
Dowlatabad · Sar-e Pol · Aq Kopruk · Aybak · **Baghlan** · Shahr-e Monjan
Belcheragh · Dahaneh-ye Ghowri · Nahrin
Meymaneh · Qal'eh-ye Sarkari · Pol-e Khomri
Balamorghab · Qeysar · Teylan · Dowshi · Banow · Deh Khavak
Golran · Koshk-e Kohneh · 3494 · Tarkhoj · Do Ab-e Mikh-e Zarrin · 5011 · Jabal os Saraj · Asmar
Tir Pol · Now · Qades · Morghab · Band-e Amir National Park · Kowtal-e Shebar · 4710 · Charikar · Asadabad
Ghurian · **Herat** · Karokh · Owbeh · Harirud · Dowlat Yar · Bamian · Paghman · Sarowbi · Narang
Chahar Borj · Chaghcharan · Panjab · Diwal Qol · **KABUL (KABOL)** · **Jalalabad**
Paropamisus Range · Helmand · Sheykhabad · Khyber Pass
Yazdān · Adraskan · Tulak · Shahrak · Gizab · Ghazni · Pol-e 'Alam
Mandel · Shindand · 3857 · Farsi · 3741 · Kuh-e Sangan · Sang-e Masheh · Wazay · Gardiz · Khost
Khvosh · Por Chaman · Qarah Bagh · Soltan Bagh
Asia · Sakhar · Moqor · Zarghun · Shahr · Orgun
Karizak · Farah · Now Zad · Tarīn Kowt · 3807 · Shah Juy · Gowmal Kalay
Soltan-e Bakva · Delaram · Nawah · Mashuray
Dasht-e Khash · Kajaki · Arghandab Dam · Qalat · Shinkay
Lash-e Joveyn · Khash · Lashkar Gah · Gereshk · Darakht-e Yahya
Sistan Basin · Chakhansur · **Kandahar** · Ma'ruf
Zaranj · Shah Malan · Spin Buldak
Chehar Borjak · Landay · Rigestan
Rudbar · Deh Shu · Towrzi
Helmand · Pishin Lora

SCALE: 0 · 100 · 200 MILES / 0 · 100 · 200 KILOMETERS

DIGITAL TRAVELER!

What large animals do you think live in Afghanistan? Use the Internet to find out and to learn in what part of the country each lives.

NATIONAL BIRD:
spotted eagle

NATIONAL FLOWER:
tulip

NATIONAL MAMMAL:
snow leopard

AFGHANISTAN

A Landlocked, Mountainous COUNTRY

Afghanistan has deserts, rolling plains, and the high Hindu Kush mountains, which rise along the border with Pakistan. The country has ancient ruins, historic routes such as the Khyber Pass, and fertile valleys, where village farmers grow crops. Nomads herd Karakul sheep, prized for hides and wool. Kabul is the biggest city in Afghanistan, which has been troubled by war since the 1980s.

Globetrotter Attractions

KHYBER PASS
Roads, hiking paths, and trains use this pass through the Khyber Hills to go from Afghanistan to Pakistan.

HINDU KUSH
The Hindu Kush is a Central Asian mountain system in both Pakistan and Afghanistan. In Afghanistan, lower rounded mountains are in the west with higher mountains to the east.

BAND-E AMIR NATIONAL PARK
This chain of six deep lakes was formed when minerals created natural dams to hold back the water in this desert region.

ASIA

5 WATCH KITE-FIGHTING
Kabul

Cheer the colorful kites controlled from the ground by boys and men. Watch kites crash to the ground when the specially prepared strings of one kite cut another's strings. Find the kite-flyers on rooftops and in the nearby hills. Catch a falling kite to become a kite runner.

4 TRACE TILES AT TOWERS
Ghazni

Locate the Ghazni towers as they rise above the barren plain. The outsides of the towers are covered with intricate tile decorations. The towers were built during the Ghaznavid Empire in the 1200s.

ID CARD
COUNTRY FACTS

Size: 251,827 sq mi (652,230 sq km)
Population: 30,552,000
Capital: Kabul
Official languages: Afghan Persian (Dari) and Pashto
Currency: afghani
Highest point: Nowshak, 24,580 ft (7,492 m)
Life expectancy: 60.0 years

135

NATIONAL BIRD: chukar partridge

NATIONAL FLOWER: poet's jasmine

NATIONAL MAMMAL: markhor

PAKISTAN

A Mix of LANDSCAPES

Separated from British India in 1947, Pakistan has northern mountains where the Hindu Kush and Karakoram ranges meet the Himalaya. Central and southern plains are watered by the Indus and other rivers. Baluchistan in the west is arid, and so is the Thar Desert in the southeast. Most cities, including Islamabad and Lahore, are in the greener, wetter north, but the biggest is Karachi on the Arabian Sea.

5 EAT POTATOES MASALA
Islamabad

Smell the spices. Make your own masala, which is a mix of local spices—any that you like. Each region and house has its own favorite combination. It may include coriander, cumin, and cinnamon.

Globetrotter Attractions

KARAKORAM HIGHWAY

This highway from China to Pakistan is about 500 miles (800 km) long. It goes across high mountains and deep valleys.

PUNJAB PROVINCE

Most of this province is on a plain used to grow crops. The Indus River and four others flow across it and often change course due to annual floods.

MOHENJO-DARO

This was once the largest city of the Indus civilization. Its ruins show well-planned streets and a drainage system built nearly 4,500 years ago. It is located in the southeastern part of Pakistan near the city of Larkana.

DIGITAL TRAVELER!
Five of the fourteen highest mountains in the world are found in Pakistan. Use the Internet to find these mountains. Make a list from highest to lowest, in both meters and feet.

136

5 COOL THINGS TO DO HERE

0   100   200 MILES
0   100   200 KILOMETERS

1 TOUR A SALT MINE
Khewra

Ride a train through the second largest salt mine in the world. Travel into the mines used by Alexander the Great 2,300 years ago. See bridges of rock salt stretching across ponds.

2 FIGURE OUT A FORT
Lahore

View the marble palaces and mosques inside the fort. Compare the red sandstone, baked bricks, and marble that were used for the buildings. Examine the elaborate mosaics. Wander in the elegant water gardens with terraces, waterfalls, and ponds.

ASIA

3 WATCH A CRICKET MATCH
Multan

Cheer your favorite team on the lush green field at the Multan Cricket Stadium. Watch them play along with more than 30,000 other spectators.

4 GO TURTLE SPOTTING
Karachi

Identify the two types of sea turtles that nest on Karachi's beaches. Watch them come ashore from August to February when they nest in the sand. Keep the beach clean for the turtles.

ID CARD
COUNTRY FACTS

Size: 307,374 sq mi (796,095 sq km)
Population: 190,709,000
Capital: Islamabad
Official languages: Urdu and English
Currency: Pakistani rupee
Highest point: K2 (Mt. Godwin-Austen), 28,251 ft (8,611 m)
Life expectancy: 66.0 years

137

CENTRAL ASIA

Mountain Passes to Vast DESERTS

Five republics formerly in the Soviet Union are neighbors in Central Asia. They are Kazakhstan, Kyrgyzstan, Tajikistan, Turkmenistan, and Uzbekistan. The thinly populated region has two seas, the Caspian and Aral, but mountains and mostly grassy plains, dotted with lakes and rivers, stretch as far as the eye can see. Central Asian nomads make portable tentlike homes, but many people now live in cities.

5 WONDER AT THE WALLS
Shahristan

Take a ride to reach Tajikistan's ancient town, Shahristan. Examine the ruins of castles, a fort, and a moat. Discover the wall paintings that still exist.

Globetrotter Attractions

ARAL SEA
Once the world's fourth largest salt lake, the Aral Sea is disappearing. Located on the Kazakhstan–Uzbekistan border, it is now reduced to several smaller lakes.

PAMIR MOUNTAINS
In Tajikistan, many mountain ranges meet at the Pamirs. The longest glacier valley outside the polar region is here.

ALTYN-EMEL STATE NATIONAL PARK
This park in Kazakhstan includes the Singing Dunes, where the sliding grains of sand cause a humming. It has rock drawings that are thousands of years old.

ID CARD COUNTRY FACTS

Kazakhstan
Population: 17,031,000
Capital: Astana

Kyrgyzstan
Population: 5,665,000
Capital: Bishkek

Tajikistan
Population: 8,085,000
Capital: Dushanbe

Turkmenistan
Population: 5,240,000
Capital: Ashgabat

Uzbekistan
Population: 30,215,000
Capital: Tashkent

5 COOL THINGS TO DO HERE

ASIA

1 SHOP IN A GIANT TENT
Astana

Enter the clear Khan Shatyr tent to find a huge shopping mall. Ride the monorail, sit on a beach, play golf, shop, or eat. Learn about how the tent keeps the inside warm during northern Kazakhstan's very cold and very long winter.

2 CAMP IN A YURT
Alay Valley

Trek in Kyrgyzstan. Experience the life of a nomad. Herd goats in mountain pastures or hike to the snowy mountains to find wild sheep, goats, and yaks. Spend the night in a traditional, round, felt tent called a yurt. With felt rug floors, a cooking stove, and trunks for closets, whole families live in these small spaces.

3 GO ROCK CLIMBING
Tashkent

Climb over rocks and big boulders on Uzbekistan's Yangiabad Rocks. Ski or go ice-climbing if it's winter!

4 WALK WITH DINOSAURS
Kugitang Nature Reserve

Stand in the footprints of dinosaurs that lived more than 140 million years ago on the Dinosaur Plateau in Turkmenistan's Kugitang Nature Reserve. Count the park's 438 dinosaur footprints.

DIGITAL TRAVELER!
The Silk Road was an ancient trade route linking China to the West. Search the Internet to find the route's passage through Central Asia. What goods were traded in both directions?

	NATIONAL BIRD:	NATIONAL FLOWER:	NATIONAL MAMMAL:
INDIA	peacock	Indian lotus	lion
NEPAL	Himalayan monal	rhododendron	cow
MALDIVES	gray heron	pink rose	flying fox (bat)
SRI LANKA	jungle fowl	blue water lily	Sri Lankan elephant

SOUTH ASIA

Land of High Peaks and Mighty RIVERS

India, seventh largest country in area, and second biggest in population, dominates South Asia. It has mountains, deserts, plains, jungles, a long sea coast, and both historic and modern cities. The Ganges and Brahmaputra rivers rise in the Himalaya, where Nepal is India's small neighbor. Sri Lanka is an island off India's southern tip, and the Maldives are islands west of India, in the Indian Ocean.

ID CARD COUNTRY FACTS

India
Population: 1,276,508,000
Capital: New Delhi

Maldives
Population: 360,000
Capital: Male

Nepal
Population: 26,810,000
Capital: Kathmandu

Sri Lanka
Population: 20,501,000
Capital: Colombo

5 TOUR BOLLYWOOD FILM CITY
Hyderabad

Visit Ramoji Film City's sets where many of India's famous Bollywood movies are made. Watch the actors and directors working as they shoot a movie in a garden, house, or village.

DIGITAL TRAVELER!
The music of South Asia is very different from Western music. Search the Internet for songs from South Asian countries. Then see if you can find out what instruments they use.

### Map labels

Boundary claimed by India
KAS
SRINAGAR
AMRITSAR
PAKISTAN
LUDHIANA
CHANDIGARH
GHAZIABAD
DELHI
Bikaner
New Delhi
JAIPUR
GREAT INDIAN DESERT (THAR DESERT)
Jodhpur
Ajmer
Kota
Udaipur
Rann of Kutch
BHOPAL
AHMADABAD
Ujjain
Gulf of Kutch
INDORE
Narmada
RAJKOT
VADODARA
Porbandar
SURAT
AURANGABAD
Gulf of Khambhat
Jalna
THANE
KALYAN
Nanded
ARABIAN SEA
MUMBAI (BOMBAY)
PUNE
SHOLAPUR
Kolhapur
Belgaum
Hubli
Bellary
BANGALORE (BENGALURU)
Mangalore
MYSORE
LAKSHADWEEP
India
Thrissur (Trichūr)
COIMBATORE
Kochi
Nine Degree Channel
Tirunelve
Thiruvananthapuram
Eight Degree Channel
Cape Comori
LACCADIVE SEA
Male (Maale)
MALDIVES
INDIAN

5 COOL THINGS TO DO HERE

1 BE GUIDED BY SHERPAS
Kathmandu

Learn about the Sherpa culture as you hike at the base of Nepal's Mount Everest. Visit their villages that cling to the mountain slopes. Outsiders use Sherpa guides to climb the world's highest mountains.

2 VISIT THE TAJ MAHAL
Agra

Wander the gardens to reach the beautiful Taj Mahal memorial, opened in 1648. Admire the buildings that blend Indian, Persian, and Islamic styles.

3 PHOTOGRAPH ELEPHANTS
Minneriya

Watch Sri Lanka's Gathering. This is when hundreds of wild Asian elephants come to the Minneriya National Park to find water and food.

4 SNORKEL AT A CORAL REEF
Maldives

Wonder at the colorful fish, other underwater creatures, and the coral reefs around these islands.

Globetrotter Attractions

THAR DESERT
This desert crosses the India and Pakistan border. Its sand dunes are often very tall or move in the wind, taking different shapes.

CHITWAN NATIONAL PARK
This Nepal park has wild Bengal tigers and the last population of horned Asiatic rhinoceroses.

GANGES RIVER
The Ganges begins in the high Himalaya and crosses a fertile region of India until it reaches the Bay of Bengal.

ASIA

| BANGLADESH BHUTAN | NATIONAL BIRD: magpie-robin raven | NATIONAL FLOWER: shapia blue poppy | NATIONAL MAMMAL: royal Bengal tiger takin |

BANGLADESH AND BHUTAN

From Mangrove Forests to a MOUNTAIN NATION

East of India is Bangladesh, so flat and low-lying that cyclone storms cause floods as the sea surges inland from the Bay of Bengal. The Ganges and Brahmaputra rivers flow into the bay, forming a vast delta. Bangladeshi people farm, fish, and work in factories. In Dhaka city, "baby taxis" jostle for passengers. Bhutan is a rugged Himalayan mountain kingdom, between India and Chinese-ruled Tibet.

DIGITAL TRAVELER!
Weather in Bangladesh is influenced by monsoons— wind systems that change directions on a seasonal basis. Find out when the monsoons come to Bangladesh. Which month gets the highest average rainfall in Dhaka? On average, how much rain falls during that month?

5 COOL THINGS TO DO HERE

1 HIKE A HOLY TRAIL
Paro

Climb from the valley floor along the cliff to find Bhutan's small Paro Taktsang or Tiger's Nest Monastery. Admire the views across the canyon before you take the trail down the cliff to a waterfall.

2 WATCH AN ARCHERY COMPETITION
Tashigang

Watch the archers in any village in Bhutan. Archery is the national sport and this small country is proud to take part in only one Olympic sport: archery.

Globetrotter Attractions

THE SUNDARBANS

This mangrove forest in Bangladesh is one of the largest in the world. It extends across islands and along waterways that empty into the Bay of Bengal.

JIGME DORJI NATIONAL PARK

Snow leopards and tigers live in this Bhutan protected area. Meltwater from mountain glaciers fills lakes and rivers.

GANGES DELTA

The Ganges and Brahmaputra rivers flow into the Bay of Bengal. The Ganges Delta is where the rivers' flowing waters have left fertile land. It is the largest delta in the world.

5 TASTE TASTY TEA
Sylhet

Drive through lush, green tea gardens near Sylhet. See how the tea growers have made terraces on the hillside. At the Bangladesh Tea Research Institute, taste teas and learn how tea is grown and processed.

3 RIDE A CYCLE RICKSHAW
Dhaka

Choose a cycle rickshaw to get around Bangladesh's capital, called "The Rickshaw Capital of the World." While stuck in a rickshaw traffic jam, admire the paintings on those rickshaws nearby.

4 PLAY ON THE BEACH
Cox's Bazar

Play games or sun yourself on the beach in this town in Bangladesh. Enjoy the tropical weather and sandy shore on this, the world's longest uninterrupted natural beach.

ID CARD COUNTRY FACTS

BANGLADESH
Population: 156,595,000
Capital: Dhaka

BHUTAN
Population: 733,000
Capital: Thimphu

ASIA

INDIA

BANGLADESH

MYANMAR (BURMA)

Rangpur
Dinajpur
Nawabganj
Joypurhat
Naogaon
Bogra
Jamalpur
Ishwardi
Pabna
Mymensingh
Tangail
Kushtia
Tongi
DHAKA
NARAYANGANJ
Madaripur
Jessore
KHULNA
Pirojpur
Patuakhali
Koyra
Barisal
Chandpur
Comilla
Feni
Magdhara
Sandwip
South Hatia
CHITTAGONG
Rangamati
Bandarban
Satkania
Chakaria
Ramu
Cox's Bazar
Maiskhal
Kutubdia
Ukhiya
Teknaf
Sylhet
Jaintiapur
Kulaura
Habiganj
Brahmanbaria
Bhairab Bazar
Jamalpur

Chittagong Hills
Karnaphuli Res.
Ganges
Ganges Delta
Bhairab
Sundarbans
Mouths of the Ganges
BAY OF BENGAL
Dakhin Shahbazpur
Donmanick Islands
Rabnabad Islands
TROPIC OF CANCER

5 COOL THINGS TO DO HERE

1 SEE THE TERRA-COTTA ARMY
Xi'an

Admire the Terra-cotta Army buried about 2,200 years ago. See how workers today have pieced together the broken bits of clay to rebuild the warriors, their horses, and chariots. Hundreds of warriors with different faces but the same body stand in rows, protecting China's first emperor.

2 HIKE ALONG A GREAT WALL
Badaling

Hike along the Great Wall of China. Built over hundreds of years, the wall protected China. Imagine the soldiers marching along the steep winding path that is high on the mountain ridge.

ID CARD
COUNTRY FACTS

Size: 3,705,407 sq mi (9,596,961 sq km)
Population: 1,357,372,000
Capital: Beijing
Official language: Standard Chinese or Mandarin
Currency: renminbi (yuan)
Highest point: Mount Everest, 29,035 ft (8,850 m)
Life expectancy: 75.0 years

CHINA
Land of the GREAT WALL

No country has more people than China. Civilization in the ancient land of fabled dragons grew around rivers, such as the Huang He and Yangtze. To the west are Tibet and the Himalaya. To the north lie the Tien Shan and Altai mountains, and the Gobi Desert. Ships ply the Yellow, East China, and South China seas. Northern winters are cold, but south China is subtropical, with monsoon rains.

3 ENTER A FORBIDDEN CITY
Beijing

Wander through this huge palace complex where emperors and their families lived. Search for designs using animals and flowers.

4 FEED A GIANT PANDA
Chengdu

Admire, photograph, and feed a giant panda. In Southwest China the Chengdu Research Base of Giant Panda Breeding allows visitors to meet the giant pandas in their specially designed environment.

5 VISIT DISNEYLAND
Hong Kong

In this Chinese city, visit the Wild West in Grizzly Gulch. Enjoy Mystic Manor. Play in Toy Story Land. Journey into the jungle.

DIGITAL TRAVELER!
Yaks are important animals for the people of Tibet, an autonomous region of China. Search the Internet to learn how Tibetans use the yak.

Globetrotter Attractions

THE GOBI
This desert, shared with Mongolia, is mostly bare rock. Very little water is found here, except deep underground. Parts of the Gobi get less than four inches (102 mm) of rain a year. It is a very cold desert in winter, but has very hot summers.

HONG KONG
A view from the hills shows the city's skyscrapers, its excellent harbor, and the New Territories in the distance.

THREE GORGES DAM
This concrete dam on the Yangtze River creates electricity and protects many people from river flooding.

NATIONAL BIRD:
green pheasant

NATIONAL FLOWER:
chrysanthemum

NATIONAL MAMMAL:
raccoon dog

JAPAN

A Rugged ISLAND CHAIN

Japan is a country of islands in the Pacific Ocean. The islands lie on the Pacific "Ring of Fire" where earthquakes, tsunamis, and volcanic eruptions occur. The four main islands are Honshu, Hokkaido, Kyushu, and Shikoku. The capital, Tokyo, is on Honshu, as is Mount Fuji. About 80 percent of Japan is mountain and forest, so most people live in cities along the coastal plains.

DIGITAL TRAVELER!
Manga comics are popular in Japan among people of all ages. Use your digital device to look for manga kids' comics and choose your favorites to read.

5 COOL THINGS TO DO HERE

1 VISIT A PEACE MEMORIAL
Hiroshima

At Hiroshima Peace Memorial Park, remember those who died from the nuclear bomb attack in 1945 at the end of World War II.

2 SOAK IN HOT SPRINGS
Beppu

Go to a resort or public bath to relax in pools of hot water. Hot volcanic water gushes into hot springs throughout Beppu. People also use this resource for heating buildings.

## Map labels

La Perouse Strait
Rebun
Rishiri
Wakkanai
45°
45°
SEA OF OKHOTSK
Nayoro
Abashiri Wan
145°
RUSSIA
Asahikawa
+2290
Kitami
140°
HOKKAIDO
Ishikari Wan
Kushiro Shitsugen
National Park
Kamui Misaki
Otaru
SAPPORO
Obihiro
Kushiro
Tomakomai
145°
Okushiri
Hakodate
Cape Erimo
Uchiura Bay
Shirakami Misaki
Tsugaru Strait
O C E A N
Aomori
Hachinohe
Hirosaki
J A P A N
40°
40°
Nyūdō Zaki
Morioka
Akita
Kamaishi
Tobi Shima
Sakata
Ishinomaki
Yamagata
SENDAI
Sado
Ishinomaki Wan
Niigata
Fukushima
Toyama Wan
Jōetsu
H U A
Nasuhiobara
Toyama
Nagano
Utsunomiya
Kanazawa
S P
SAITAMA
Matsumoto
Maebashi
TOKYO (TŌKYŌ)
N
Kōfu
YOKOHAMA
KAWASAKI
NAGOYA
3776 + Fuji
Shizuoka
Tokyo Wan
35°
Toyohashi
Sagami Nada
Hamamatsu
A
Ise Wan
Miyake Jima
S E A
Hachijo
P A C I F I C
Aoga
Beyonēsu Retsugan
Izu
Smith Island
Islands
Tori
30°
Sōfu-gan
140°

Globetrotter Attractions

MOUNT FUJI
Japan's highest mountain is called an active volcano, though it last erupted in 1707. Its cone-shaped peak is visible from Tokyo and Yokohama.

LAKE BIWA
Japan's largest lake is most likely the oldest one. It probably is more than five million years old.

KUSHIRO–SHITSUGEN NATIONAL PARK
Endangered Japanese cranes are protected here. You may see pairs of cranes dancing together.

3 MAKE YOUR OWN NOODLES
Yokohama

Create your own ramen noodles at the Cupnoodle Museum. Learn how Momofuku Ando invented his first instant meal in 1958 and ramen for space flights in 2005.

4 HOLD ON TO YOUR SEAT!
Tokyo

Speed from Tokyo to Aomori at 199 miles an hour (320 kph) on the super-fast Shinkansen train. The train's pointy front prevents "tunnel boom" caused by air pressure changing as the train enters a tunnel at high speed.

5 CROSS SWORDS WITH SAMURAI
Himeji

Discover one of the few surviving wooden castles in Japan. With watchtowers, moats, and residences for samurai warriors, Himeji Castle protected this area in the 1600s.

ASIA

ID CARD
COUNTRY FACTS

Size: 145,913 sq mi (377,915 sq km)
Population: 127,301,000
Capital: Tokyo
Official language: Japanese
Currency: yen
Highest point: Fuji, 12,388 ft (3,776 m)
Life expectancy: 83.0 years

5 COOL THINGS TO DO HERE

1 GET TO GRIPS WITH GIANTS
Erdenet

Wrestling is the country's most popular sport. Fans watch competitions in stadiums and on television. The wrestler who wins the most rounds in a competition is ranked "Giant."

2 DON'T GET THE HUMP!
Yol Valley

Explore the Gobi desert by camel. Guided camel rides take you over the desert's highest sand dunes. The two-humped camels are unique to this region.

5 WALK WITH DINOSAURS
Nemegt Basin

Explore the land where dinosaurs once roamed. See fossils and footprints here. A great collection of dinosaur eggs and nests were sent to a museum in Ulaanbaatar.

4 SLEEP IN A GER
Terelj

Stay with a nomadic family and learn about their lives. Many Mongolians still live in *gers*. These are sturdy tents that can be built and taken down in under an hour.

### Map labels

RUSSIA

Turt
Renchinlhumbe
+3351
Hövsgöl Nuur
Hatgal
Egiyn
Bulgan
Sühbaatar
Uldz
Ulaangom
Uvs Nuur
Tavan Bogd Uul +4374
Tsagaannuur
Halban
Mörön
Ingettolgoy
Hutag
Darhan
Selenge
Onon
Bilüü
Ölgiy
Hyargas Nuur
Hödrögö
Baruunharaa
Hentiyn Nuruu
Onon
Uldz
Tolbo
Har Us Nuur
Har Nuur
Ideriyn
Orhon
Bulgan
Erdenet
Mandal
Choybalsan
Herlen
Hovd
Tsahir
+3130
Hanuy
Teel
Dzaanhushuu
Dund-Urt
Terelj
Hentiy
Uliastay
Hunt
Hustai National Park
Ulaanbaatar
Tsonjin Boldog
Undurhaan
ALTAY MOUNTAINS
Hangay Mountains
+3905
Dzavhan
Buyanbat
Dzag
Tsetserleg
Tsetsegnuur
MONGOLIA
Bumbat
Baruun Urt
Altay
Bayanhongor
Arvayheer
Ulaan-Uul
MONGOLIAN
Choyr
Buyant
Tamch
Bayan
Jargalant
Bööntsagaan Nuur
Bodĭ
Arguut
Mandalgovĭ
Har Ayrag
Shireet
Hongor
Talshand
3957+
PLATEAU
Hashaat
Saynshand
Ovoot
+3802
2076 +
Edrengiyn Nuruu
Bulgan
Gurvan Bogd Uul
+3590
Sharhulsan
Baruunsuu
Borhoyn Tal
Hövsgöl
+2695
Nemegt Uul +2768
2825 +
Gurvan Sayhan Uul
Dalanzadgad
Yol Valley
Tsagaan Bogd Uul +2480
Bayandalay
Nemegt Basin
Nomgon
Sulanheer
CHINA

0   100   200 MILES
0   100   200 KILOMETERS

NATIONAL BIRD:
Saker falcon

NATIONAL TREE:
saxaul

NATIONAL MAMMAL:
Bactrian camel

MONGOLIA
A Vast and Barren LAND

Warm clothes and hats are essential in windswept Mongolia. In the Gobi Desert it can get very cold, and very hot. Though smaller than neighbors Russia and China, Mongolia is a vast country, sparsely populated, with few cities. Most of the land is treeless steppe plains, where nomads herd livestock, and there is little farmland. The snow-topped Altay Mountains rise in western Mongolia, where there are many lakes.

50°

Buir Nuur

Jargalant
Tamsagbulag

120°

Chonogol

Globetrotter Attractions

ALTAY RANGE
This mountain range stretches through China, Mongolia, Russia, and Kazakhstan. Humans lived in this region more than a million years ago. Many small groups of people still live here

THE GOBI
In Mongolian, *gobi* means "waterless place." Much of the Gobi desert is covered in rocks, not sand. There are even a few ice-filled canyons.

HUSTAI NATIONAL PARK
The protected grasslands here made this a suitable place to reintroduce wild Przewalski's horses. The endangered horse is Mongolia's national symbol.

3 ENTER A GIANT HORSE
Tsonjin Boldog

Take an elevator to the horse's head and see a beautiful view. The 131-foot (40-m) Genghis Khan statue is one of the world's largest equestrian statues.

ID CARD
COUNTRY FACTS

Size: 603,908 sq mi (1,564,116 sq km)
Population: 2,792,000
Capital: Ulaanbaatar
Official language: Khalkha Mongol
Currency: togrog (tugrik)
Highest point: Tavan Bogd Uul, 14,350 ft (4,374 m)
Life expectancy: 69.0 years

DIGITAL TRAVELER!
Mongolia is one of the most sparsely populated countries in the world. Use the Internet to find out its population density. How does that compare to the population density in the United States and other highly populated countries, such as India and Brazil?

NORTH AND SOUTH KOREA

A Rugged PENINSULA

NORTH KOREA
SOUTH KOREA

NATIONAL BIRD:
meadow bunting
Korean magpie

NATIONAL FLOWER:
magnolia
rose of Sharon

NATIONAL MAMMAL:
chollima (mythical animal)
Siberian tiger

The Korean Peninsula, shared by communist North Korea and democratic South Korea, has the Yellow Sea to the west, and the Sea of Japan to the east. Korea has been divided since 1948. The landscape is a mix of coastal plains that are good for farming, and bleak mountains. The South has more industries and cities. China lies beyond the Yalu River of North Korea, while the Korea Strait separates South Korea from Japan.

2 CLAP FOR YOUNG STARS
Pyongyang

Enjoy a performance by children at Mangyongdae Children's Palace. Children come here after school to learn music, martial arts, gymnastics, computer skills, languages, sports, and theater. They give performances for visitors.

DIGITAL TRAVELER!
Kimchi is a traditional food in Korean meals. Use the Internet to find out more about kimchi. What is it made of?

5 COOL THINGS TO DO HERE

1 GO BAREFOOT IN A PARK
Seoul

Ride a roller coaster, check out Elephant World at the zoo, and walk barefoot through the squishy walking path.

4 GUARD THE GATES!
Suwon

Walk along a city wall fortified with towers and gates that was built more than 200 years ago to protect the town and the king's palace. Traffic now flows through the gates.

ID CARD
COUNTRY FACTS

NORTH KOREA
Population: 24,720,000
Capital: Pyongyang

SOUTH KOREA
Population: 50,220,000
Capital: Seoul

5 SEE A WATERFALL
Jeju

Stand below the cliffs and look up at Jeongbang Waterfall. It is the only waterfall in Asia that falls into the ocean.

3 WHIZ DOWN A WATERSLIDE
Asan

Spend all day at the water park, slipping down waterslides and floating through artificial caves. All the water is warmed by underground hot springs.

Globetrotter Attractions

PAEKTU-SAN
North Korea's highest mountain is an extinct volcano. A deep crater lake sits at the top. It is one of the coldest lakes in the world.

SONGNISAN NATIONAL PARK
Hiking trails wind through a granite mountain—Songni—and its valleys. On the mountain is a temple with one of the world's largest Buddha statues.

OEDO ISLAND
Two people took 30 years to grow beautiful gardens all over the island. You can visit the gardens.

ASIA

SOUTH KOREA

NORTH KOREA

SEA OF JAPAN (EAST SEA)

YELLOW SEA

EAST CHINA SEA

KOREA STRAIT

Jeju Strait

Sobaek Sanmaek

Haeju-man

KOREA BAY

Military Demarcation Line, July 27, 1953

Liancourt Rocks

Ulleung Island

PYONGYANG (P'YONGYANG)
Wŏnsan
Anbyŏn
Sep'o
Ich'ŏn
Songnim
Sariwŏn
Namp'o
Anak
Changyŏn
Haeju
Ongjin
Kimhwa (Gimhwa)
P'yŏnggang
Kaesŏng
Changsan-got
Baengnyeongdo
Daecheongdo
Sokcho
Chuncheon
Gangneung
Donghae
Samcheok
SEOUL
SEONGNAM
GOYANG
INCHEON
Ansan
SUWON
Anseong
Cheonan
Asan
Seosan
Wonju
Jecheon
Cheongju
Songni Mountain National Park
DAEJEON
Iksan
Jeonju
Gunsan
Ganggyeong
GWANGJU
Hampyeong
Mokpo
Boseong
Gangjin
Haenam
Wando
Jindo
Gageodo
Namwon
Gochang
Andong
Uiseong
Gumi
DAEGU
Jinju
Changwon
Suncheon
Yeosu
Goseong
Masan
BUSAN
Ulsan
Kyŏngju (Gyeongju)
Gatbawi Statue
Pohang
Hupo
Geoje
Geojedo
Oedo Island
Hallim
Jeju
Hallasan
1950
Seogwipo
Jeju Island

130°
125°
35°
35°

151

NATIONAL BIRD:
Burmese peacock
Siamese fireback

NATIONAL FLOWER:
paduak
rachapruek

NATIONAL MAMMAL:
elephant
Thai elephant

MYANMAR AND THAILAND

The Heart of SOUTHEAST ASIA

Myanmar, also known as Burma, is a mountainous, forested country with rice-growing lowlands such as the Irrawaddy Delta. To the south and east is Thailand, called Siam until 1939. Northern Thailand is hilly, but the southern plains offer rich farmland. The main river is the Chao Phraya. People use the rivers for transportation. Monsoon rains sweep both these countries in the rainy season. Away from the cities, tribal groups live in mountain villages.

DIGITAL TRAVELER!

Pad Thai is a popular food eaten throughout Thailand. Go online to find out what this is and how to cook it. Ask your family to help you prepare it at home.

5 COOL THINGS TO DO HERE

1 BE A NIGHT OWL
Chiang Mai

Find out what the animals at the Chiang Mai Zoo do after the sun goes down. Walk along the Jaguar Trail. Or, ride in a tram through the Savannah Safari and the Predator Prowl. Zebras, giraffes, and tigers will be waiting for you.

2 SLINK WITH SNAKES
Bangkok

Get acquainted with snakes of all kinds, including a poisonous king cobra. Staff at Bangkok Snake Farm will show you how they handle snakes safely. Learn which snakes are dangerous.

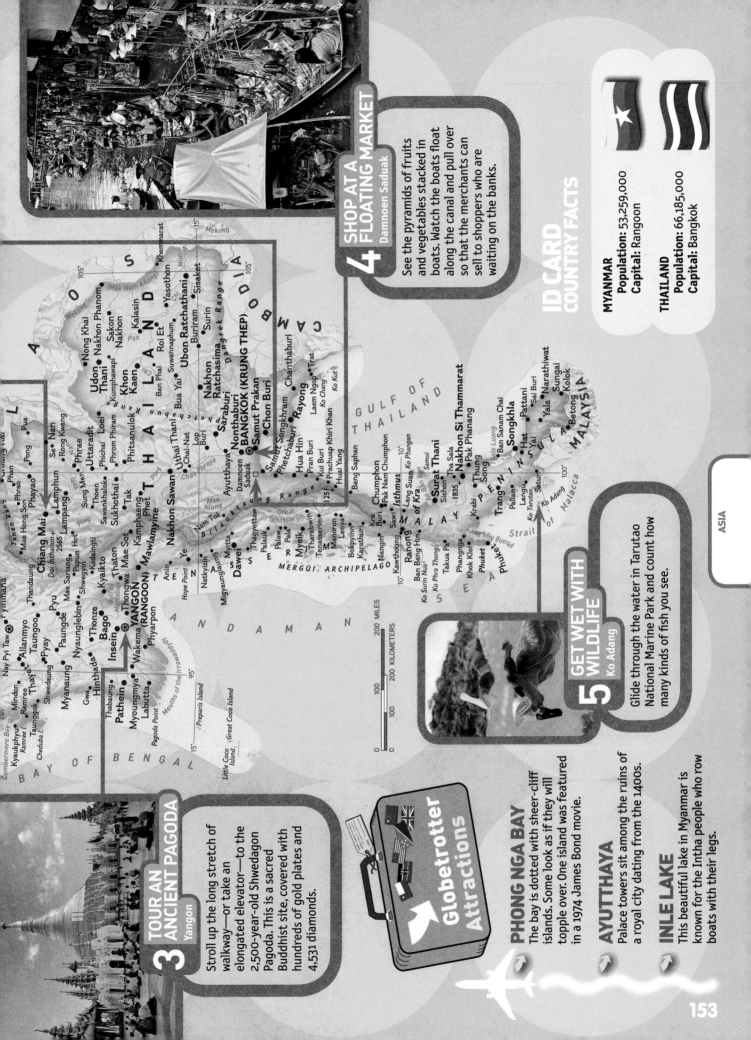

3 TOUR AN ANCIENT PAGODA
Yangon

Stroll up the long stretch of walkway—or take an elongated elevator—to the 2,500-year-old Shwedagon Pagoda. This is a sacred Buddhist site, covered with hundreds of gold plates and 4,531 diamonds.

4 SHOP AT A FLOATING MARKET
Damnoen Saduak

See the pyramids of fruits and vegetables stacked in boats. Watch the boats float along the canal and pull over so that the merchants can sell to shoppers who are waiting on the banks.

5 GET WET WITH WILDLIFE
Ko Adang

Glide through the water in Tarutao National Marine Park and count how many kinds of fish you see.

Globetrotter Attractions

PHONG NGA BAY
The bay is dotted with sheer-cliff islands. Some look as if they will topple over. One island was featured in a 1974 James Bond movie.

AYUTTHAYA
Palace towers sit among the ruins of a royal city dating from the 1400s.

INLE LAKE
This beautiful lake in Myanmar is known for the Intha people who row boats with their legs.

ID CARD
COUNTRY FACTS

MYANMAR
Population: 53,259,000
Capital: Rangoon

THAILAND
Population: 66,185,000
Capital: Bangkok

### Map labels

LAOS

Mekong

(Mae Nam Khong)

THAILAND

Chiang Mai
Doi Inthanon 2565
Mae Hong Son
Phrao
Phayao
Pua
Nan
Sa
Phrae
Pong
Rong Kwang
Lamphun
Lampang
Thoen
Sung Men
Phichai
Uttaradit
Loei
Phrom Phiram
Phitsanulok
Sawankhalok
Sukhothai
Phet
Tak
Kamphaeng
Nakhon Sawan
Uthai Thani
Chai-Nat
Lop Buri
Ayutthaya
Saraburi
Nakhon Ratchasima
Nonthaburi
BANGKOK (KRUNG THEP)
Samut Prakan
Chon Buri
Rayong
Chanthaburi
Trat
Ko Chang
Ko Kut

Nong Khai
Nakhon Phanom
Udon Thani
Sakon Nakhon
Kalasin
Roi Et
Yasothon
Sisaket
Ubon Ratchathani
Khon Kaen
Kumphawapi
Ban Phai
Bua Yai
Surin
Buriram
Ban Sang
Suwannaphum

Chi
Pao
Mun
Chi

Dangrek Range

CAMBODIA

GULF OF THAILAND

Samut Songkhram
Phetchaburi
Hua Hin
Pran Buri
Prachuap Khiri Khan
Huai Yang
Bang Saphan
Chumphon
Pak Nam Chumphon
Lang Suan
Ko Pha Ngan
Ko Samui
Isthmus of Kra
Ranong
Ban Bang Hin
Takua Pa
Ko Phra Thong
Ko Surin Nua
Phangnga
Khok Kloi
Phuket
Krabi
Trang
Pak Phanang
Nakhon Si Thammarat
Surat Thani
Thung Song
Sichon
Phatthalung
Songkhla
Hat Yai
Pattani
Sai Buri
Yala
Narathiwat
Sungai Kolok
Betong
Satun
Ko Tarutao
Ko Adang
Langu
Pallian
Thale Luang

MALAY PENINSULA

MALAYSIA

Strait of Malacca

Phong Nga Bay

Chao Phraya

Bilauktaung Range

Nam Tok
Mae Klong
Great Tenasserim
Palaw
Pala
Myitta
Tavoy
Dawei
Ye
Thagyettaw
Natkyizin
Migyaunglaung
Agang
Thayetchaung
Tenasserim
Lenya
Bokpyinn
Karathuri

MERGUI ARCHIPELAGO

ANDAMAN SEA

TENASSERIM

Manoron

Mawlamyine
Thaton
Kyaikto
Mae Sot
Thongwa
YANGON (RANGOON)
Phyarpon
Wakema
Insein
Bago
Thonze
Pyu
Taungoo
Nyaunglebin
Shwegyin
Kadaingti
Hinthada

Nay Pyi Taw
Mindon
Allanmyo
Thayet
Taunggok
Ramree I.
Kyaukphyu
Gwa
Pathein
Myoungmya
Labutta
Myanaung
Pyay
Paungde
Shwedaung

Mouths of the Irrawaddy

BAY OF BENGAL

Preparis Island
Great Coco Island
Little Coco Island
Pagoda Point
Cheduba I.
Combermere Bay

Scale
0   100   200 MILES
0   100   200 KILOMETERS

	NATIONAL BIRD:	NATIONAL FLOWER:	NATIONAL MAMMAL:
LAOS	bare-faced bulbul	plumeria	Indian elephant
VIETNAM	Vietnamese waterbird	red lotus	water buffalo
CAMBODIA	giant ibis	romduol	kouprey

LAOS, VIETNAM, AND CAMBODIA

Ancient Temples, Powerful Rains, and AMAZING FOOD

In these Southeast Asian countries, forested uplands, plateaus, and mountains rise above lowland plains. The people of Laos, Vietnam, and Cambodia (formerly Kampuchea) rely on seasonal rains and the Mekong and other rivers for rice-growing. Houses are built on stilts beside rivers. Cambodia has a lake-river, the Tonle Sap, while Vietnam's long coastline extends from the Gulf of Tonkin in the north to the South China Sea.

5 COOL THINGS TO DO HERE

1 GO BOATING ON A BAY
Ha Long Bay

Float by some of the thousands of jungle islands. Some are hollow with huge caves. About 1,000 people live in the bay on boats and floating houses. They support themselves by fishing.

2 HARVEST RICE
Louangphrabang

Visit a farm and help cut the rice stalks and separate the grains. Learn about the tools farmers use in the rice paddies. Your host may cook a delicious dish for you to eat.

DIGITAL TRAVELER!

Buddhism is an important religion in Laos, Vietnam, and Cambodia. Use the Internet to find out more about Buddha. Who was Buddha, and when did he live? What are some main beliefs of the faith?

4 SWIM, SLIP, AND SLIDE
Ho Chi Minh City

Ride on a turtle-shaped boat in Suoi Tien Cultural Theme Park, a water park devoted to Buddhism. Swim in a pool surrounded by dragon statues. Climb up the face of a Buddhist sage figure and slip down a waterslide.

ID CARD
COUNTRY FACTS

LAOS
Population: 6,736,000
Capital: Vientiane

VIETNAM
Population: 89,721,000
Capital: Hanoi

CAMBODIA
Population: 14,406,000
Capital: Phnom Penh

3 MEANDER WITH MYTHS
Angkor

Walk through the remains of temples dating back to the 800s. Angkor Wat Temple has stone carvings of mythological stories and historic events.

Globetrotter Attractions

ANNAMESE CORDILLERA

This beautiful mountain range forms the boundary between Laos and Vietnam. Its forests are home to the long-horned Vu Quang ox.

PLAIN OF JARS

Stone jars are scattered in these fields in Laos, sometimes in clusters of several hundred. Scientists think these prehistoric jars may have been part of local burial customs.

TONLE SAP

This lake in Cambodia increases in size and flows into a river after the rainy monsoon season.

5 EXPLORE UNDERGROUND TUNNELS
Cu Chi

Crawl through a tunnel as a guide explains how the Viet Cong lived here during the 1960s war. The tunnels had meeting rooms, hospitals, and sleeping quarters.

5 COOL THINGS TO DO HERE

Globetrotter Attractions

MOUNT KINABALU

Strong mountain climbers hike to the top of Malaysia's highest mountain. Other visitors have fun below, walking across swinging bridges and soaking in hot springs.

TAMAN NEGARA NATIONAL PARK

People say that Malaysia's largest national park is also the world's oldest jungle. The plants and animals have survived the Ice Age and other major world changes.

TASEK MERIMBUN

Brunei's largest lake has black water. The tannin from falling leaves stains the water. Scientists found rare white-collared fruit bats near the lake.

1 TOUR GIANT TWIN TOWERS
Kuala Lumpur

The Petronas Twin Towers are among the tallest buildings in the world. They are 1,483 feet (452 m) high. There are 88 floors in each building. The Skybridge connects the two towers on the 42nd floor.

2 STEP BACK IN TIME
Singapore

Walk around the Chinatown Heritage Center and see kitchens, bedrooms, and streets that have been re-created to look like the past.

3 CLIMB 272 STEPS
Selangor

Explore the three Batu Caves where you'll probably see monkeys frolicking. The main cave can be found at the top of the tall staircase. You won't miss the huge Hindu statue outside.

4 PARTY WITH PINK DOLPHINS
Sentosa

Watch pink dolphins perform at a water show. Stand at underwater level and follow the sharks on the other side of the glass. Wade into a pool and swim with shovel-nosed rays. It's all at Underwater World and Dolphin Lagoon.

**Map labels:**

THAILAND · MALAY · SOUTH CHINA SEA · PENINSULA · MALAYA · STRAIT OF MALACCA · NATUNA SEA · INDONESIA

Langkawi · 881 · Kangar · Kuala Nerang · Alor Setar · Sungai Petani · George Town · Pinang · Kampung Ayer · Butterworth · Kuala Berang · Taiping · Gua Musang · Ipoh · Kampar · Benta · Raub · Kota Baharu · Redang · Kampong Kuala Besut · Kuala Terengganu · Taman Negara National Park · Chukai · Maran · Pahang · Kuantan · Temerloh · Pekan · Batu Caves · SELANGOR · KUALA LUMPUR · KELANG · Seremban · Segamat · Malacca · Muar · Batu Pahat · Keluang · Johor Bahru · SINGAPORE · Tioman · Singapore Strait · Sentosa · Pulau Perak

0 100 200 MILES
0 100 200 KILOMETERS

	NATIONAL BIRD:	NATIONAL FLOWER:	NATIONAL MAMMAL:
BRUNEI	crested fireback	simpoh ayer	pygmy treeshrew
MALAYSIA	rhinoceros hornbill	Chinese hibiscus	Malayan tiger
SINGAPORE	crimson sunbird	vanda "Miss Joaquim"	merlion (mythical animal)

BRUNEI, MALAYSIA, AND SINGAPORE

Lowlands and Mountains Surrounded by WATER

Forested west Malaysia occupies most of the Malay Peninsula, shared with Thailand. To the west across the Strait of Malacca is Sumatra, part of Indonesia. In the far south is Singapore, a city-state with a busy trade port, which separated from Malaysia in 1965. Travelers cross the South China Sea to the island of Borneo to reach east Malaysia, including Sarawak and Sabah. Also on Borneo is the small oil-rich state of Brunei.

DIGITAL TRAVELER!

Singapore is both a country and a city. Search the Internet to find the distance between Singapore and these other Southeast Asian cities: Kuala Lumpur, Manila, Ho Chi Minh City, and Bangkok.

5 WALK ON STILTS
Bandar Seri Begawan

Ride a tour boat to these water villages where more than 30,000 people live. Their houses sit above the river on stilts. Wooden bridges connect the homes, schools, shops, and restaurants.

ID CARD
COUNTRY FACTS

BRUNEI
Population: 407,000
Capital: Bandar Seri Begawan

MALAYSIA
Population: 29,794,000
Capital: Kuala Lumpur

SINGAPORE
Population: 5,444,000
Capital: Singapore

ASIA

5 COOL THINGS TO DO HERE

1 TIE-DYE A T-SHIRT
Yogyakarta

Learn to make a batik pattern on a shirt. Batiks have been around for centuries. Trace a pattern with glue or wax. Then paint over it. When you wash off the glue or wax, the pattern shows up.

2 HANG IN A HAMMOCK
Atauro Island

Ride a ferry to the island for a quiet vacation. Islanders built eco-friendly bamboo cabins that encourage tourists to relax without disturbing the natural beauty.

3 SEE AN ORANGUTAN
Palangkaraya

Learn about orangutans and how the B.O.S. Nyaru Menteng Reintroduction Center saves and cares for injured and orphaned animals. It is the world's largest orangutan conservation facility. Since the animals are wild, people cannot stand close to them.

4 GO NUTS UP A TREE
Bali

Stand back from the palm trees and shout when you see a coconut drop. Workers climb the tall trees to chop down the coconuts. Indonesia is one of the world's top producers of coconuts. Coconut is a popular food by itself and in sauces and desserts.

	NATIONAL BIRD:	NATIONAL FLOWER:	NATIONAL MAMMAL:
TIMOR-LESTE	iris lorikeet	puspa pesona	crocodile
INDONESIA	Javan hawk-eagle	jasminum sambac	Asian palm civet

TIMOR-LESTE AND INDONESIA

Wildlife, Islands, and RAIN FORESTS

ndonesia has more than 13,000 islands, including Java, Sumatra, and Sulawesi. Parts of New Guinea and Borneo are also in Indonesia. About half the islands are inhabited. Java has most of Indonesia's cities and industries. The island of Timor is shared between Indonesia and independent Timor-Leste (East Timor). The rugged landscape includes volcanoes, mountains, and rain forests with rare animals, like orangutans, but also fertile farmlands.

Globetrotter Attractions

PUNCAK MANDALA

This mountain peak in Papua, Indonesia, is popular with mountain climbers and scientists. The peak's melting ice cap was last seen in 1989.

DIENG PLATEAU

This land in Java, Indonesia, was once a sacred Hindu temple complex. Eight temples still stand there today. The plateau is a volcano's crater that was once filled with water.

NINO KONIS SANTANA NATIONAL PARK

Timor-Leste's first national park is home for several endangered birds, such as the yellow-crested cockatoo and the Timor green-pigeon.

5 GO WHALE WATCHING
Dili

Stand at the railing of a tour boat and look for pilot whales, melon-headed whales, and many other kinds. The coast of Timor-Leste has one of the world's highest concentrations of whales.

DIGITAL TRAVELER!

One of the world's greatest volcanic eruptions took place in Indonesia, on the island of Krakatau. Search the Internet to find out more about this eruption. When did it happen? What happened to the island? How did the eruption affect the world?

159

NATIONAL BIRD: Philippine eagle

NATIONAL FLOWER: sampaguita

NATIONAL MAMMAL: swamp water buffalo

PHILIPPINES

An Archipelago NATION

Like its neighbor Indonesia, the Philippines has many islands. It's an archipelago, or chain, of more than 7,000 islands. Eleven large islands are where most Filipino people live. The capital, Manila, and most other major cities are on Luzon island. There are mountains and volcanoes, and earthquakes sometimes occur. Dense forest formerly covered most islands, but much of it has been cut for lumber and cleared for farmland.

Globetrotter Attractions

CHOCOLATE HILLS (CHOCLOATE HILLS)
There are at least 1,260 nearly identical dirt hills in Bohol. Scientists can't agree how they got here. Legends say that two giants threw sand and stones at each other.

MOUNT MAYON
The most active volcano in the Philippines is also called the world's most symmetrical volcano. Mount Mayon in Luzon has erupted 47 times in the last 400 years.

BANAUE RICE TERRACES
Almost 2,000 years ago, the Ifugao people carved out giant, steplike layers of rice fields. How they did so remains a mystery. The Ifugao continue to grow rice here.

5 TOUR AN OLD-WORLD CITY
Vigan

Step back in time in a city that people from Spain settled in 1572. Ride in a horse-drawn carriage. See how old-world houses are now museums, inns, and stores. Churches and the Archbishop's Palace are as splendid as ever.

4 GET INTERACTIVE AND INSIDE
Manila

Pick up a magnifying glass and examine an ant colony. Crawl through models of body organs to understand how they work. The Museo Pambata wants you to get up close and touch the exhibits.

160

5 COOL THINGS TO DO HERE

1 BEWARE 'TITES AND 'MITES!
Penablanca

Climb 200 steps and start exploring the seven chambers of the Callao Cave. The sun pokes through natural cracks to let you see the stalactites and stalagmites. Local people have turned one chamber into a religious chapel.

2 SQUISH, SPLISH, AND SPLASH
Boracy Island

Squish your toes in the softest sand you've ever felt! White Beach is famous for its powdery sand. When you want to cool off, take a sail along the island in a boat called a paraw.

3 TAKE A LOOK AT THOSE TEETH!
Davao

Meet Crocodile Park's biggest resident, a 19-foot (5.8-m)-long crocodile named Pangil. Learn how the staff care for newborn crocodiles.

ASIA

## Map labels

'Ami
ISLANDS
Batan
Basco
btang
Channel
Babuyan
ISLANDS
Camiguin
Channel
Santa Ana
enablanca
Ilagan
Casiguran
Polillo
Islands
San Miguel Bay
Naga
Virac
Catanduanes
Lucena
Mayon Volcano
Marinduque
2462
Legazpi
Sibuyan Sea
Bulan
Burias
San Bernardino Str.
Catarman
125°
Masbate
Tablas
MASBATE
850
SAMAR
Sibuyan
Boracy
Visayan Sea
Calbayog
Roxas
Tacloban
2117 Mt. Nangtud
Ormoc
1350 Leyte Gulf
PANAY
Cadiz
908
LEYTE
Iloilo
Dinagat
Bacolod
Cebu
10°
San Carlos
BOHOL
Siargao
NEGROS
Chocloate Hills
Bohol Sea
Surigao
1903
Camiguin
Butuan
Siquijor
Gingoog
Cagayan de Oro
Malaybalay
Bislig
Iligan
MINDANAO
Pagadian
Cateel
Sibuco
Cotabato
Tagum
Zamboanga
DAVAO
Isabela
Datu Piang
2954
Digos
Mati
Lamitan
Lebak
Governor Generoso
Basilan
Koronadal
Tupi
Cape San Agustin
General Santos
Davao Gulf
CELEBES SEA
Tinaca Point
Sarangani Islands
125°
5°

DIGITAL TRAVELER!
The word *yo-yo* may have come from the Philippines. Use the Internet to find out when and how people in the Philippines first used yo-yos.

ID CARD
COUNTRY FACTS

Size: 115,831 sq mi (300,001 sq km)
Population: 96,209,000
Capital: Manila
Official languages: Filipino and English
Currency: Philippine peso
Highest point: Mount Apo, 9,692 ft (2,954 m)
Life expectancy: 69.0 years

AFRICA

A Banded Continent Straddling the Equator

Seen from space, Africa is marked by the Great Rift Valley—an enormous 3,700-mile (5,955-km)-long trench in the continent created by a fault in Earth's crust. Its landscape changes in bands, with a Mediterranean coastline and mountains in the north, then desert, grassland, tropical rain forest, and more grassland and desert in the south. There are mighty rivers, giant waterfalls, and huge lakes. Second only to Asia in size, Africa stretches some 4,600 miles (7,400 km) east to west and 5,000 miles (8,050 km) north to south.

In the background is Mount Kilimanjaro, the highest point in Africa. In the foreground, a herd of elephants migrates across the African savanna, which is also home to fierce members of the cat family, including lions, leopards, and cheetahs.

163

AFRICA

A Diverse GIANT

Africa has more countries (54), cultures, and languages (some 1,600) than any other continent. Most of the people live in small villages and towns, but there are booming cities such as Cairo, Lagos, and Johannesburg. Africa is the poorest continent, and many of its countries suffer unrest, corruption, and disease. In the last few years, several of the countries in the northwest and northeast regions of Africa have been troubled by civil wars and ethnic tensions.

Globetrotter Attractions

✈ AUNT BERTHA'S
TRAVEL TIPS

▸ ### TASTY TREATS
Sample dates, olives, and rice dishes in North Africa, millet (cereal), cassava (also known as manioc), and plantain (bananas) in East and West Africa, and sweet potatoes in southern Africa.

▸ ### WILDLIFE WONDERS
Go on safari in one of eastern or southern Africa's national parks to see some of the world's greatest concentrations of wildlife.

▸ ### SHOPPING
Railway stations and road junctions are often packed with booths and stalls where local farmers and traders sell to visitors and passersby. These are great places to buy handicrafts and souvenirs.

NORTHWEST
From the Atlas Mountains in the north to the Gulf of Guinea coast in the south, this region has lots of natural resources such as oil and natural gas. At its center is the Sahara—the world's largest desert. This region also has many countries with fast-growing populations.

CENTRAL
The Congo, the region's longest river and major transportation route, flows through rain forest. To the east are Africa's great lakes and the savanna with its rich diversity of wildlife.

GREAT CITIES
Nairobi

Nairobi is one of Africa's most modern cities. Skyscrapers fill the center of the city.

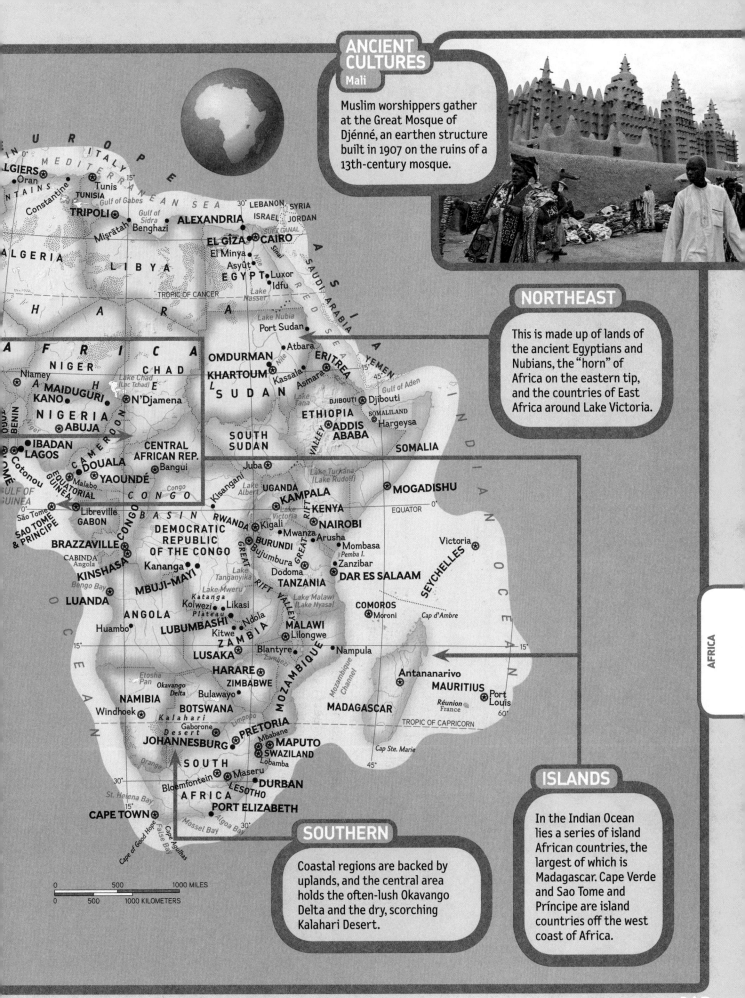

ANCIENT CULTURES
Mali

Muslim worshippers gather at the Great Mosque of Djénné, an earthen structure built in 1907 on the ruins of a 13th-century mosque.

NORTHEAST

This is made up of lands of the ancient Egyptians and Nubians, the "horn" of Africa on the eastern tip, and the countries of East Africa around Lake Victoria.

ISLANDS

In the Indian Ocean lies a series of island African countries, the largest of which is Madagascar. Cape Verde and Sao Tome and Príncipe are island countries off the west coast of Africa.

SOUTHERN

Coastal regions are backed by uplands, and the central area holds the often-lush Okavango Delta and the dry, scorching Kalahari Desert.

165

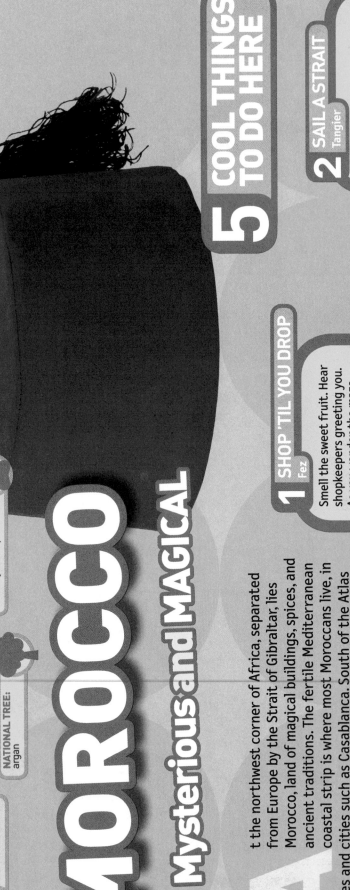

NATIONAL BIRD:
northern bald ibis

NATIONAL TREE:
argan

NATIONAL MAMMAL:
Barbary macaque

MOROCCO
Mysterious and MAGICAL

At the northwest corner of Africa, separated from Europe by the Strait of Gibraltar, lies Morocco, land of magical buildings, spices, and ancient traditions. The fertile Mediterranean coastal strip is where most Moroccans live, in villages and cities such as Casablanca. South of the Atlas Mountains that rise to more than 13,000 feet (3,962 m), the vast Sahara desert begins. Here are rocky plains, giant sand dunes, and oases. Western Sahara is a disputed desert region, claimed by Morocco.

ID CARD
COUNTRY FACTS

Size: 275,117 sq mi (712,550 sq km)*
Population: 32,950,000
Capital: Rabat
Official language: Arabic
Currency: Moroccan dirham
Highest point: Jebel Toubkal, 13,665 ft (4,165 m)
Life expectancy: 70.0 years
* includes Western Sahara

5
COOL THINGS TO DO HERE

1 SHOP 'TIL YOU DROP
Fez

Smell the sweet fruit. Hear shopkeepers greeting you. As you wander the maze-like streets, you can shop for everything from candy to carpets.

2 SAIL A STRAIT
Tangier

You can take a one-hour ferry ride from the northern tip of Africa to Spain in Europe. You'll cross the Strait of Gibraltar, where the Atlantic Ocean meets the Mediterranean Sea.

SPAIN
MEDITERRANEAN SEA
Strait of Gibraltar
(Tanger) Tangier
Ceuta Spain
Tétouan
Melilla Spain
Chechaouene
Larache
Ksar e Kebir
Ouezzane
Taza
Oujda
Kenitra
Meknès
FEZ (FÈS)
Midelt
Er Rachidia
Erfoud
RABAT
Rommani
Figuig
CASABLANCA
Berrechid
Settat
El Jadida
Benguerir
Safi
Marrakech
Ras Cantin
Gordes

3 SEEK OUT SNAKE CHARMERS
Marrakech

Go to a busy marketplace and watch snake charmers perform their acts. They pretend to hypnotize their snakes by playing music. You will probably see fortune-tellers and jugglers, too.

WESTERN SAHARA
Western Sahara, formerly Spanish Sahara, was divided by Morocco and Mauritania in 1976. Morocco has administered the territory since Mauritania's withdrawal in August 1979. The United Nations does not recognize this annexation, and Western Sahara remains in dispute.

4 GO BLUE FOR A DAY
Chechaouene

Stroll through the old streets in this town and snap photos of the blue houses. Stop in a blue-tinted cafe and sip a cup of famous Moroccan mint tea.

Globetrotter Attractions

GORGES DU TODRHA
In the High Atlas Mountains, a hiking trail stretches between steep cliff walls.

HASSAN II MOSQUE
About 25,000 worshippers can fit in this beautiful Casablanca mosque.

KASBAH AT AÏT BEN HADDOU
This is Morocco's most famous and oldest kasbah (old city). Visitors can see earthen homes, stores, and mosques. *Lawrence of Arabia* and other movies were filmed here.

5 RIDE A CAMEL
Merzouga

Sit tall on the back of a camel as it ambles through the sand in the Sahara. Camels are the main way to travel in the Sahara, a desert almost the size of the United States.

DIGITAL TRAVELER!

In Morocco, you may see a man wearing a *fez*. This is a round, red, felt hat. It often has a tassel on top. Where do you think the hat originated? Go on the Internet to check.

200 MILES
200 KILOMETERS
0 100
0 100

TROPIC OF CANCER

WESTERN SAHARA

ALGERIA AND TUNISIA

Hot Desert DESTINATIONS

Both Algeria and Tunisia have a Mediterranean coast with a pleasant climate and fertile farmland. Along the coast are many seaside resorts popular with tourists. Most Algerians and Tunisians live along the coast, in cities such as Algiers and Tunis. Here, too, are ruins of ancient towns. Algeria—Africa's largest country—features the High Atlas Mountains and the rock, sand, and scattered oases of the vast Sahara.

Globetrotter Attractions

5 HAVE A SWEET DATE
M'Zab Valley

Taste a date that was just picked off the date palm tree. Enjoy this tiny, sweet fruit. Northern Africa has just the right warm, sunny climate to grow dates. One tree can produce 180 pounds (82 kg) of dates each year.

TASSILI-N-AJJER
Between 8,000 and 1,000 years ago, cave-dwellers drew pictures on cave walls in what is now south-eastern Algeria. Today, you can still see more than 15,000 of these drawings.

MONUMENT DES MARTYRS
An eternal flame sits in the center of this monument in Algiers that honors soldiers who fought in Algeria's war for independence.

EL JEMM
In A.D. 238, El Jemm, Tunisia, was a small Roman village with one of the world's largest amphitheaters. More than 35,000 people gathered for sporting events with animals and gladiators.

ID CARD COUNTRY FACTS

ALGERIA
Population: 38,290,000
Capital: Algiers

TUNISIA
Population: 10,882,000
Capital: Tunis

DIGITAL TRAVELER!
Search the Internet for a map of the Sahara. List all the countries that the Sahara crosses.

168

5 COOL THINGS TO DO HERE

1 SMELL SPICES
Algiers

Wander the Africaine Market and see if your nose knows the difference between ginger and cinnamon.

2 CRISS-CROSS CLIFF BRIDGES
Constantine

Cross some of Constantine's many bridges. The Rhumel River has carved a deep gorge through the city. The bridges allow cars and people to cross the gorge. Some bridges are suspended from cliffs.

3 GO FISHING
Tabarqa

See what you catch when you ride in a fishing boat from Tabarqa's harbor. Learn about coral fishing as you watch divers drag small nets to pick up pieces from coral reefs.

4 STEP INTO THE STAR WARS SET
Shott el Jerid

Visit the place where Luke Skywalker grew up. In 1977, George Lucas picked the desert of Tunisia for his *Star Wars* setting.

AFRICA

*Map labels:*

MEDITERRANEAN SEA
ALGIERS (ALGER)
Oran
Sídi Bel Abbès
Tiaret
Constantine
Skikda
Annaba
Tabarqa
Bizerte
Cape Bon
Tunis
ATLAS MOUNTAINS
Sétif
Batna
Tébessa
Jebel ech Chambi 1544
El Jemm
Sfax
Gulf of Gabes
Jerba Island
Gabes
TUNISIA
SAHARAN ATLAS
Djelfa
Biskra
Chott Melrhir
Shott el Jerid
Laghouat
El Oued
Touggourt
M'Zab
Ghardaïa
Ouargla
Great Western Erg
Great Eastern Erg
ALGERIA
El Golea
Timimoun
Hamada de Tinrhert
I-n-Amenas
LIBYA
Tademaït Plateau
Chech
I-n-Salah
SAHARA
Reggane
Tassili-n-Ajjer
Illizi
Tadjmout
Tanezrouft
TROPIC OF CANCER
Tahat 3,003
Ahaggar Mountains
Tamanrasset
Tassili Oua-n-Ahaggar
Ti-n-Zaouâtene
MALI
NIGER

0   150   300 MILES
0   150   300 KILOMETERS

NATIONAL BIRD:
rough-legged hawk

NATIONAL TREE:
date palm

NATIONAL MAMMAL:
dromedary camel

LIBYA
Vast Deserts and SEASHORES

1 YOU RULE THE TOWN!
Tripoli

Stand on the balcony of the historic Yusuf Karamanli House. This was once the home of Tripoli's ruling family. Now it is a museum where you can see clothing, furniture, and everyday objects from the 1800s.

L ike its neighbors, Libya is a land of contrasts. Most Libyans farm or live in cities in the coastal regions of Cyrenaica and Tripolitania, on either side of the Gulf of Sidra. Very few people live in the other 90 percent of Libya—mostly the Libyan Desert of the Sahara, with vast tracts of sand dunes and low mountains. Even oases are scarce, but beneath the sand are rich reserves of oil.

5 FLOAT IN SALTY LAKES
Ubari Sand Sea

Splash in a lake in the middle of the Sahara. Because of the high level of carbonation and salt in the water, swimmers can float easily. The water is five times saltier than ocean water.

DIGITAL TRAVELER!
Among the early people of Libya were Berbers. They were nomads, moving with their herds of sheep and goats to find new grazing land. Berbers are well known for making dishes in a pot called a tajine. Look on the Internet for pictures of tajines and find a recipe you would like to make.

4 SEE 12,000-YEAR-OLD PAINTINGS
Jebel Acacus

Take a tour through a cave in the Jebel Acacus mountain range. Look at the prehistoric rock paintings and carvings and try to retell their stories.

5 COOL THINGS TO DO HERE

2 TAKE TEA AND TUNES
Tripoli

Nibble on a date and sip a cup of tea at Magha as-Sa'a, a popular teahouse. Sit outdoors, but be sure to go inside to see the collection of musical items, such as an old electric guitar and jukebox.

ID CARD
COUNTRY FACTS

Size: 679,362 sq mi (1,759,540 sq km)
Population: 6,518,000
Capital: Tripoli
Official language: Arabic
Currency: Libyan dinar
Highest point: Bikku Bitti, 7,434 ft (2,166 m)
Life expectancy: 75.0 years

3 VAMOOSE TO SEE ZEUS
Shaḥḥāt

Imagine how the Greeks built this Temple of Zeus in the fifth century B.C. It was even bigger than the Parthenon in Athens. It was part of the ancient city of Cyrene.

Globetrotter Attractions

LEPTIS MAGNA
Here are the ruins of one of the most beautiful cities of the Roman Empire. In 190 B.C. the city had a harbor, monuments, stores, and homes.

GURGI MOSQUE
The main prayer hall of this mosque in Tripoli is decorated with marble from Italy, tiles from Tunisia, and carved stones from Morocco.

WĀW-AN-NĀMŪS CRATER
This prehistoric volcano is located in the Sahara, surrounded by lakes.

AFRICA

NATIONAL BIRD:
golden eagle

NATIONAL FLOWER:
Egyptian lotus

NATIONAL MAMMAL:
fennec fox

EGYPT

Crossroads of CONTINENTS

1 OPEN A BOOK TO HISTORY
Alexandria

Stand in this library and look up through the high glass-panelled roof. The shelves can hold eight million books. The first library here was destroyed in a war in the third century B.C.

The Nile River and its delta nurture Egypt's farmland and cities, as they have since the time of the pyramids. The Aswan Dam's Lake Nasser provides extra irrigation for a hot, dry land. To the west of the Nile is the Libyan Desert, to the east are the Red Sea and the Sinai Peninsula joining Asia and Africa. The Suez Canal links the Red Sea to the Mediterranean, providing a route between Europe and Asia.

Globetrotter Attractions

5 SNORKEL IN THE RED SEA
Dahab

Put on a mask and fins and wade into the water of the Red Sea. The coral reefs are home to colorful fish, dolphins, and turtles.

MEDITERR

Maṭrûḥ•

Libyan Plateau

Qattara Depression

30°

–133

Sîwa•

Western

Baḥari
Oasi

Qaṣr Farâfra • Farâfra
Oasis

E   G

Desert

Dakhla
Oasis

+682   +Abu Ballâs
467

*Gilf Kebîr
Plateau*

S A H A

+Gebel Kâmil
785

➥ PYRAMIDS OF GIZA
More than 4,500 years ago, three Egyptian rulers ordered these pyramids built. After the rulers died, their bodies were placed inside their pyramids.

➥ VALLEY OF THE KINGS
Egyptians built underground tombs for their kings. People placed clothes, furniture, and food next to the kings' bodies for the afterlife.

➥ CAIRO MUSEUM
King Tutankhamun's mask (see above) and mummies of other kings are in the museum.

DIGITAL TRAVELER!
The Suez Canal is an important modern transportation route in Egypt. Go online and find a picture of the canal. Then read how long it takes ships to sail through the canal.

5 COOL THINGS TO DO HERE

2 RIDE A CAMEL TO THE SPHINX
El Gîza

Ride from the pyramids to the biggest and oldest statue in Egypt. Decide where the lion's body ends and the human head begins. The Sphinx is 66 feet (20 m) high and 240 feet (73 m) long.

3 CLIMB MOSES' MOUNTAIN
Mount Sinai

Hike in a special place to Muslims, Christians, and Jews. Traditionally, some people call this the place in the Bible where Moses received the Ten Commandments.

ID CARD
COUNTRY FACTS

Size: 386,662 sq mi (1,001,450 sq km)
Population: 84,667,000
Capital: Cairo
Official language: Arabic
Currency: Egyptian pound
Highest point: Mount Catherine, 8,652 ft (2,637 m)
Life expectancy: 70.0 years

4 SAIL ON A SLOW BOAT
Aswân

Feel the wind take your felucca sailboat along the Nile River, the longest river in the world. Sail by the Tombs of the Nobles and stop at the Aswân Botanic Gardens.

### Map labels

MEDITERRANEAN SEA
ALEXANDRIA (EL ISKANDARÎYA)
Nile Delta
Port Said (Bûr Sa'îd)
GAZA STRIP
ISRAEL
Ṭanṭa
Ismâ'îlîya
Suez Canal
EL GÎZA
SHUBRA EL KHEIMA
CAIRO (EL QÂHIRA)
Pyramids of Giza
SINAI
30°
JORDAN
El Faiyûm
Gulf of Suez
Gulf of Aqaba
Gebel el Galâla el Qiblîya 1218
Mt. Sinai 2285
Dahab
SAUDI ARABIA
El Minya
Mt. Catherine 2637
Gebel Ghârib 1751
Sharm el Sheikh
Râs Muḥammad
Mallawi
Nile (An Nîl)
Eastern Desert
Asyûṭ
Gebel Shâyib el Banât 2187
Hurghada
RED SEA
EGYPT
Bûr Safâga
Girga
Quṣeir
Valley of the Kings
Gebel el Sibâ'i 1484
El Khârga
Luxor
Khârga Oasis
Idfu
Gebel Nugruṣ 1505
Gebel Hamâta 1977
Aswân
1st Cataract
Aswan High Dam
Berenice
Râs Banâs
Foul Bay
Gebel el Farâid 1366
TROPIC OF CANCER
Lake Nasser
Marsa Sha'ab
Siyal Islands
Boundary claimed by Sudan
Gebel Siri 420
Halayeb
Cape Elba (Râs Hadarba)
SUDAN
Nile
30°

0   100   200 MILES
0   100   200 KILOMETERS

5 COOL THINGS TO DO HERE

1 WELCOME THE FISHING BOATS
Nouakchott

Hurry to the water in the late afternoon and watch the fishermen unload their fish-filled nets. Children scurry to help by sorting the fish on trays.

2 THUMP A DRUM
Dakar

Follow the beat of your drumming teacher. One kind of African drum is called a *djembe*. Use your hands to slap and tap your djembe.

3 LEARN KITE SURFING
Cape Verde Islands

Let the wind fill your kite, and hold on tight! The kite will carry you through the water. After you take a lesson, relax on the beach.

4 CHECK OUT CROCODILES
Serekunda

Stand by the Kachikally Crocodile Pool and watch the 80 or so adult crocodiles. Many people believe the pool has supernatural healing powers and the water can bring good luck.

NORTHERN WEST AFRICA

The Atlantic Meets the SAHARA

Mauritania is bigger than its southern neighbors, Senegal and Gambia. Most of Mauritania is in the Sahara, with southern grasslands near the Senegal River. The river forms a border with Senegal, which has desert, forest, and savanna. Gambia, named for the Gambia River, is enclosed by Senegal, but has an Atlantic coast. Some 400 miles (643 km) west, the dry, volcanic Cape Verde islands rise from the ocean.

ID CARD COUNTRY FACTS

CAPE VERDE
Population: 515,000
Capital: Praia

GAMBIA
Population: 1,884,000
Capital: Banjul

MAURITANIA
Population: 3,712,000
Capital: Nouakchott

SENEGAL
Population: 13,497,000
Capital: Dakar

Globetrotter Attractions

CHÃ DAS CALDEIRAS
This village is set inside a volcano's crater on Fogo Island in Cape Verde. Villagers grow grapes in the rich volcanic soil. The steaming volcano peak is almost always in view.

HOUSE OF SLAVES
In the late 1700s, thousands of captured Africans were forced into this Goree Island (Île de Gorée) building in chains. They left Senegal through the Door of No Return to become slaves in the Americas.

BANC D'ARGUIN NATIONAL PARK
Mauritania's island beaches and sand dunes attract migrating sandpipers, pelicans, and flamingos to spend the winter.

AFRICA

5 TWEET ABOUT WILD BIRDS
Gambia River

Listen to bird calls as your *pirogue* glides on the Gambia River. A pirogue is like a canoe. This colorful bird is called a malachite kingfisher.

DIGITAL TRAVELER!
Kora, tabala, and *balafon* are three kinds of African instruments. Do some digital research to find out what each instrument looks and sounds like.

CENTRAL WEST AFRICA

Wetlands and WILDLIFE

Five states occupy the Atlantic coast of West Africa from Senegal south and then east to the Gulf of Guinea. They are Guinea-Bissau, Guinea, Sierra Leone, Liberia (Africa's oldest republic), and Côte d'Ivoire (Ivory Coast). Central West Africa is warm and wet, with coastal forest and mangrove swamps, rivers flowing through coastal plains, and amazing wildlife. Inland are savanna grasslands and mountains rising more than 6,000 feet (1,829 m).

ID CARD COUNTRY FACTS

CÔTE D'IVOIRE (IVORY COAST)
Population: 21,142,000
Capital: Yamoussoukro

GUINEA
Population: 11,793,000
Capital: Conakry

GUINEA-BISSAU
Population: 1,677,000
Capital: Bissau

LIBERIA
Population: 4,357,000
Capital: Monrovia

SIERRA LEONE
Population: 6,242,000
Capital: Freetown

Globetrotter Attractions

ORANGO ISLANDS NATIONAL PARK
The park in Guinea-Bissau covers several islands. A rare kind of saltwater hippo lives here.

YAMOUSSOUKRO BASILICA
This church in Côte d'Ivoire may be the largest Christian house of worship in the world. It can hold 18,000 people inside and 300,000 outside.

NIMBA MOUNTAINS
Some unusual animals live here, including goliath frogs, which can weigh seven pounds (3 kg). The mountains straddle Guinea, Liberia, and Côte d'Ivoire.

5 FLIP OUT!
Conakry

Catch a performance by the children of Conakry. After school, many of them learn acrobatics. They perform in parks and in their gym. Some have become circus stars.

DIGITAL TRAVELER!
When Ellen Johnson Sirleaf was elected president of Liberia in 2005, she was the first woman president of any African country. Use your electronic device to find out how many other countries have had women presidents.

Map labels: São Domingos, Cacheu, Farim, Mansabá, Bafatá, 12°, GUINEA-BIS, Bissau, Formosa, Fulacunda, Bissagos Islands, Bolama, Buba, Bubaque, Catió, Orango Islands National Park, Roxa, Kanfarande, Kamsar, Monchor, Cacine, 15°, ATLANTIC, Orango

5 COOL THINGS TO DO HERE

1 BUY KORHOGO CLOTH
Korhogo

Choose the pictures that you like best. Artists paint large scenes on cloth. People hang the cloths on their walls or sew them into shirts and jackets.

2 KEEP YOUR EYES ON THE BALL
Abidjan

See teams play at the stadium called "Le Felicia," which also hosts athletic events. The Ivory Coast soccer team often plays here.

4 CHECK OUT THE CHIMPS
Bossou Forest

Visit the chimpanzee research station and find out why studies show that these chimps are the smartest in the world.

3 LOOK FOR RUBBER TREES
Buchanan

Visit a rubber farm and watch the milky latex drip from the trees. Workers collect the latex and turn it into rubber for tires and other products.

EASTERN WEST AFRICA

Warm and WELCOMING

Ghana, Togo, and Benin have coasts on the Gulf of Guinea. To the north is landlocked Burkina Faso. These four warm countries share historic cultures and a landscape of mostly plains and forest plateaus. The highest peak (in Togo) is only 3,235 feet (986 m). Building the Akosombo Dam in the 1960s created Lake Volta and many rivers that water land for farming. English is the official language of Ghana, but French is spoken in Benin, Burkina Faso, and Togo.

ID CARD COUNTRY FACTS

BENIN
Population: 9,645,000
Capital: Porto-Novo

BURKINA FASO
Population: 18,015,000
Capital: Ouagadougou

GHANA
Population: 26,088,000
Capital: Accra

TOGO
Population: 6,168,000
Capital: Lomé

DIGITAL TRAVELER!
A lithophone is a traditional percussion instrument in Togo and other African places. Search the Internet to find a picture of a lithophone. Then find a sample of lithophone music.

Globetrotter Attractions

STONE SCULPTURES OF LAONGO
Sculptors from around the world come to Laongo, in Burkina Faso, to carve the large granite stones.

LAKE VOLTA
This is one of the world's largest artificial lakes. It provides much of the water for Ghana and serves as a transportation route, a source of electric power, and a resource for fishing.

OUIDAH MUSEUM OF HISTORY
The museum tells the story of slave trading. It is located by the Benin port where slaves were forced onto ships.

Nouna
Tougan
Dédougou
BURKI
Boromo
Bobo Dioulasso
Banfora
Lawra
Gaoua
Logoniégué
Batié
CÔTE D'IVOIRE
(IVORY COAST)

5 COOL THINGS TO DO HERE

1 SPOT A HIPPO
Wechiau

Peer through binoculars to spot the hippos at the Wechiau Community Hippo Sanctuary. This river is home to one of the two remaining hippo groups in Ghana.

2 SHOP AT THE MARKETPLACE
Ouagadougou

Join the crowds of locals and tourists at the market where you'll find vegetables and fruits, pottery and baskets, clothing, and jewelry. Musicians often entertain the shoppers.

3 SPLASH UNDER WATERFALLS
Badou

Let the Akloa Falls gush down around you as you cool off in its natural pool. The falls drop down from a cliff that is 115 feet (35 m) above the pool.

4 LIVE LIKE ROYALTY
Abomey

Learn about the powerful Benin Empire and the kings who ruled it from these palaces from 1695 to 1900. In addition to being homes for the kings, the ten palaces stored the treasures of the kingdom. Modern reenactments show how the royal families lived.

5 HANG ON TIGHT!
Cape Coast region

Step carefully on this rope bridge suspended 98 feet (30 m) above the forest floor in Kakum National Park.

AFRICA

179

MALI

Land of Music and MASKS

NATIONAL BIRD:
Nubian bustard

NATIONAL TREE:
nere

NATIONAL MAMMAL:
African wild frog

Mali has no seacoast, is mostly flat, and has two distinct regions. In the hot, dry north, the Sahara merges into the Sahel, a drought-prone, treeless expanse where nomads herd livestock. In the south, the Niger River waters the landscape for trees and crops. Mali, once a rich empire, has a fascinating culture, and ancient trade routes link historic cities such as Timbuktu.

ID CARD
COUNTRY FACTS

Size: 478,841 sq mi (1,240,192 sq km)
Population: 15,461,000
Capital: Bamako
Official language: French
Currency: Communaute Africaine Financiere franc
Highest point: Hombori Tondo, 3,789 ft (1,155 m)
Life expectancy: 54.0 years

5 COOL THINGS TO DO HERE

1 MEET PEOPLE ON THEIR WAY TO MARKET
Mopti

Greet the Fulani people as they go to trade goods at the market. The people are nomadic. They move from place to place with their cattle. The women and girls wear colorful clothing.

2 FOLLOW THE HUMPBACK ROAD
Timbuktu

Pretend you are a trader crossing the Sahara. Tourists can take short camel rides, but real traders still travel on camels to make deliveries from the salt mines.

3 SIP FLOWER JUICE
Bamako

Drop by a restaurant and enjoy a djablani drink. It is made from the petals of a hibiscus flower.

4 MAKE BEAUTIFUL MUD CLOTHS
Ségou

Start with a colorful fabric. Use a stick and mud to draw pictures that tell a story. The Mali people will show you how to dry the mud and rinse it off. Then your mud cloth will be ready!

Globetrotter Attractions

ETHNOLOGICAL MUSEUM

The collections of clothing, jewelry, games, and musical instruments tell what life was like in Timbuktu hundreds of years ago.

GREAT MOSQUE OF DJENNÉ

It is said that this Islamic house of worship is the largest mud-built structure in the world.

BANDIAGARA CLIFFS

More than 600 years ago, the Dogon people carved their villages into the cliffs of Bandiagara. These communities are still alive today.

5 MARVEL AT MASKED DANCERS
Bandiagara

Celebrate with the Dogon people as they put on masks and colorful clothes and dance on stilts during religious ceremonies and festivals.

DIGITAL TRAVELER!
Bright, colorful fabrics are everywhere in Mali. Take photographs of the fabrics you like best and use them in a scrapbook about your globetrotter journey.

NIGER
Land of Rivers and SAND DUNES

The sand dunes of the Sahara spread into northern Niger, but nomads travel with their livestock in the cooler Air Mountains. Most people live in the south, where there is farmland, savanna grassland with scattered trees, and the country's only big river, the Niger. In the south, too, is Niger's largest city, Niamey. Part of Lake Chad, a shrinking but still vital water resource, is in southeast Niger.

2 GET THUMPING AND MASHING
Maradi

Follow the sound of thump, thump, thump, and find villagers grinding flour by hand. A mortar is a bowl. A pestle is a thick rod with a rounded end used to mash or grind food.

5 COOL THINGS TO DO HERE

1 GO BATS ABOUT BATS
Niamey

At nighttime, check the sky for soaring fruit bats. During the day, you may find these large creatures hanging in trees in the Place de la République. They sleep during the day.

3 FOLLOW GIRAFFES
Dosso

Try to spot a giraffe at the Dosso Reserve. This place protects endangered West African giraffes. The giraffes migrate into the park from Mali after the rainy season.

4 GET LOST IN THE MOSQUE
Agadez

Climb the steps to the top of this tower. You'll see a spectacular view of the town and the desert. This is one of the most famous buildings in Niger. Muslims have been praying here since the 1500s.

Globetrotter Attractions

NATIONAL MUSEUM OF NIGER, NIAMEY
The Tree of Tenere, no longer alive, is on display here. Until a truck hit it in 1973, it was the last tree standing in the Sahara.

"W" NATIONAL PARK
The park is named for the double bend in the Niger River, which borders it. It is home to gazelles, elephants, and cheetahs.

YAAMA MOSQUE
In the early 1960s, everyone in the community helped build this mosque by making mud bricks or carrying water and wood.

ID CARD
COUNTRY FACTS

Size: 489,076 sq mi (1,266,700 sq km)
Population: 16,916,000
Capital: Niamey
Official language: French
Currency: Communaute Africaine Financiere franc
Highest point: Idoukal-n-Taghes, 6,634 ft (2,022 m)
Life expectancy: 57.0 years

AFRICA

5 ACT LIKE ZINDER-ELLA
Zinder

Take a tour of the home of Zinder's ruler. You'll find out that the building was a prison hundreds of years ago. Pictures drawn by prisoners are still on the walls.

DIGITAL TRAVELER!
About 65 years ago, scientists found dinosaur fossils in Niger. They reconstructed the dinosaur called *Nigersaurus*. Go online and get information about this dinosaur.

5 COOL THINGS TO DO HERE

1 SEE GODDESS SCULPTURES
Oshogbo

Follow the forest path into this sacred grove. The Yoruba people have made shrines, statues, and artwork for the goddesses they believe in.

2 STOP AT THE STONE
Abuja

Shout out when the rock comes into view! This huge boulder is called the "Gateway to Abuja." Its picture is on the 100 naira bill, Nigerian money.

3 RIDE A BOAT TO THE BEACH
Lagos

Head for Tarkwa Beach, one of the most popular beaches in Lagos. You can only reach it by boat, but the ride is worth it for a fun day of swimming.

4 SPOT A CUTE CRITTER
Rhoko Forest

Look out for bush babies jumping from tree to tree. These nocturnal primates are about the size of a squirrel and have supersharp night vision.

Map of Nigeria

NIGER

CHAD

Lake Chad (Lac Tchad)

240

Gashagar
Geidam
Ngala
Dikwa
Bama
MAIDUGURI
Damboa
Gwoza
Biu
Mubi
Numan

Sokoto
Birnin Kebbi
Kaura-Namoda
Gusau
Jega
Gummi
Koko
Zuru
Yelwa
Katsina
KANO
Nguru
Gashua
Potiskum
Gaya
Azare
Kari
Funtua
Zaria
KADUNA
Bauchi
Gombe
Kumo
Jos
Yankari National Park
Kontagora
Kainji Reservoir
Kaiama
Minna
Jebba
Bida
ABUJA
Baro
Abaji
Nasarawa
Shendam
Jalingo
Yola
Mayo Faran
Toungo
ILORIN
Ogbomosho
Oyo
Iwo
Oshogbo
Ife
Ikare
Owo
Lokoja
Wukari
Donga
Serti
IBADAN
Abeokuta
Ondo
Idah
Makurdi
Otukpo
Chappal Waddi 2419
Mayo Ndaga
Ikorodu
LAGOS
Slave Coast
Bight of Benin
Sapele
Warri
BENIN CITY
Onitsha
Nsukka
Ogoja
Enugu
Umuahia
ABA
PORT HARCOURT
Rhoko Forest
Calabar
Niger
Palm Point
Niger Delta
Bight of Benin
GULF OF GUINEA
Sokoto
Niger
Borgou
BENIN
CAMEROON
Mandara Mts.
Gongola
Benue

0   100   200 MILES
0   100   200 KILOMETERS

NATIONAL BIRD:
black crowned crane

NATIONAL FLOWER:
costus

NATIONAL MAMMAL:
Cross River gorilla

NIGERIA

Africa's Most Populated COUNTRY

Africa's population giant, Nigeria, is a prosperous country, thanks to oil fields in the south and offshore in the Gulf of Guinea. The country has distinct regions, each with its own cultures and wildlife, and large, lively cities. The landscape includes grassy plains and highlands, rivers, lakes including artificial Kainji Reservoir, rocky mountains, lowland forest, and mangrove swamps in the Niger River Delta. Northern Nigeria is hotter and drier than the south.

5 READ MESSAGES FROM MONKEYS
Calabar

Try to figure out what these animals are communicating to one another at the Drill Monkey Rehab Center. A grin usually is a friendly gesture. They make sounds to keep their group together and rub their chests on trees to keep others away.

Globetrotter Attractions

ABUJA NATIONAL MOSQUE
This gold-domed mosque attracts worshippers and visitors throughout the year.

OLUMO ROCK
During an 1830s war, the Egba people hid from their enemies by this rock. After the war, the rock became a sacred place. Visitors can reach the top of the 449-foot (137-m)-high rock in Abeokuta by elevator or stairs.

YANKARI NATIONAL PARK
This large park has swamps, floodplains, bush, and grasslands—a comfortable home for baboons, giraffes, hyenas, hippos, and others.

AFRICA

ID CARD
COUNTRY FACTS

Size: 356,669 sq mi (923,768 sq km)
Population: 173,615,000
Capital: Abuja
Official language: English
Currency: naira
Highest point: Chappal Waddi, 7,936 ft (2,419 m)
Life expectancy: 52.0 years

DIGITAL TRAVELER!
The currency of Nigeria is *naira* and *kobo*, with 100 kobo to 1 naira. Find a website that converts 10 U.S. dollars into Nigerian money. How many naira and kobo would you have?

CHAD

From Desert to SAVANNA

Northern deserts and central savanna grasslands where elephants roam —that's most of Chad. Only in the south of this sub-Saharan country is there land suitable for farming. It's still hot in the south, though in the highlands of the Tibesti Mountains it is cool, and the Ennedi Plateau is temperate. Chad's farmers and herders rely on rivers such as the Chari and Logone, and on Lake Chad, which is shallow and shrinking so fast it may disappear.

Globetrotter Attractions

GUELTA D'ARCHEI
Far out in the Sahara is this *guelta*, or oasis. Between canyon walls, water bubbles up to form a pool. Camels drink near the home of the last Nile crocodiles.

LAKE CHAD
The size of this large lake changes with each season but is getting smaller.

EMI KOUSSI
This large and broad volcano is the highest mountain in the Sahara, but it no longer erupts.

ID CARD
COUNTRY FACTS

Size: 495,755 sq mi (1,284,000 sq km)
Population: 12,209,000
Capital: N'Djamena
Official languages: French and Arabic
Currency: Cooperacion Financière en Afrique Central franc
Highest point: Emi Koussi, 11,204 ft (3,415 m)
Life expectancy: 50.0 years

5 COOL THINGS TO DO HERE

1 GET INTO MUSIC AND MASKS
N'Djamena

Examine this museum's many musical instruments used by Chad's people over the years. Find the masks people used throughout Chad's history.

4 TREK OVER AN OLD VOLCANO
Tibesti Massif

Walk the Tibesti Mountains and see several inactive volcanoes. Visit canyons and hot springs. Find the rock paintings and carvings made long ago. Meet the Toubou people who now live on oases in the nearby desert.

5 BE AN ELEPHANT CONSERVATIONIST
Zakouma National Park

Watch rangers protect the elephants in Chad's first national park. Elephants almost disappeared until better protection allowed their numbers and those of other wild animals to increase.

2 TAKE A WALK ON SANDY STREETS
Mao

Wander the sandy streets and meet with friendly children. Admire the bright clothes worn by girls. Visit their one-room school. Travel down the dusty streets on a horse. Shop at street vendors.

3 GET WATER FROM A WELL
Ati

Join villagers as they get the water they need for drinking, cooking, and washing from the local well. Try carrying water in a jug on your head.

DIGITAL TRAVELER!

Lake Chad provides water to millions of people in Chad and three other neighboring countries. Go online to figure out which countries these are. Then see if you can find out how deep Lake Chad is.

SUDAN AND SOUTH SUDAN

Desert, Rivers, and the RED SEA

South Sudan broke from Sudan in 2011. Until the split, Sudan was Africa's biggest country. It's mostly desert. To the west is the Sahara, while the Nubian Desert borders the Red Sea.

Yet through this hot land of sand and camels flows the Nile, Africa's mightiest river. On its banks stands Khartoum, capital of Sudan. In South Sudan is a vast wetland formed by the White Nile, known as the Sudd.

NATIONAL BIRD:
SUDAN secretary bird
SOUTH SUDAN African fish eagle

NATIONAL FLOWER:
oleander
Bidens chipli

NATIONAL MAMMAL:
Burton's gerbil
kob

ID CARD
COUNTRY FACTS

SUDAN
Population: 34,186,000
Capital: Khartoum

SOUTH SUDAN
Population: 9,782,000
Capital: Juba

5 COOL THINGS TO DO HERE

1 GET THE POINT OF PYRAMIDS
Meroë

Visit Sudan's Meroë, once the capital of the Kingdom of Kush. Wander through its royal cemetery, which includes about 100 small pyramids.

### Map labels

RED SEA

Ras Abu Shagara
Salala
Muhammad Qol
Sanganeb Lighthouse
Port Sudan
Suakin
Sinkat
Haiya
Musmar
Tokar
Aqiq
Ras Kasar
Deruded
Berber
Atbara
Ad Damer
Meroë
5th Cataract
Abu Hamed
Shereiq
Keheili
Merowe
Korti
4th Cataract
Ed Debba
El Khandaq
Argo
Dongola
Delgo
3rd Cataract
Wadi Halfa
2nd Cataract
Nile (an Nil)
Nubian Desert
EGYPT
Selima Oasis
+654
Jebel 'Uweinat 1893
LIBYA
Libyan Desert
SAHARA
Boundary claimed by Sudan

400 MILES
400 KILOMETERS
0 200
0 200

.704

Globetrotter Attractions

SANGANEB LIGHTHOUSE
This Sudan lighthouse stands on a coral reef in the Red Sea. There are great views from the top.

DINDER NATIONAL PARK
Many different animals live on the grasslands and in woodlands and forests of this park in Sudan.

AL-MOGRAN PARK
This Sudan amusement park is where the Blue Nile and White Nile rivers come together.

---

2 TOUR TEMPLES AND TOMBS
Khartoum
Visit ancient temples and tombs outside the Sudan National Museum. These buildings and ruins were moved from where the Nubia area was flooded for Egypt's Aswan High Dam.

3 SAIL FOR A MILE ON THE BLUE NILE
Wad Medani
Hop a boat to travel on the Blue Nile in Sudan's Wad Medani. Take a boat to the beach just across the river from the city. Explore the city, which is a favorite with visitors and honeymooning couples.

4 WATCH WATER MAKE ELECTRICITY
Ed Damazin
Watch the water move through the Ar-Rusayris Dam. Enjoy the green land it waters and the electricity its hydroelectric plant creates.

5 PACK UP A CAMEL
Omdurman
Admire camels from South Sudan that are for sale in this camel market. Find one that is fast, one that can carry a heavy load, or one that can do both!

DIGITAL TRAVELER!
Do online research to learn about the traditional foods in Sudan and South Sudan. What would you eat if you traveled there?

AFRICA

189

*Map labels:*

ERITREA

Atbara · Kassala · Gedaref · Qallabat · Galegu · Dinder National Park

KHARTOUM · Khartoum North · OMDURMAN · Wad Medani · Es Suki · Singa · Sennar · Blue Nile (Al Bahr al Azraq) · Ed Damazin · Qeissan

Kagmar · Bara · Er Rahad · Rashad · Kaka · Kodok · Malakal · Abwong · Nasir · Akobo

ETHIOPIA

Sodiri · Mazrub · El Obeid · Abu Zabad · Dilling · Kadugli · Talodi · Tonga · Fangak · Nyerol · Akobo · Pibor Post

En Nahud · Ogr · El Odaiya · Muglad · Muglad Basin · ABYEI · Wang Kai · Bentiu · Ler · Kongor · Mongalla · Juba

Babanūsah · Abu Matariq · Gabras · Aweil · Gogrial · Rumbek · Amadi · Yei

Nyala · 'Iddel Ghanam · Kubbum · El Fifi · Deim Zubeir · Tambura · Li Yubu · Maridi · Yambio

Tundubai · Kutum · El Fasher · Kas · Jebel Marra 3088 · Geneina · DARFUR · Kafia Kingi · Raga

SUDAN · SAHEL · S O U T H   S U D A N · Sue · Kuru · Lol · Nyamlell

Wadi Howar · Wadi el Milk · Wadi Ibra · 6th Cataract · White Nile (Al Bahr al Abyad) · Mountain Nile (Bahr el Jebel)

CENTRAL AFRICAN REP. · DEMOCRATIC REPUBLIC OF THE CONGO · UGANDA · KENYA

Kapoeta · ILEMI TRIANGLE Administered by Kenya (claimed by South Sudan)

Boundary claimed by South Sudan · Boundary claimed by Sudan

"HORN" OF DARFUR: Southern South Darfur an area referred to by some as the "Horn" of Darfur, is marginally administered by both Sudan and South Sudan. The future of this resource-rich area is subject to further Sudanese and South Sudanese negotiations.

ERITREA
ETHIOPIA

NATIONAL BIRD:
lemon dove
African firefinch

NATIONAL FLOWER:
prickly acacia
calla lily

NATIONAL MAMMAL:
Arabian camel
lion

ERITREA AND ETHIOPIA

Two Contrasting COUNTRIES

Eritrea separated from Ethiopia in 1993. Ethiopia, one of Africa's oldest countries, is almost ten times larger than Eritrea, which occupies a strip of Red Sea coast. In the mountains and plateaus of the Great Rift Valley are grasslands, forests, and many farms. There is also a wealth of wildlife. Rivers rise here, including the Blue Nile, and Tana is a large lake in Ethiopia. The lowlands are hot and barren, with severe droughts.

5 COUNT THE CHERUBS
Gonder

Look up from the wall paintings to find the cherubs painted on the ceiling of Debre Berhan Selassie, an Ethiopian church.

Globetrotter Attractions

SIMIEN MOUNTAINS NATIONAL PARK

This Ethiopian national park has many animals found nowhere else in the world. The weather has shaped its mountains, deep valleys, and high sharp cliffs.

THE ROYAL ENCLOSURE

The Ethiopian fortress-city of Fasil Ghebbi in Gonder has several castles surrounded by a wall. Ethiopian emperors of the 1600s and 1700s built these unique palaces and churches.

DAHLAK ARCHIPELAGO

Only 4 of these 210 Eritrean islands have people living on them. Many divers come to explore the Red Sea around them with its many fish and birds.

4 INSPECT WAR TANKS
Taulud Island

Wander around Eritrea's Massawa War Memorial. Visit the three captured tanks and see the fountain spouting water.

ID CARD COUNTRY FACTS

ERITREA
Population: 5,765,000
Capital: Asmara

ETHIOPIA
Population: 89,209,000
Capital: Addis Ababa

Āsosa
Mendī
Tulu Welel + 3312
Dembi Dolo
Gorē
Majī
ILEMI TRIANGLE
Administered by Keny
claimed by South Sudan
Boundary claimed by Kenya
Lake Rudolf
(Lake Turkana)

5 COOL THINGS TO DO HERE

1 SNAP A FUTURISTIC GAS STATION
Asmara

Admire this unusual service station in Eritrea, built in the shape of a 1930s airplane.

2 EAT YOUR PLATE
Adi Ugri

Sit around a table in Eritrea. Eat the stew that comes on a spongy pancake called *injera*. Tear a piece of injera and wrap it around the meat. No forks, just pop it into your mouth!

3 EXPLORE CAVE CHURCHES
Lalibela

Look down into a pit to find a church carved from one piece of rock. See all 11 of Lalibela, Ethiopia's rock cave churches. Admire how the rock was cut away for doors and windows.

AFRICA

DIGITAL TRAVELER!
Go online to search for the languages spoken in Eritrea and Ethiopia. Find out how to say "Hello" in both countries.

NATIONAL BIRD:
Djibouti francolin
Somali lark

NATIONAL FLOWER:
Egyptian starcluster
Euphorbia noxia

NATIONAL MAMMAL:
gerenuk
leopard

HORN OF AFRICA

Neighbors by the SEA

N eighbors on the jutting Horn of Africa are Djibouti and Somalia. The climate is hot and dry, and there are few rivers. Tiny Djibouti is separated from the Arabian Peninsula by a narrow seaway, part of the Red Sea and Gulf of Aden. To the east, Somalia, possibly the "Land of Punt" of legend, stretches south from Cape Gwardafuy along the Indian Ocean. Somalia has been strife-torn, with civil war and piracy.

5 COOL THINGS TO DO HERE

2 JOIN IN A JAM SESSION
Berbera

Instead of walking through the streets of Berbera in Somalia, ride in a *bajaj*, a three-wheeled motorized rickshaw. Listen for music and street singers, and hear songs that tell a story.

1 WATCH WHALE SHARKS
Gulf of Tadjoura

See the world's largest fish when it comes to feed on tiny plankton in this Djibouti gulf. Some whale sharks weigh more than an elephant but they don't bite, even though they are sharks not whales.

5 IMAGINE YOU ARE ON THE MOON
Abhé Bid Háyk'

Wander between the limestone chimneys that dot this flat plain in Djibouti. Wake early to see flocks of pink flamingos on the shores of the lake. Maybe they'll take off to fly over the tall pillars and dry land.

Cape Gwardafuy
Xaafuun
Caluula
Bargaal
Hurdiyo
Qandala
50°
2200
Boosaaso
Laasqoray
Ceerigaabo
45°
Maydh
Berbera

YEMEN
Bab el Mandeb
Gulf of Tadjoura
RED SEA
ERITREA
DJIBOUTI
Djibouti
Saylac
Day Forest National Park
Lake Assal
Lake Abbe

ID CARD
COUNTRY FACTS

DJIBOUTI
Population: 939,000
Capital: Djibouti

SOMALIA
Population: 10,383,000
Capital: Mogadishu

3 BE ARTISTIC IN CAVES
Laas Geel

See some of Africa's best-preserved cave paintings on a guided tour of Laas Geel in Somalia. The paintings were made between 7,000 and 5,000 years ago and show people and both domesticated and wild animals.

Globetrotter Attractions

LAKE ASSAL
When the warm, salty water of Djibouti's Lake Assal (Lac 'Assal) dries, it leaves a crust of salt. The lake is in one of the hottest places on Earth.

DAY FOREST NATIONAL PARK
This ancient forest in northern Djibouti has a variety of trees and birds. The land is very different from the semi-desert and deserts nearby.

SINBUSI BEACH
The coastline near Marka has many small beach resorts where tourists can do various watersports.

DIGITAL TRAVELER!
Parts of the original *Planet of the Apes* movie of 1968 were filmed in Djibouti. Do an Internet search for scenes from the movie.

4 SHOP AT THE MARKET
Djibouti City

Buy what you need at the Central Market in the city of Djibouti in Djibouti. Visit stores and street vendors with their goods spread out under an umbrella. Go in the morning, as it gets very hot and quiet in the afternoon.

### Map labels

SOMALILAND
In 1991 the Somali National Movement declared Somaliland an independent republic with Hargeysa as the capital. It is not internationally recognized.

Boundary Undemarcated and in Dispute

ETHIOPIA

SOMALILAND

PUNTLAND

Boorama
Laas Geel Caves
Hargeysa
Burco
Xudun
Caynabo
Laascaanood
Qardho
Bandarbeyla
Xalin
Garoowe
Eyl
Eyl
Garacad
Bacaadweyn
Gaalkacyo
Hobyo
Dhuusa Marreeb
Ceelbuur
Xarardheere
Mereeg
Buulobarde
Jawhar
Shebele
Beledweyne
Xuddur
Buurhakaba
Wanlaweyn
MOGADISHU (MUQDISHO)
Marka
Luuq
Baydhabo
Baardheere
Baraawe
Jubba
Sarinleey
Afmadow
Jilib
Jamaame
Kismaayo
Buur Gaabo
Kaambooni

EQUATOR

KENYA

INDIAN OCEAN

200 MILES
100
200 KILOMETERS
100

AFRICA

193

5 COOL THINGS TO DO HERE

1 COUNT FLAMINGOS
Lake Nakuru

Count the thousands of flamingos eating in the lake. Search for the other 450 types of birds found here. Watch for rhinoceroses and giraffes.

2 GREET A GIRAFFE
Nairobi National Park

Watch these gentle-looking giants stretch their long tongues to reach the best leaves at the top of trees. See zebras, lions, baboons, and hippopotamuses as you are guided through this park of grasslands. All these animals live very close to Kenya's capital city of Nairobi.

Boundary claimed by Kenya

ILEMI TRIANGLE
Administered by Kenya
(claimed by South Sudan)

0   100   200 MILES
0   100   200 KILOMETERS

SOUTH SUDAN

ETHIOPIA

Todenyang
Lake Ch'ew Bahir
Lokichokio
Lokitaung
Sabarei
Kakuma
Lake Turkana (Lake Rudolf)
Lokwakangole
North Horr
Lodwar
Chalbi Desert

Mandera
Banissa
Ramu
Sololo
Moyale
Takaba
Geilo Hills

UGANDA

Lorukumu
Loperot
Maikona
Buna
El Wak
Kaputirr
Mt. Nyiru 2752
South Horr
Marsabit
Bute Helu
Tarbaj
Khorof Harar
Bokol
Baragoi 2534
Laisamis
Wajir
Kapenguria
Mathews Peak 2375

K E N Y A

Kitale
Kapedo
Kinyang
Maralal
Archers Post
Merti
Habaswein
Dif
Kapsowar
Rumuruti
Samburu National Reserve
Mado Gashi
Bungoma
Eldoret
Kabarnet
K E N Y A
Isiolo
Garba Tula
Liboi
Busia
Kapsabet
Nyahururu
Meru
EQUATOR
Hagadera
Kisumu
Molo
Kericho
Nanyuki
+ Mt. Kenya 5199
Mbalambala
Saka
Homa Bay
Lake Nakuru
Nakuru
Nyeri
Garissa
Victoria
Kisii
Sotik
Naivasha
Murang'a
Nguni
Bura
Karungu
Migori
Narok
Ruiru
Thika
Mwingi
Kolbio
Lolgorien
HIGHLANDS
Hola
Masai Mara National Reserve
NAIROBI
Kitui
Endau
Ijara
Nairobi National Park
Machakos
Voo
Bodhei
Magadi
Kajiado
Konza
Mutha
Ikutha
Garsen
Lamu
Pate Island
Manda Island
Sultan Hamud
Kibwezi
Witu
Kipini
Namanga
Mtito Andei
Ungama Bay
Lake Amboseli
Malindi
Mambrui
Tsavo
Voi
Gede Ruins
Taveta
Kilifi
Mwatate
Takaungu
Mackinnon Road
Mariakani
Mombasa
Kwale
Gazi
Vanga
Shimoni

T A N Z A N I A

S O M A L I A

ID CARD
COUNTRY FACTS

Size: 224,081 sq mi (580,367 sq km)
Population: 44,184,000
Capital: Nairobi
Official languages: English and Kiswahili
Currency: Kenyan shilling
Highest point: Mount Kenya, 17,057 ft (5,199 m)
Life expectancy: 60.0 years

KENYA

Sand, Cities, and SAFARIS

Wildlife-rich savanna plains, forest highlands, desert scrub, the Great Rift Valley, Indian Ocean beaches, and mangrove swamps make Kenya a globetrotter's delight. Nairobi and other cities, and most big farms, are in the southern highlands, topped by Mount Kenya. Mombasa on the coast is popular with tourists. Kenya's main lake is Turkana (formerly called Lake Rudolf), though it shares Africa's largest lake, Victoria, with Tanzania and Uganda.

3 DANCE TO THE BEAT
Samburu National Reserve

Enjoy watching the Samburu people dance in circles. Men and women dance separately to singing, not instruments. Admire the elaborate beaded necklaces used in their dances.

4 WATCH SNAPPERS SNAP
Mombasa

Watch the crocodiles at Mamba Village jump high into the air to snap meat at feeding time. Learn as you see crocs at different ages.

5 IMAGINE GHOSTS OF GEDE
Gede Ruins

Wander through the palace, mosque, and houses built of coral bricks. Puzzle over why the people abandoned the town hundreds of years ago.

Globetrotter Attractions

MASAI MARA NATIONAL RESERVE
This preserve is home to the biggest and wildest animals in Africa, including the Cape buffalo, elephant, leopard, lion, and rhinoceros.

LAKE TURKANA
This lake is the largest desert lake in the world. Little lives in the desert around it, but some hippopotamuses and crocodiles live in or near its salty water.

MOUNT KENYA
This ancient extinct, or dead, volcano is Africa's second highest mountain. It is near the Equator with glaciers at its top.

DIGITAL TRAVELER!
Take a digital safari. Go online and find photographs of some of the most popular animals native to Kenya: elephants, Cape buffalo, lions, leopards, and rhinoceroses.

AFRICA

NATIONAL BIRD:
ostrich

NATIONAL FLOWER:
African blackwood

NATIONAL MAMMAL:
giraffe

TANZANIA

From Mountains to GRASSLANDS

0   100   200 MILES
0   100   200 KILOMETERS

I n Tanzania snow-topped Mount Kilimanjaro towers above the Serengeti Plains, teeming with big game. Most of the country is high plateau, with western lakes including Tanganyika, Malawi (Nyasa), and Rukwa. Tanzania also shares Lake Victoria, on its northern border. In the Indian Ocean, the islands of Zanzibar and Pemba are part of Tanzania. Most people are farmers, but minerals and tourism are vital to the economy.

Globetrotter Attractions

5 SPOT LIONS IN THE TREES
Lake Manyara National Park

Drive along the rugged roads to see baboons and hear birds. Continue through the woodland where lions hang out in trees and elephants trumpet. Watch for the hippo pools.

MOUNT KILIMANJARO
The highest mountain in Africa is also the tallest in the world that is not part of a mountain chain. Its weather is tropical at the bottom and arctic at the top.

NGORONGORO CRATER
A large volcano exploded and left this bowl-shaped depression. Today, many African animals and the cattle of the Maasai people live on its grasslands.

SELOUS GAME RESERVE
This huge game reserve protects many elephants, lions, and other big animals.

ID CARD
COUNTRY FACTS

Size: 365,754 sq mi (947,300 sq km)
Population: 49,122,000
Capital: Dar es Salaam
Official languages: Kiswahili and English
Currency: Tanzanian shilling
Highest point: Kilimanjaro, 19,340 ft (5,895 m)
Life expectancy: 60.0 years

Map labels: UGANDA, Kagera, Bukoba, RWANDA, Ngara, Geita, BURUNDI, Moyowosi, Kigoma, Uvinza, Malagarasi, Ugalla, LAKE TANGANYIKA, Mpanda, Kafufu, DEM. REP. OF THE CONGO, Kipili, Sumbawanga, ZAMBIA

5 COOL THINGS TO DO HERE

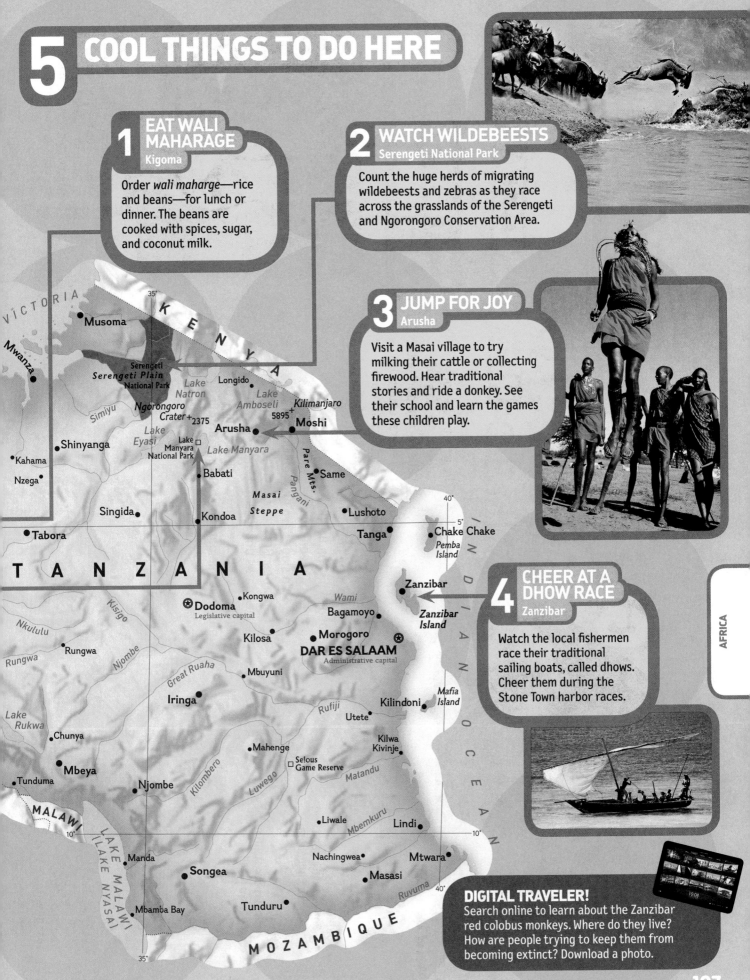

1 EAT WALI MAHARAGE
Kigoma

Order *wali maharge*—rice and beans—for lunch or dinner. The beans are cooked with spices, sugar, and coconut milk.

2 WATCH WILDEBEESTS
Serengeti National Park

Count the huge herds of migrating wildebeests and zebras as they race across the grasslands of the Serengeti and Ngorongoro Conservation Area.

3 JUMP FOR JOY
Arusha

Visit a Masai village to try milking their cattle or collecting firewood. Hear traditional stories and ride a donkey. See their school and learn the games these children play.

4 CHEER AT A DHOW RACE
Zanzibar

Watch the local fishermen race their traditional sailing boats, called dhows. Cheer them during the Stone Town harbor races.

DIGITAL TRAVELER!
Search online to learn about the Zanzibar red colobus monkeys. Where do they live? How are people trying to keep them from becoming extinct? Download a photo.

GREAT LAKES REGION

A Nature-Rich LANDSCAPE

T he great lakes of Central Africa's Rift Valley are important to several countries, including Burundi, Rwanda, and Uganda. Lake Victoria is partly in southern Uganda, Lake Tanganyika on Burundi's southwest border, and Lac Kivu on Rwanda's western border. Mountain slopes are planted with coffee and other crops. Gorillas survive in forests, and game roams Uganda's northern savanna. Uganda is on the Equator but the altitude means it's seldom too hot for comfort.

ID CARD
COUNTRY FACTS

BURUNDI
Population: 10,892,000
Capital: Bujumbura

RWANDA
Population: 11,116,000
Capital: Kigali

UGANDA
Population: 36,890,000
Capital: Kampala

5 COOL THINGS TO DO HERE

1 VIEW CHEETAHS
Kidepo Valley National Park

Locate lions, leopards, and cheetahs on the grasslands of Uganda's isolated park. When water is scarce, find the animals near wetlands and pools.

2 FIND FRESH TEA AND COFFEE
Rubavu

Walk through a tea or coffee field in Rwanda. Visit one of the thousands of small farms that grow these crops.

4 CANOE PAST BIRD PARADISE
Lac Ruhondo

Travel on this Rwandan lake in a canoe carved from one piece of wood. Admire the rare water birds. Enjoy a picnic on one of its islands.

Globetrotter Attractions

LAKE VICTORIA
Uganda, Tanzania, and Kenya border this lake, the largest lake in Africa. Its waters flow into the Nile River.

PARC NATIONAL DES VOLCANS
This park in Rwanda has beautiful scenery, active volcanoes, and mountain gorillas.

"MOUNTAINS OF THE MOON"
In Uganda, the Ruwenzori Mountains, with their glaciers and lakes, descend into the Rift Valley. Their tops are often covered in clouds and are always snow-covered.

5 LIVE LIKE KINGS AND QUEENS
Nyanza

Imagine the king on his huge bed in this replica of a traditional palace in Nyanza, Rwanda. Photo the huge horns on the royal cattle that live there. Visit the newer palace nearby. No one has ever lived here, but today it has a special art museum.

3 SPEND A DAY BY THE SEA
Bujumbura

Visit the capital of Burundi at the northeast end of this lake, the longest freshwater lake in the world. Enjoy the sun and water at its beaches, but watch for a hippo walking on the beach!

DIGITAL TRAVELER!
Burundi drummers are famous for the music they play at festivals and other important events. Search the Internet to find a video clip of the Drummers of Burundi. They are also called *Les Tambourinaires.*

AFRICA

199

	NATIONAL BIRD:	NATIONAL FLOWER:	NATIONAL MAMMAL:
CEN. AF. REPUB.	Sangha Forest robin	*Pleiocarpa mutica*	African elephant
CONGO	Ituri batis	orchid	lion
D.R. CONGO	Congo peafowl	coffee flower	okapi

CENTRAL AFRICA

The Heart of the CONTINENT

T he mighty Congo River, and other rivers such as the Ubangi (or Oubangui), flow across Central Africa. Two countries use the name Congo: Congo (Congo-Brazzaville) and the Democratic Republic of the Congo (Dem. Rep. Congo, or Congo-Kinshasa, formerly Zaire). Their northern neighbor is the Central African Republic (Cen. Af. Rep.). There are equatorial rain forests and savanna, and grassy plateaus in the drier north. The Democratic Republic of the Congo's eastern border passes through several of Africa's great lakes.

5 EAT FRIED BANANAS
Pointe-Noire

Order fried plantains, a type of banana. In the Congo enjoy them with meat, often goat. Eat plantains fried, boiled, or baked, but not raw.

Globetrotter Attractions

CONGO RIVER
This river, the second longest in Africa, forms the border between the Democratic Republic of the Congo and Congo. Its waters take six months to go from its source to the Atlantic Ocean.

DZANGA-SANGHA SPECIAL RESERVE
This rain forest reserve in the Central African Republic is home to many lowland gorillas and forest elephants.

VOLCAN NYIROGONGO
The city of Goma in the Democratic Republic of the Congo lies in the path of lava from this very active volcano.

4 MEET MANATEES
Conkouati-Douli National Park

Watch the manatees in the lagoons of this Congo park. The manatee is the park's symbol because this endangered animal is protected here.

5 COOL THINGS TO DO HERE

1 SPOT ELEPHANTS
Nouabalé-Ndoki National Park

Explore this Congo park to find forest elephants. Count the different kinds of apes and antelopes you can find.

2 HAVE A FISH FEAST
Brazzaville

Watch the Congo River that flows alongside Brazzaville in the Congo. Eat fish from the river's waters. Take a water taxi across the river to Kinshasa in another country!

3 PLAY BASKETBALL
Kinshasa

Cheer the women and men as they play basketball in the Dem. Rep. Congo. Meet the boys and girls who practice in the hope of joining international basketball teams.

ID CARD
COUNTRY FACTS

CENTRAL AFRICAN REPUBLIC
Population: 4,476,000
Capital: Bangui

CONGO
Population: 4,355,000
Capital: Brazzaville

DEMOCRATIC REPUBLIC OF THE CONGO
Population: 71,128,000
Capital: Kinshasa

DIGITAL TRAVELER!
Hundreds of kinds of butterflies live in Central African Republic. Go online and find photographs of the country's butterflies. Compare them to photographs of butterflies where you live.

AFRICA

201

EQUATORIAL AFRICA

Land of Varied LANDSCAPES

C ountries in West Africa crossed by the Equator (0° latitude) are Cameroon, Equatorial Guinea (including Bioko), Gabon, and Sao Tome and Principe, islands about 125 miles (201 km) west of Gabon. The islands are volcanic; the mainland is a mix of landscapes—rain forest, rivers, plateaus, mountains (the highest Mount Cameroon), savanna, and coastal plains. Most people in Equatorial Africa are farmers, but mineral wealth includes aluminum ore and oil.

Globetrotter Attractions

MINDO NATIONAL PARK
Because of the dense rain forest in this park in Gabon, many apes and monkeys live here. There are also three beautiful waterfalls on the park's rivers.

WAZA NATIONAL PARK
In this Cameroon park you'll find big cats such as lions and exotic birds like ostriches.

PICO DE SÃO TOMÉ
This rain forest–covered volcanic mountain is at the center of the island country of Sao Tome and Principe.

5 COOL THINGS TO DO HERE

1 ENJOY BAMILEKE DANCING
Batié

Catch some of the 200 or more traditional Cameroon dances as people celebrate events, such as a birth or wedding. Admire the leather fans, masks, or long sticks some dancers use as they move in a circle.

Map labels: C H A D, Lake Chad (Lac Tchad), Fotokol, Waza National Park, Maroua, Kaélé, Rey Bouba, Garoua, Lagdo Reservoir, Mbé, 1960, Mbang Mts., Tchabal, Gangdaba, Ngaoundéré, Meiganga

3 ADMIRE THE MASKS
Yaoundé

Marvel at the masks and carvings made with dried fruit skins in this Cameroon Benedictine monastery. See the art museum's traditional pipes, musical instruments, and beaded statues, too.

4 GET A TASTE OF CHOCOLATE
São Tomé

Visit a cocoa plantation on the island of São Tomé, a major exporter of cocoa. Watch how cocoa is grown and then follow it being made into chocolate, which you can taste. Both small and large plantations grow cocoa.

ID CARD
COUNTRY FACTS

CAMEROON
Population: 21,491,000
Capital: Yaoundé

EQUATORIAL GUINEA
Population: 761,000
Capital: Malabo

GABON
Population: 1,601,000
Capital: Libreville

SAO TOME & PRINCIPE
Population: 188,000
Capital: São Tomé

2 SEE SEA TURTLE NESTS
Ureca

Patrol the sand beaches together with the local villagers to protect the nesting sea turtles in Ureca in Equatorial Guinea.

5 WATCH SURFING HIPPOS
Loango National Park

Walk this park's beaches carefully or you may run into a hippo in the ocean surf or a buffalo walking along the beach. In Gabon, experience what happens when the rain forest meets the ocean.

DIGITAL TRAVELER!

In the town of Tourou in Cameroon, the women design hats from a gourd called a calabash. Search the Internet for a photo of a calabash tree. Then find photos of the calabash hats worn in Cameroon.

ID CARD
COUNTRY FACTS

Size: 481,354 sq mi (1,246,700 sq km)
Population: 21,635,000
Capital: Luanda
Official language: Portuguese
Currency: kwanza
Highest point: Morro de Moco, 8,596 ft (2,620 m)
Life expectancy: 51.0 years

5 AMUSE AN ANTELOPE
Quiçama National Park

Find the secretive giant sable antelope in Angola's national parks. Once thought extinct, this antelope with long horns that curve toward its back has been spotted by researchers.

4 SNIFF A SPICY FLOWER
N'dalatando

Check out the Porcelain Rose, a sweet-smelling ginger plant that is unique to the region. Wander under giant bamboo plants that grow in the botanical garden just outside this small city.

3 GO FISHING
Namibe

Observe the fishermen who bring in most of the fish Angolans love to eat. Identify the factories where the fish are processed.

NATIONAL BIRD:
peregrine falcon

NATIONAL TREE:
acacia

NATIONAL MAMMAL:
leopard

ANGOLA

Building a BRIGHT FUTURE

Angola is a land of hills, rivers, and grasslands, with forests in the north and desert in the south toward Namibia. Separate, but part of Angola, is Cabinda to the north. Portuguese sailors explored this coast in the 1500s, and today Angola's national capital Luanda is an international port. Portuguese is the official language. Natural resources include diamonds and oil, but most Angolans are village farmers.

5 COOL THINGS TO DO HERE

1 VISIT AN AMAZING WATERFALL
Calandula Falls

Admire the horseshoe-shaped Calandula Falls on the Lucala River. It usually spans 1,300 feet (396 m) but after seasonal floods stretches 2,000 feet (606 m).

2 GET ON TRACK
Huambo

Ride the only train that goes from the Atlantic Coast to central Africa. This train, built in 1929, needed major repairs. It is now carrying goods and passengers once again.

DIGITAL TRAVELER!
People in Angola enjoy eating fish *calulu*, or fish stew. Do an Internet search for a fish calulu recipe and find out its ingredients. Is this something you would order in Angola?

Globetrotter Attractions

THE BLACK ROCKS
These huge rocks near Pungo Andongo are more than 656 feet (200 m) high and are unlike the rest of the grassland region where they are found.

SHIPWRECK BEACH
The shore of Bengo Bay (Baía do Bengo), north of Angola's capital, Luanda, is home to old, rusting ships. Huge metal ships stand at a tilt along the beach or on their side in the water.

FORTALEZA DE SÃO MIGUEL
This star-shaped fort was built by the Portuguese in 1576. It's the oldest building in the city and still watches over the port of Luanda. It now houses the Museum of the Armed Forces.

AFRICA

205

NATIONAL BIRD:
African fish eagle
bar-tailed trogon

NATIONAL FLOWER:
mangrove flower
water mint

NATIONAL MAMMAL:
black rhinoceros
Thomson's gazelle

ZAMBIA AND MALAWI

Buffalo, Bats, and MONKEY BREAD

Much of Zambia is high plateau, with the Muchinga Mountains near the border with Malawi, which is a land of forests and savanna. There are large lakes, including Bangweulu in Zambia and Malawi (Nyasa) on Malawi's eastern border with Tanzania. Zambia has copper mines, but farming is the chief activity in both countries. The Victoria Falls on the Zambezi River, the Kariba Dam, and amazing wildlife attract tourists.

3 MEET MILLIONS OF BATS
Kasanka National Park

Observe the largest mammal migration in the world. Each October, about eight million fruit bats arrive. They swarm the sky and hang upside down in trees.

Globetrotter Attractions

LAKE MALAWI
This is one of the African Great Lakes and one of the deepest lakes in the world. It is home to hundreds of colorful cichlid fish, called *mbuna*.

KAFUE NATIONAL PARK
Whether you go on a night drive or daytime boat cruise here in Zambia, there is a good chance you will see elephants, leopards, crocodiles, rhinos, and much more.

VICTORIA FALLS
Some people call this the "Greatest Curtain of Falling Water in the World." It is on the Zambia–Zimbabwe border.

5 COOL THINGS TO DO HERE

1 CANOE PAST BUFFALO
Lower Zambezi National Park

Snap lots of photos on your canoe tour of the Zambezi River. You may see Cape buffalo quenching their thirst or hippos taking a bath. Keep your distance!

2 EAT MONKEY BREAD
Likoma Island

Taste the coconut-looking fruit of the baobab tree. Its nickname is "monkey bread." It tastes like a mix of pear, grapefruit, and vanilla.

4 CELEBRATE WITH THE CHEWA
Lilongwe

See the men of the Chewa tribe tell stories and teach lessons at festivals and celebrations. They dress in costumes and masks made of wood and straw. They dance as characters, such as wild animals, slave traders, and the spirits of those who have died.

ID CARD
COUNTRY FACTS

ZAMBIA
Population: 14,187,000
Capital: Lusaka

MALAWI
Population: 16,338,000
Capital: Lilongwe

DIGITAL TRAVELER!
A popular food in Zambia is *nshima*. It is made with cornmeal. Search the Internet to find pictures, a recipe, and what it is typically eaten with. Try a meal with nshima and find out if you like it.

5 KEEP SCORE AT A NETBALL GAME
Blantyre

Hear the crowd roar when the ball swishes through the hoop! Malawi's national women's netball team has played in international games. Netball is like basketball.

AFRICA

### Map labels
NGO
LAKE TANGANYIKA
Mbala
TANZANIA
Chitipa
Karonga
Isoka
Chilumba
Kasama
Chinsali
Lake Bangweulu
Chambeshi
Muchinga Mountains
Mzuzu
LAKE MALAWI (LAKE NYASA)
Nkhata Bay
Mpika
+1850
Kasanka National Park
Lundazi
Likoma Island
Luangwa
Nkhotakota
MALAWI
MOZAMBIQUE
Chipata
Mchinji
Salima
Lilongwe
Mangochi
ZAMBIA
I A
MOZAMBIQUE
Liwonde
Lake Chilwa
Luangwa
Lower Zambezi National Park
Zomba
Blantyre
+3002
Shire
Chiromo
Zambezi

0   100   200 MILES
0   100   200 KILOMETERS

207

MOZAMBIQUE
Land of Sky-Blue WATERS

NATIONAL BIRD: flamingo

NATIONAL TREE: baobab

NATIONAL MAMMAL: African elephant

M ozambique is a land of sand and water: It has plains, swamps, grassy plateaus, and forested hills. There are rivers such as the Limpopo and the Zambezi, which fills a lake behind the Cahora Bassa Dam. Lake Malawi (Nyasa) in the north is one of Africa's great natural lakes. Mozambique, with its valuable fisheries, borders the warm, blue Indian Ocean. The seaway off the coast is called the Mozambique Channel.

ID CARD
COUNTRY FACTS

Size: 308,642 sq mi (799,380 sq km)
Population: 24,336,000
Capital: Maputo
Official language: Portuguese
Currency: metical
Highest point: Monte Binga, 7,992 ft (2,436 m)
Life expectancy: 50.0 years

5 COOL THINGS TO DO HERE

1 GO ISLAND HOPPING
Quirimbas Archipelago

Sail on a boat called a dhow to some of the 12 islands in this archipelago. Ibo Island was a trading post in the 1500s. Now it has resorts.

2 TAKE A TRAIN RIDE
Nampula

Travel from Nampula to Cuamba on one of the country's few railroad routes. Recently there have been big improvements in reducing the trip from 10 hours to 7 (27 stops to 9). The distance is the same as Boston to New York.

3 SEARCH FOR DUGONGS
Nyati Beach

Stay in the shallow water and you could see a huge dugong poke its head up for air. Dugongs are also called sea cows because they walk on the ocean floor and pull up grass to eat.

Globetrotter Attractions

NATIONAL MUSEUM OF ART
Mozambique's artists express the country's pain and joy. In this museum in Maputo you can see some artists at work.

CAHORA BASSA DAM
There are rumors that a colony of sharks became trapped behind the dam when it was built across the Zambezi River in 1974.

TOFO BEACH
There's something for everyone here—swimming, scuba diving, and dolphin watching from the sand.

5 SPICE UP YOUR DAY
Maputo

Taste the spicy chile sauce in the piri-piri chicken. When the Portuguese came to Mozambique to try to rule the land in the 1500s, they introduced chile peppers (called *piri-piri* in Swahili). They also introduced cashew nuts, corn, potatoes, and paprika.

4 FIND YOUR FAVORITE ANIMAL
Beira

Stroll through a marketplace where artists display their work. Wood carving is an old craft that Africans have taught their children. They start with a piece of a tree and use a knife to carve it into animal and human shapes.

DIGITAL TRAVELER!
Use the Internet to find out what day and time it is in Mozambique right now. How many hours is it ahead of your time zone?

ZIMBABWE

Ruins, Rhinos, and WATERFALLS

Zimbabwe is a land of ancient history, traditional crafts, modern cities and farms, and wildlife roaming national parks. The central highlands, or high veld, rise to rocky hills in the south. In the north, Zimbabwe shares with Zambia the hydroelectric dam and lake at Kariba on the Zambezi River. The spectacular Victoria Falls in the northwest have the African name Mosi oa Tunya ("Smoke that Thunders").

5 CRAFT WITH CLAY
Bulawayo

Watch the pottery wheel spin as people shape soft clay into bowls. The Mzilikazi Art and Crafts Center trained many famous African artists.

4 SEE ANCIENT FINGERPRINTS
Sentinel Ranch

Explore a cave and see clay bins where people kept their grain safe from enemies thousands of years ago. You can see ancient fingerprints on the bins.

ID CARD
COUNTRY FACTS

Size: 150,872 sq mi (390,757 sq km)
Population: 13,038,000
Capital: Harare
Official language: English
Currency: Zimbabwean dollar
Highest point: Mt. Inyangani, 8,504 ft (2,592 m)
Life expectancy: 56.0 years

DIGITAL TRAVELER!
Search online to learn about the name of Zimbabwe. What does it mean? What other name did the country have from the 1890s to 1980? How did it get that name?

Map labels: NAMIBIA, ZAMBIA, LAKE KARIBA, Victoria Falls, Hwange, Shangani, Sengwa, Gwayi, Hwange National Park, Gwai, BOTSWANA, Mzilikazi Arts & Crafts Center, Bulawayo, Plumtree, Matopos Hills, Shashe, ZI, 25°, 20°

5 COOL THINGS TO DO HERE

1 BRIDGE THAT GAP
Victoria Falls

Start at Victoria Falls, Zimbabwe, and walk the bridge over the Zambezi River. At the other end, you will be in Livingston, Zambia. Enjoy the view of rushing water at Victoria Falls.

GREAT ZIMBABWE
Massive stone walls remind us of a great city built about A.D. 1200 to 1400 with more than 10,000 people.

MATOPOS HILLS
Awesome shapes of boulders stretch for miles. Stone Age people lived here and left an abundance of rock paintings.

HWANGE NATIONAL PARK
More than 35,000 elephants live here. Each year people must pump water into dry waterholes so that there is enough for the elephants to drink.

2 FOLLOW BLACK RHINOCEROSES
Matusadona National Park

See this endangered rhino in the wild. Learn how the park is trying to protect the rhinos from hunters and increase the population. The park also has the second largest group of wild lions in Africa.

AFRICA

3 BUY A COLORFUL BASKET
Harare

Arrive early at the Mbare flea market and look at the woven baskets. Craftspeople are proud of their work.

0   50   100 MILES
0   50   100 KILOMETERS

	NATIONAL BIRD:	NATIONAL FLOWER:	NATIONAL MAMMAL:
BOTSWANA	lilac-breasted roller	red spiderling	zebra
NAMIBIA	African fish eagle	welwitschia	oryx

BOTSWANA AND NAMIBIA

Sparkling Sea, Sunshine, and DESERT SANDS

Botswana's rolling-hill landscapes are fine for cattle-raising, while in the north the Okavango River floods wetlands. It is much more barren in the southwestern Kalahari Desert. In mineral-rich Namibia, the Namib Desert receives hardly any rain. The bleak Atlantic coastline was called by early sailors the "Skeleton Coast." Wildlife herds make seasonal migrations, and many people travel outside the country, too, finding jobs in the cities of neighboring South Africa.

Globetrotter Attractions

SKELETON COAST PARK
Through history, this Namibia beach was littered—first with whalebones, and later shipwrecks.

CENTRAL KALAHARI GAME RESERVE
Twice the size of Massachusetts, this park's grasslands seem to go on forever. After a strong rain the wild animals flock to the watering holes.

TULI BLOCK FARMS
This narrow piece of Botswana has beautiful views, especially from a cliff called Solomon's Wall.

5 STROLL AROUND A METEORITE
Grootfontein

See Earth's largest meteorite, the Hoba. Scientists say it fell to Earth less than 80,000 years ago. A farmer found it in 1920.

4 CLIMB A SAND DUNE
Sossusvlei

Enjoy the soft, deep sand as you climb up Dune 45 for a spectacular view of the sand and water. Some people sand-ski down the steep slope by zigzagging. Others sit down and slide.

Map labels: ANGOLA, Kunene, Opuwo, Ondangwa, OVAMBO, Etosha Pan, Kaokoland, Sesfontein, Okaukuejo, Namutoni, Hoanib, Skeleton Coast Park, Ugab, Outjo, Otjiwarongo, Anixab, NAMIB, NAM, Usakos, Okahandja, DAMARA, Swakopmund, Windhoek, Swakop, Kuiseb, Walvis Bay, Rehoboth, DESERT, Sossusvlei, Maltahöhe, Hottentot Bay, GREAT, Lüderitz, Garub, Aus, Cape Dernberg, Oranjemund, ATLANTIC Coast, OCEAN

212

5 COOL THINGS TO DO HERE

ID CARD
COUNTRY FACTS

BOTSWANA
Population: 1,866,000
Capital: Gaborone

NAMIBIA
Population: 2,410,000
Capital: Windhoek

1 DELVE IN A DELTA
Okavango Delta

Step into a canoe, called a *mokoro*. Glide through the water and look for some of the 122 kinds of mammals and 64 kinds of reptiles in the delta. Some of the islands there have been built by termites.

2 ZOOM IN ON ZEBRAS
Makgadikgadi Pans Game Reserve

Observe the zebras that migrate to the rivers after heavy rain. In prehistoric time the park was a giant lake, but it has dried up.

DIGITAL TRAVELER!
Search the Internet for photographs of sand dunes in Namibia. How many different shapes can you find? Make a drawing or painting of your favorite sand-dune photo.

3 GO ON A QUIVER TREE QUEST
Keetmanshoop

Walk among trees that store water in their trunks. Past hunters made quivers (bags to hold arrows) from the branches.

AFRICA

Map

LA LAND
Rundu •
Okavango
CAPRIVI STRIP
Schuckmannsburg
ZAMBIA 25°
Zambezi
Muhembo •
Kasane •
Karakuwisa •
Sepupa •
Mpandamatenga •
• Tsumeb
Okavango Delta
Nokaneng •
• Shorobe
20°
• Otavi
• Grootfontein
Tsau •
Maun •
Nata •
ZIMBABWE
IBIA LAND
• Epukiro
Lake Ngami
• Toteng
Makgadikgadi Pans Game Reserve
Makgadikgadi Pans
Rakops •
Lake Xau
Francistown
Shashe
Ghanzi •
Central Kalahari Game Reserve
Serowe •
• Palapye
Tuli Block Farms
• Tshootsha
Okwa
BOTSWANA
Limpopo
• Gobabis
Kule •
Mahalapye •
KALAHARI
TROPIC OF CAPRICORN
Aminuis •
Lehututu •
• Tshane
Mochudi •
• Narib
Lokhwabe •
Molepolole •
• Salzbrunn
DESERT
Kanye •
• Mariental
Gaborone ⊛
25°
Fish
• Gibeon
Lobatse •
Tses • Köes •
Tshabong •
Nossob
Molopo
NAMALAND
• Bethanie
Keetmanshoop •
Seeheim
• Aroab
25°
Gawachab •
SOUTH **AFRICA**
• Karasburg
Warmbad •
Orange
20°

200 MILES
200 KILOMETERS

213

Globetrotter Attractions

NGYWENYA MINE
The iron ore mine in Swaziland is the world's oldest mine. People began using the mine's iron about 43,000 years ago. Ngywenya locally means "crocodile," and that is the shape of the mountain above the valley.

KRUGER NATIONAL PARK
This South African park, a leader in protecting animals and the environment, is home to 34 kinds of amphibians, 114 reptiles, and 147 mammals.

CAPE OF GOOD HOPE
Sir Francis Drake passed the Cape of Good Hope when he sailed around the world in 1580. To get a good view of it today, people can ride cable cars to the top of Table Mountain.

5 COOL THINGS TO DO HERE

DIGITAL TRAVELER!
Find a map online that shows the most southern point of South Africa. What is the name of that cape? How far away is it from where you live?

1 WATCH A RUGBY MATCH
Johannesburg

See the Springboks, South Africa's team, play top-notch rugby at Ellis Park Stadium.

2 LISTEN TO PENGUINS
Boulders Beach

Listen for the braying sound of these African penguins. They sound like donkeys. The colony of black-and-white birds lives on the beach, but residents can hear the noise in their homes nearby.

### Map labels

BOTSWANA
NAMIBIA
LESOTHO
SOUTH AFRICA

Thabazimbi
PRETORIA — Administrative capital
JOHANNESBURG
Mmabatho
SOWETO
Klerksdorp
Vereeniging
Tosca
Severn
Vryburg
Pudimoe
Kroonstad
Aansluit
Kuruman
Bloemhof
Welkom
Bethlehem
Warrenton
Brandfort
Olifantshoek
Upington
Kimberley
Brandfort
Griquatown
Bloemfontein — Judicial capital
Maseru
Kakamas
Edenburg
Alexander Bay
Kenhardt
Hopetown
Malealea
Goodhouse
Priska
Philippolis
Port Nolloth
Okiep
Colesberg
Quthing
Springbok
De Aar
Aliwal North
Matatiele
Kamieskroon
Brandvlei
Britstown
Maclear
Garies
Carnarvon
Richmond
Middelburg
Mthatha
Bitterfontein
Calvinia
Fraserburg
Queenstown
Vanrhynsdorp
Tarkastad
Gcuwa
Klawer
Beaufort West
Graaff-Reinet
Cradock
Lambert's Bay
Sutherland
Bhisho
Saldanha
Porterville
Laingsburg
Jansenville
Malmesbury
Touwsrivier
Prince Albert
Grahamstown
East London
CAPE TOWN — Legislative capital
Worcester
Oudtshoorn
Uitenhage
Paarl
Port Alfred
Boulders Beach
Swellendam
Cape Recife
Cape of Good Hope
Hermanus
George
Knysna
Cape Seal
PORT ELIZABETH
Cape Agulhas
Bredasdorp
Port Beaufort
Mossel Bay
Humansdorp

Orange
Molopo
Vaal
Augrabies Falls
Cape Columbine
St. Helena Bay

100   200 MILES
0   100   200 KILOMETERS

	NATIONAL BIRD:	NATIONAL FLOWER:	NATIONAL MAMMAL:
LESOTHO	African rock pipit	spiral aloe	black rhinoceros
SOUTH AFRICA	blue crane	king protea	springbok
SWAZILAND	purple turaco	sugarbush	Thomson's gazelle

SOUTHERN AFRICA

The Tip of a Vast CONTINENT

South Africa surrounds its mountainous neighbor, Lesotho, and almost envelops Swaziland's grassland and forests. It lies at Africa's tip, and ships sail east around the Cape of Good Hope from the Atlantic into the Indian Ocean. The interior is a saucer-shaped plateau, with veld or grassy plains behind coastal mountains, including the Drakensberg. Rivers include the Orange, Limpopo, and Tugela. Major cities include Cape Town, Johannesburg, and Pretoria.

5 BUY SWAZI CANDLES
Mbabane

Discover that no two Swazi candles are alike. In the candle shop, see the variety of colorful patterns. More than 200 local candle-makers produce candles that are sent all over the world.

4 RIDE A PONY ON A TREK
Maiealea

Enjoy the scenery as you ride a pony along the trail. Teenagers from local villages will walk beside the ponies to help you and they will point out the sites.

3 BE A FOSSIL HUNTER
Quthing

Look carefully on the road to Quthing and you could find dinosaur footprints. These are tracks of many different dinosaurs.

ID CARD
COUNTRY FACTS

LESOTHO
Population: 2,242,000
Capital: Maseru

SOUTH AFRICA
Population: 52,982,000
Capital: Pretoria

SWAZILAND
Population: 1,238,000
Capital: Mbabane

215

AFRICAN ISLANDS
Jewels in the INDIAN OCEAN

A frica's Indian Ocean islands were stopovers for old-time sailors, and today are glittering tourist destinations. The island countries are Madagascar (the largest African island), Mauritius, Seychelles, and Comoros. These are precious natural jewels, for their stunning wildlife is threatened as the island ecosystems are unbalanced. Madagascar's lemurs, for example, are unique to the island, but much of their forest habitat has been felled for farms and development.

Globetrotter Attractions

STONE FOREST
At the heart of Tsingy de Bemaraha National Park on Madagascar is a labyrinth of knife-edged stone towers, canyons, and wet caves. The stone forest is home to many unusual plants and animals.

KARTHALA
Here on Comoros, one of the world's largest active volcanoes also has one of the largest craters.

COUSIN ISLAND
Many rare birds live here in Seychelles. Sometimes the sky gets dark because of all the birds soaring together.

5 STOP AND SMELL YLANG YLANG
Mohéli

Sniff the sweet smell of the ylang ylang flower. Comoros exports most of the world's supply of ylang ylang oil. It is the main ingredient of many fine perfumes.

DIGITAL TRAVELER!
There are about 115 islands in Seychelles. Go online and find a list of these islands. Are there any island names that start with the same letter as your first name?

SEY
Aldabra Islands
Cosmoledo Group
Grande Comore (N'gazidja)
Moroni
2361
Karthala
Mohéli
Glorieuses Islands France
Anjouan (Ndzuwani)
Cap d'Ambre
Antsirañana
Mamoudzou
Mayotte France
Andoany
Ambanja
Maromokotro 2876
Sambava
Antsohihy
Antalaha
Maroantsetra
Mahajanga
Marovoay
Mandritsara
Antongila Bay
Juan de Nova Island France
Besalampy
Ikopa
Lac Alaotra
Ambatondrazaka
Maintirano
Tsingy de Bemaraha National Park
1303
Toamasina
Miandrivazo
ANTANANARIVO
Antsirabe
Avenue of the Baobabs
Morondava
Mania
Mananjary
Manja
Mangoky
Fianarantsoa
Morombe
Boby Peak 2658
Europa Island France
Ihosy
Farafangana
Toliara
TROPIC OF CAPRICORN
Onilahy
1637
Bekily
Androka
Tôlañaro
Cap Ste. Marie
MADAGASCAR
COMOROS
Mozambique Channel

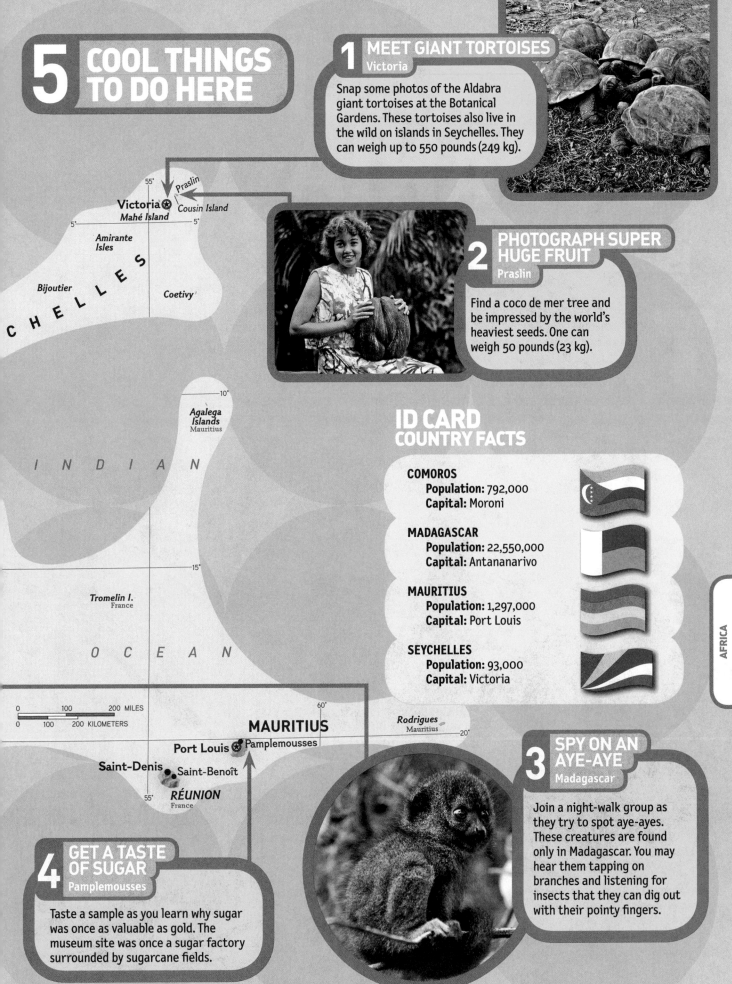

5 COOL THINGS TO DO HERE

1 MEET GIANT TORTOISES
Victoria

Snap some photos of the Aldabra giant tortoises at the Botanical Gardens. These tortoises also live in the wild on islands in Seychelles. They can weigh up to 550 pounds (249 kg).

2 PHOTOGRAPH SUPER HUGE FRUIT
Praslin

Find a coco de mer tree and be impressed by the world's heaviest seeds. One can weigh 50 pounds (23 kg).

ID CARD
COUNTRY FACTS

COMOROS
Population: 792,000
Capital: Moroni

MADAGASCAR
Population: 22,550,000
Capital: Antananarivo

MAURITIUS
Population: 1,297,000
Capital: Port Louis

SEYCHELLES
Population: 93,000
Capital: Victoria

3 SPY ON AN AYE-AYE
Madagascar

Join a night-walk group as they try to spot aye-ayes. These creatures are found only in Madagascar. You may hear them tapping on branches and listening for insects that they can dig out with their pointy fingers.

4 GET A TASTE OF SUGAR
Pamplemousses

Taste a sample as you learn why sugar was once as valuable as gold. The museum site was once a sugar factory surrounded by sugarcane fields.

AFRICA

Map labels: Praslin · Cousin Island · Victoria · Mahé Island · Amirante Isles · Bijoutier · Coetivy · CHELLES · Agalega Islands Mauritius · INDIAN · Tromelin I. France · OCEAN · MAURITIUS · Rodrigues Mauritius · Port Louis · Pamplemousses · Saint-Denis · Saint-Benoît · RÉUNION France

0 100 200 MILES
0 100 200 KILOMETERS

AUSTRALIA AND OCEANIA

Islands of all SIZES

This vast region includes Australia—a huge island continent—New Zealand, Papua New Guinea, and about 25,000 islands scattered across the Pacific Ocean. These islands make up the cultural areas of Melanesia, Micronesia, and Polynesia. While Australia, New Zealand, and Papua New Guinea have mountain ranges, many of the other islands are low-lying. Stretching in an arc from the north island of New Zealand to Papua New Guinea is a series of volcanoes, many of them active.

The dry, inland plains of Australia are home to kangaroos, the world's largest pouched mammals. The huge Uluru, also called Ayers Rock, is a sacred place for the Aboriginal people.

AUSTRALIA AND OCEANIA

From Ancient Peoples to Modern CULTURES

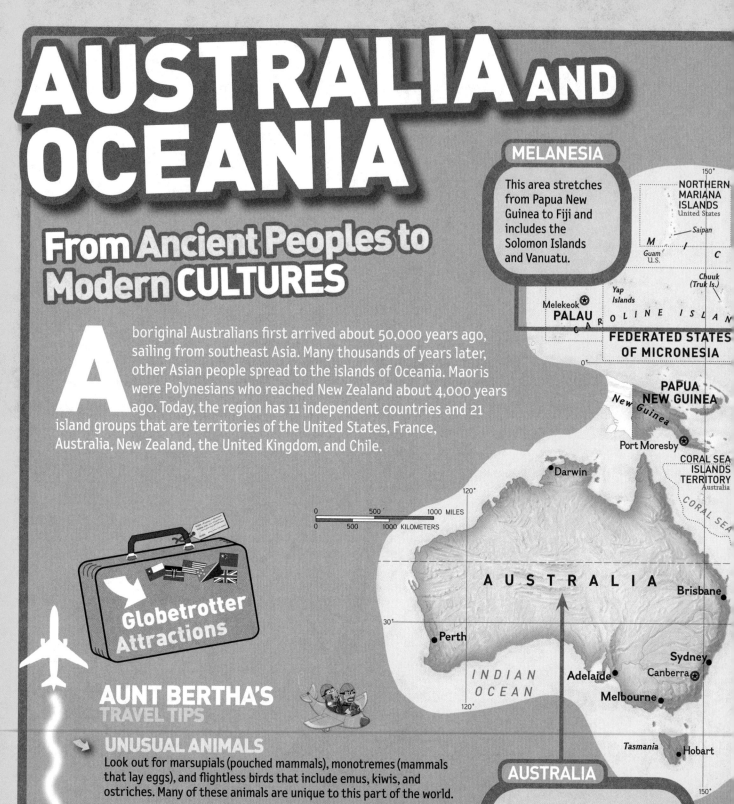

Aboriginal Australians first arrived about 50,000 years ago, sailing from southeast Asia. Many thousands of years later, other Asian people spread to the islands of Oceania. Maoris were Polynesians who reached New Zealand about 4,000 years ago. Today, the region has 11 independent countries and 21 island groups that are territories of the United States, France, Australia, New Zealand, the United Kingdom, and Chile.

MELANESIA

This area stretches from Papua New Guinea to Fiji and includes the Solomon Islands and Vanuatu.

150°

NORTHERN MARIANA ISLANDS
United States

Saipan

M

Guam
U.S.

I

C

Chuuk
(Truk Is.)

Yap Islands

Melekeok
PALAU

C A R O L I N E   I S L A N

FEDERATED STATES OF MICRONESIA

0°

PAPUA NEW GUINEA

New Guinea

Port Moresby

CORAL SEA ISLANDS TERRITORY
Australia

CORAL SEA

Darwin

120°

0   500   1000 MILES
0   500   1000 KILOMETERS

A U S T R A L I A

Brisbane

30°

Perth

Sydney
Canberra

INDIAN OCEAN

Adelaide

Melbourne

120°

Tasmania

Hobart

150°

AUSTRALIA

This is the world's smallest continent and its largest island. Most of the cities lie along the coast. The remote, sparsely populated interior is called the Outback. The Great Barrier Reef is off the northeast coast.

Globetrotter Attractions

AUNT BERTHA'S TRAVEL TIPS

UNUSUAL ANIMALS
Look out for marsupials (pouched mammals), monotremes (mammals that lay eggs), and flightless birds that include emus, kiwis, and ostriches. Many of these animals are unique to this part of the world.

DOWN UNDER
Australia and New Zealand are often said to be "Lands Down Under." Being in the Southern Hemisphere, their seasons are reversed, so summer begins in December and winter begins in June.

"HAVING A BAR-B"
Particularly in Australia, where the climate is mostly tropical, people love to have their meals outdoors. They often use barbecues for cooking meat and fish.

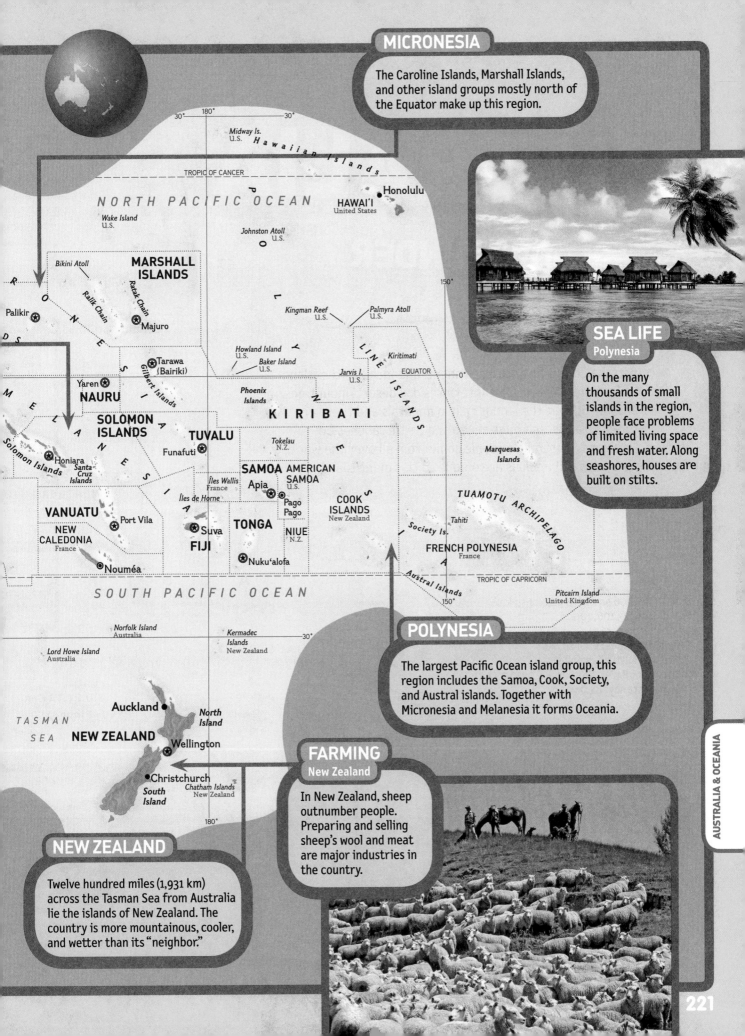

MICRONESIA

The Caroline Islands, Marshall Islands, and other island groups mostly north of the Equator make up this region.

**Map labels:**

- Midway Is. U.S.
- Hawaiian Islands
- TROPIC OF CANCER
- NORTH PACIFIC OCEAN
- Wake Island U.S.
- Johnston Atoll U.S.
- HAWAI'I United States
- Honolulu
- MICRONESIA
- Bikini Atoll
- MARSHALL ISLANDS
- Ratak Chain
- Ralik Chain
- Palikir
- Majuro
- Kingman Reef U.S.
- Palmyra Atoll U.S.
- LINE ISLANDS
- POLYNESIA
- 150°
- Tarawa (Bairiki)
- Gilbert Islands
- Howland Island U.S.
- Baker Island U.S.
- Kiritimati
- Yaren
- NAURU
- Phoenix Islands
- Jarvis I. U.S.
- EQUATOR 0°
- MELANESIA
- SOLOMON ISLANDS
- TUVALU
- Tokelau N.Z.
- KIRIBATI
- Marquesas Islands
- Solomon Islands
- Honiara
- Santa Cruz Islands
- Funafuti
- SAMOA
- AMERICAN SAMOA U.S.
- Îles Wallis France
- Apia
- MICRONESIA
- TUAMOTU ARCHIPELAGO
- VANUATU
- Port Vila
- Îles de Horne France
- Pago Pago
- COOK ISLANDS New Zealand
- Tahiti
- Society Is.
- NEW CALEDONIA France
- Suva
- TONGA
- NIUE N.Z.
- FRENCH POLYNESIA France
- FIJI
- Nouméa
- Nuku'alofa
- Austral Islands
- TROPIC OF CAPRICORN
- SOUTH PACIFIC OCEAN
- 150°
- Pitcairn Island United Kingdom
- Norfolk Island Australia
- Kermadec Islands New Zealand
- 30°
- Lord Howe Island Australia
- TASMAN SEA
- Auckland
- North Island
- NEW ZEALAND
- Wellington
- Christchurch
- Chatham Islands New Zealand
- South Island
- 180°

SEA LIFE
Polynesia

On the many thousands of small islands in the region, people face problems of limited living space and fresh water. Along seashores, houses are built on stilts.

POLYNESIA

The largest Pacific Ocean island group, this region includes the Samoa, Cook, Society, and Austral islands. Together with Micronesia and Melanesia it forms Oceania.

FARMING
New Zealand

In New Zealand, sheep outnumber people. Preparing and selling sheep's wool and meat are major industries in the country.

NEW ZEALAND

Twelve hundred miles (1,931 km) across the Tasman Sea from Australia lie the islands of New Zealand. The country is more mountainous, cooler, and wetter than its "neighbor."

221

NATIONAL BIRD:
emu

NATIONAL TREE:
golden wattle

NATIONAL MAMMAL:
red kangaroo

AUSTRALIA
A Land DOWN UNDER

Australia covers an entire continent, and includes the island of Tasmania. Much of the interior is dry desert, mountains, and "bush," but the land is rich in minerals and there are forests, farms, and huge sheep and cattle ranches or "stations." Australia's people come from all over the world, but many of its plants and animals are unique to this giant island.

ID CARD
COUNTRY FACTS

Size: 2,969,906 sq mi (7,692,024 sq km)
Population: 23,106,000
Capital: Canberra
Official language: English
Currency: Australian dollar
Highest point: Mt. Kosciuszko, 7,310 ft (2,215 m)
Life expectancy: 82.0 years

5 START A LONG TRAIN RIDE
Perth

The 2,704-mile (4,352-km)-long Indian Pacific passenger train journey from Perth to Sydney takes 65 hours. It runs along coasts and across deserts.

DIGITAL TRAVELER!
Australians drive on the left-hand side of the road. Surf the Internet to find other countries that do this.

(Map of Australia showing labels:)

TIMOR SEA
Joseph Bonaparte Gulf
Darwin
Melville Island
Cobourg Peninsula
Wessel Islands
Nhulunbuy
Jabiru
Pine Creek
Alyangula
Katherine
Groote Eylandt
Wadeye
Kununurra
Wyndham
Cape Leveque
Dampier Land
Derby
Mt. Ord 937
Lake Argyle
Victoria
Borroloola
Daly Waters
Newcastle Waters
Broome
Halls Creek
Fitzroy Crossing
Lagrange
Fitzroy
NORTHERN
Tanami Desert
Tennant Creek
GREAT SANDY DESERT
TERRITORY
Barrow Creek
INDIAN OCEAN
Port Hedland
Karratha
Roebourne
Onslow
Mt. Bruce 1235
Exmouth
Tom Price
Paraburdoo
Newman
AUSTRAL
Alice Springs
TROPIC OF CAPRICORN
Uluru (Ayers Rock) 863
Sim
De
Carnarvon
Dirk Hartog I.
Denham
WESTERN
Gibson Desert
Mt. Aloysius 1085
Musgrave Ranges
Finke
Meekatharra
Wiluna
AUSTRALIA
Oodnadatta
SOUTH
Mount Magnet
Great Victoria Desert
Coober Pedy
Lake Eyre North
Geraldton
Leonora
Laverton
AUSTRALIA
Dongara
Menzies
Moora
Bullfinch
Kalgoorlie
Nullarbor Plain
Tarcoola
Merredin
Coolgardie
Haig
Eucla Motel
Ceduna
Woomera
PERTH
Northam
Norseman
Streaky Bay
Whyalla
Geographe Bay
Cape Naturaliste
Bunbury
Hyden
Hopetoun
Rocky Point
Elliston
Eyre Peninsula
Augusta
Bluff Knoll 1096
Esperance
Great Australian Bight
Port Lincoln
Albany
Kangaroo I.

0   200   400 MILES
0   200   400 KILOMETERS

ARA

5 COOL THINGS TO DO HERE

Globetrotter Attractions

1 GO UNDERGROUND
Coober Pedy

Visit opal miners' homes called "dugouts." They are built underground so families can escape outside temperatures of more than 120°F (48.9°C).

SYDNEY OPERA HOUSE
This is one of the most photographed buildings in the world. It took 30 years to figure out how to build the "sails" on the roof.

ULURU
Rising 1,142 feet (348 m), this huge mass of sandstone is the largest single slab of rock in the world.

AUSTRALIA ZOO
Many of the world's pouched mammals can be seen at this zoo in Beerwah, Queensland. They include kangaroos, possums, bandicoots, and koalas.

2 SEE GREAT WHITE SHARKS
Great Barrier Reef

The 1,429-mile (2,300 km)-long coral reef off the east coast is the world's largest living structure. It is home to several kinds of sharks.

3 RIDE THE WAVES
Boomerang Beach

Some of the world's best surfing beaches are along the coast of New South Wales. Like a boomerang, the waves always come back to you!

4 WALK ON GLASS
Melbourne

At the Eureka Tower, you can step into a glass cube almost 1,000 feet (305 m) above street level for a bird's-eye view of the city.

Map labels:

PAPUA NEW GUINEA

URA A
140°
Cape York
10°
Weipa
Iron Range
Aurukun
Cape York Coen
Gulf of Peninsula
Cape Melville
arpentaria Edward River
Wellesley Islands
Cooktown
CORAL
Normanton
Cairns
Innisfail
SEA
Burketown
Croydon
Camooweal
Forsayth
Charters Towers
Townsville
Great Barrier Reef
Mount Isa
Hughenden
Bowen
150°
20°
Boulia
Mackay
Emerald
Rockhampton
TROPIC OF CAPRICORN
Gladstone
IA
GREAT
QUEENSLAND
SOUTH
Windorah
Fraser Island (Great Sandy Island)
Charleville
Bundaberg
Maryborough
ARTESIAN
Roma
Gympie
PACIFIC
Quilpie
Dalby
BRISBANE
BASIN
Cunnamulla
Ipswich
OCEAN
Warwick
Gold Coast
Milparinka
Grafton
Lismore
Leigh Creek
Bourke
Walgett
Armidale
30°
Broken Hill
NEW
Tamworth
ort ugusta
Darling
Nyngan
Boomerang Beach
Taree
Lord Howe I.
160°
SOUTH
Dubbo
Port Pirie
WALES
Bathurst
Newcastle
Murray
Mildura
SYDNEY
ADELAIDE
Griffith
Wollongong
Wagga Wagga
Goulburn
Murray Bridge
Albury
Canberra
cepede Bay
AUSTRALIAN CAPITAL TERR.
VICTORIA
+ Mt. Kosciuszko 2228
Mount Gambier
Horsham
MELBOURNE
Ballarat
Portland
Geelong
Moe
150°
Warrnambool
140°
TASMAN SEA
Bass Strait
King Island
Furneaux Group
40°
40°
Hunter Islands
Burnie
Devonport
Mt. Ossa 1617 +
Launceston
TASMANIA
Hobart

5 COOL THINGS TO DO HERE

1 SOAK IN HOT SPRINGS
Great Barrier Island

Dip into the warm water of Kaitoke Hot Springs. The water is heated by thermal activity underground. It feels especially good after a hike on New Zealand's fourth largest island.

2 HANG OUT ON A HARBOR BRIDGE
Auckland

Walk across the harbor bridge for a great view of the city. Get strapped into the safety gear and stroll the walkway high above water. See how tiny the boats look!

3 FLOAT THROUGH FIORDS
Milford Sound

Take a two-hour cruise from the top of this fiord to the ocean. Stare at the sheer cliffs on both sides of your boat. Look for seals resting on cliffs.

5 FACE FACE-PAINTERS
Rotorua

Step into the re-created Tamaki Maori Village. Hear stories, watch dances, and learn about Maori body and face markings and their meanings.

NATIONAL BIRD: kiwi

NATIONAL TREE: silver fern

NATIONAL MAMMAL: long-tailed bat

NEW ZEALAND
Land of the KIWI

Unique island wildlife such as the kiwi and spectacular scenery make New Zealand (named by Dutch explorers) a land not to miss. North Island, with volcanoes, hot springs, and grassy plains, is where most New Zealanders live. South Island is rugged, with snow-capped Southern Alps' peaks, lakes, glaciers, and fiords. New Zealand has more sheep than people, and the seas around its coastline and islands are rich in fish.

4 ENJOY A SWEET PAVLOVA
Wellington

Stop in a café and order their most popular dessert. A pavlova is a crunchy, sweet shell filled with whipped cream, meringue, and delicious fruit.

ID CARD
COUNTRY FACTS

Size: 103,363 sq mi (267,710 sq km)
Population: 4,450,000
Capital: Wellington
Official languages: English and Maori
Currency: New Zealand dollar
Highest point: Aoraki (Mt. Cook), 12,316 ft (3,754 m)
Life expectancy: 81.0 years

Globetrotter Attractions

MILFORD TRACK
Hikers love this trail on South Island. To keep the crowd size down and protect the land, officials allow only 90 walkers on the trail each day.

QUEENSTOWN
Here on South Island, a sky-high gondola provides a spectacular view of this lakeside resort town. *The Lord of the Rings* trilogy was filmed here.

WAITOMO CAVES
A boat ride through these caves of North Island will remind you of a starry night. Thousands of glowworms light up the walls of the cave.

DIGITAL TRAVELER!
To a New Zealander, the word "kiwi" is used not only for a type of flightless bird. Use your digital device to find two other popular uses of the word.

AUSTRALIA & OCEANIA

225

PAPUA NEW GUINEA

Rain Forests, Beaches, and Homes on STILTS

Papua New Guinea shares the island of New Guinea with Indonesia, and also covers the islands of the Bismarck Archipelago and Bougainville. New Guinea is mountainous, with dense forests, volcanoes, swampy river valleys, and coastal beaches. Tribal peoples observe traditional cultures in farm-villages, some still making stilt-houses to keep living areas above water.

Globetrotter Attractions

VARIRATA NATIONAL PARK

With grasslands, woodlands, and rain forests, the park is ideal for many kinds of plants and animals. Bird watchers can find kingfishers, cockatoos, birds of paradise, and many others.

KIMBE BAY

The enormous coral reefs are home to about 820 kinds of fish and the world's smallest seahorse, which grows to about ¾ of an inch (19 mm).

NATIONAL PARLIAMENT HOUSE

Local artists have decorated the outside of this government building in Canberra with a mural of mosaic tiles. Enter the lobby by pulling door handles made of *kundu* hand drums.

2 SWIM IN THE BISMARCK SEA
Wewak

Take a swim at a Wewak beach. Then build a sand castle or bury your toes in the soft sand. During World War II, the Japanese built military bases here.

Map labels: 145° · Sae Is. · PAC · Ninigo Group · Hermit Is. · Admiralty Islands · Wuvulu Island · Manus · Momot · Kabuli · +718 · Lou · Vanimo · Purdy Islands · +1617 · Aitape · Schouten Islands · BISM · Lumi · Maprik · Wewak · Sepik · Ambunti · Angoram · Manam · Bogia · Ulingan · Karkar · Ramu · 1831+ · Madang · Central Range · Bismarck · Long Island · +1304 · Telefomin · Mt. Wilhelm 4509 · Saidor · Tari · Mt. Hagen · Range · Huon Pen · Kiunga · Mendi · Goroka · Aiyura · 4124 · PAPUA NEW · INDONESIA · Lake Murray · Gurimatu · Lae · Huo · Lake Murray · Kikori · Menyamya · Strickland · Kikori · Wau · Ihu · Garair · Fly · 3655 · Balimo · Tapini · Bensbach · Gesoa · 145° · Bereina · Iamara · Gulf of Papua · Mt. Victoria 4035 · Sibidiro · Daru · Kokoda Track · Port Moresby · Varirata N.P. · Rigo · 10°

5 ENJOY A SING SING SHOW
Goroka

Dance to the tribal music as people from different groups and villages share their songs, costumes, and stories.

5 COOL THINGS TO DO HERE

DIGITAL TRAVELER!
There are many annual events in Papua New Guinea that celebrate the culture of native tribes. Search online for colorful photos of events such as the Crocodile Festival and the Canoe and Kundu Drum Festival. Draw your own picture of one of these festivals.

1 OGLE AT ORCHIDS
Lae

Count all the different colors of orchids you see at Rain Forest Habitat. It was built under a cloth canopy on a college campus. Besides gardens with 10,000 plants, you'll see birds, lizards, and flying foxes.

ID CARD
COUNTRY FACTS

Size: 178,703 sq mi (462,840 sq km)
Population: 7,179,000
Capital: Port Moresby
Official languages: Tok Pisin, English, and Hiri Motu
Currency: kina
Highest point: Mt. Wilhelm, 14,793 ft (4,509 m)
Life expectancy: 63.0 years

3 VIEW VOLCANOES
Rabaul

Visit the Volcano Observatory to get a glimpse of the most active volcanoes in the country. In 1994, two volcanoes erupted at the same time and devastated the city of Rabaul.

4 SAY HI TO TREE-HUGGERS
Port Moresby

Take a video of this rare animal when you visit Port Moresby Nature Park. Tree kangaroos live in only a few rain forests in the world.

AUSTRALIA & OCEANIA

227

### Map labels

PACIFIC OCEAN
150°
Mussau Is.
Mussau — Tabalo
651
Emirau
Ysabel Channel
New Hanover
Rambutyo
Umbukul — 960 — Kavieng
Tabar Is.
Lihir Group
853 Lihir
BISMARCK
NEW IRELAND
1481
Tanga Islands
Namatanai
Nuguria Is.
Samo
Feni Islands
BISMARCK SEA
ARCHIPELAGO
Rabaul
Witu Is.
2438
2021
Green Is.
Open Bay
Mt. Ulawun
St. George's Channel
Cape St. George
2334
Kimbe Bay
Wide Bay
5°
Buka
Umboi
1655 — Gloucester
NEW BRITAIN
Wakunai
2743 — Torokina
Jacquinot Bay
Bougainville
2251
finschhafen
Kandrian — Uvol
Empress Augusta Bay
Buin
GUINEA
155°
Gulf
SOLOMON SEA
SOLOMON ISLANDS
Lusancay Is.
TROBRIAND ISLANDS
Ioma
Losuia — Kiriwina
Popondetta
Kulumadau
Tufi
Goodenough I.
Woodlark
427
Fergusson I.
Laughlan Islands
Wanigela — 2566
D'ENTRECASTEAUX IS.
Owen Stanley Range
3676
Normanby I.
10°
Bonvouloir Is.
Paili
Gurney
Gpschen Str.
LOUISIADE ARCHIPELAGO
Cape Rodney
Samarai
Misima
Conflict Group
CORAL SEA
150°
806
838
Rossel I.
Tagula

0 — 100 — 200 MILES
0 — 100 — 200 KILOMETERS

	NATIONAL BIRD:	NATIONAL FLOWER:	NATIONAL MAMMAL:
FIJI	golden fruit dove	tagimoucia	spotted dolphin
SOLOMON ISLANDS	yellow-bibbed lory	temple plant	spinner dolphin
VANUATU	Vanuatu kingfisher	*Veitchia metiti*	Vanuatu flying fox

MELANESIA

Ancient Living CULTURES

PAPUA NEW GUINEA

Choiseul · Santa Isabel · Vella Lavella · New Georgia Sound · Kolombangara · Kennedy I. · New Georgia · Savo I. · Malaita · Honiara · Guadalcanal · Solomon Sea · **SOLOMON** · San Cristobal · Rennell

160° · 10° · 160°

The Pacific islands of Melanesia include New Caledonia, Vanuatu, the Solomon Islands, and Fiji. Most islands are hilly and forested, with volcanoes and mountains. They have a tropical climate, with a rainy season from December to March. Traditional Melanesian cultures survive alongside modern life. Most islands are self-governing, but New Caledonia is French.

Globetrotter Attractions

GARDEN OF THE SLEEPING GIANT
More than 2,000 kinds of orchids grow on this Fiji plantation that was once the home of U.S. TV star Raymond Burr. It is one of the largest orchid collections in the world.

GUADALCANAL AMERICAN MEMORIAL
The United States built this to honor Americans and their allies who died in World War II battles.

SRI SIVA SUBRAMANIYA TEMPLE
Painted a rainbow of colors, this is the largest Hindu temple in the Southern Hemisphere. It is in Nadi, Fiji.

4 MIX WITH MOUND-BUILDING BIRDS
Savo Island

Stay on the beach at night to watch the megapodes build their nests. They dig down three feet (1 m), lay their eggs, and bury them. If the nests are undisturbed, the eggs will hatch in seven weeks. The babies will dig their way up.

5 SEE SPECTACULAR BIRDS
Kennedy Island

Listen to the bird calls all around this small island. It is named for U.S. President John F. Kennedy who swam ashore here after his military boat sank during WWII.

228

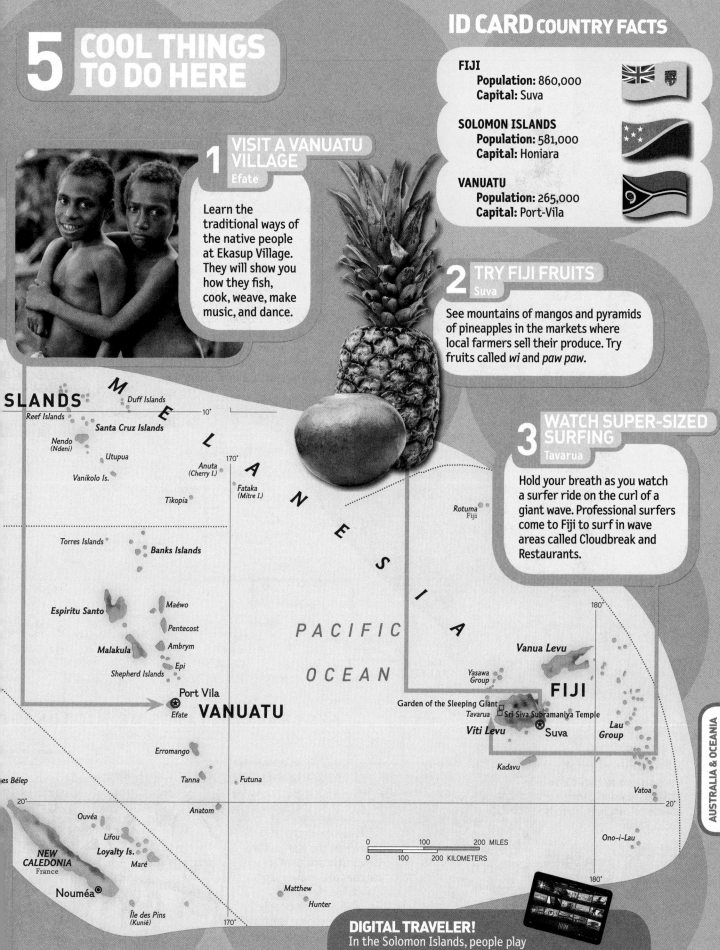

5 COOL THINGS TO DO HERE

1 VISIT A VANUATU VILLAGE
Efate

Learn the traditional ways of the native people at Ekasup Village. They will show you how they fish, cook, weave, make music, and dance.

2 TRY FIJI FRUITS
Suva

See mountains of mangos and pyramids of pineapples in the markets where local farmers sell their produce. Try fruits called *wi* and *paw paw*.

3 WATCH SUPER-SIZED SURFING
Tavarua

Hold your breath as you watch a surfer ride on the curl of a giant wave. Professional surfers come to Fiji to surf in wave areas called Cloudbreak and Restaurants.

### Map labels

SLANDS
Duff Islands
Reef Islands
Santa Cruz Islands
Nendo (Ndeni)
Utupua
Vanikolo Is.
Anuta (Cherry I.)
Fataka (Mitre I.)
Tikopia
Rotuma Fiji
MELANESIA
Torres Islands
Banks Islands
Espiritu Santo
Maéwo
Pentecost
Malakula
Ambrym
Shepherd Islands
Epi
Port Vila
Efate
VANUATU
Erromango
Tanna
Futuna
Anatom
es Bélep
Ouvéa
Lifou
Loyalty Is.
Maré
NEW CALEDONIA
France
Nouméa
Île des Pins (Kunié)
Matthew
Hunter
PACIFIC OCEAN
Vanua Levu
Yasawa Group
Garden of the Sleeping Giant
Tavarua
Sri Siva Subramaniya Temple
FIJI
Viti Levu
Suva
Lau Group
Kadavu
Vatoa
Ono-i-Lau

0   100   200 MILES
0 100 200 KILOMETERS

AUSTRALIA & OCEANIA

DIGITAL TRAVELER!
In the Solomon Islands, people play traditional music on panpipes. Go online to find a video clip of Solomon Islanders playing this instrument.

MICRONESIA

Sunny Island PARADISE

3 WALK A PATH OF STONE MONEY
Yap

Imagine using a stone the size of a car to buy food or a canoe trip. Long ago, stones with holes in the middle served as money. People did not move the largest stones. They just claimed ownership.

Micronesia is a vast island region in the northern Pacific Ocean, and boats are the best way to get around. The larger countries include Palau, Nauru, the Federated States of Micronesia, the Marshall Islands, and Kiribati. "Micro" means small, and many Micronesian islands are tiny coral atolls. Wake Island (U.S.), for instance, has fewer than 200 people on an atoll with a coastline of just 12 miles (19 km).

5 COOL THINGS TO DO HERE

Farallon de Pajaros
Asuncion
Agrihan
Pagan
Alamagan
Sarigan
Anatahan
Capital Hill · Saipan
Tinian
Rota
GUAM
U.S.

NORTHERN MARIANA ISLANDS
U.S.

200   400 MILES
200   400 KILOMETERS

M I C R O N E

Enewetak Atoll

Ulithi Atoll

Yap Islands
Woleai Atoll
Fais
Gaferut
Namonuito Atoll
Ujelar Atoll

Melekeok
Koror
Malakal I.
PALAU
Sonsorol Is.
Ngulu Atoll
Ifalik Atoll
Satawal
Hall Is.
Oroluk Atoll
Senyavin Is.
Pulap Atoll
Chuuk (Truk Is.)
Palikir · Pohnpei (Ponape)

Eauripik Atoll
Puluwat Atoll
Pulusuk
Mortlock Is.
Ngatik Atoll
Kosra (Kusaie)

Pulo Anna
Merir
Tobi
Helen I.

C A R O L I N E   I S L A N D S

Nukuoro Atoll

FEDERATED STATES OF MICRONESI

1 READ CARVED STORY BOARDS
Koror

Ask woodcarvers to tell you their stories as they carve pictures in wood. Story boards tell ancient legends about Palau.

2 INSPECT GIANT CLAMS
Malakal Island

Learn how the Mariculture Demonstration Center hatches and grows giant clams. The clams are valuable because people put them in aquariums, use their shells, and serve them for food.

ID CARD COUNTRY FACTS

FEDERATED STATES OF MICRONESIA
Population: 107,000
Capital: Palikir

KIRIBATI
Population: 106,000
Capital: Tarawa

MARSHALL ISLANDS
Population: 56,000
Capital: Majuro

NAURU
Population: 11,000
Capital: Yaren

PALAU
Population: 21,000
Capital: Melekeok

Globetrotter Attractions

NGARDMAU WATERFALLS
In the Ngardmau district of Palau, hikers reach the tallest and biggest waterfall—the Tiki Falls—by walking a path of old railroad tracks through the jungle.

ALELE MUSEUM AND LIBRARY
Here in the Marshall Islands, a collection of stick charts shows off traditional technology. Made from coconut leaves, these 3-D charts helped islanders memorize wave patterns so they could canoe the ocean safely.

KIRIBATI BATTLE SITES
World War II tanks, ships, and planes are visible on the reef at low tide.

4 REPORT ON A CANOE RACE
South Tarawa Lagoon

Find out why people say that Kiribati canoes are the fastest canoes in the Pacific Ocean. Watch the wind fill their sails as they speed through the water.

5 EXPLORE ANCIENT RUINS
Pohnpei

Ride a touring kayak to the island of Nan Madol, an ancient city now in ruins. Walk among the remains of the home and tombs of the island's kings.

### Map labels

Taongi Atoll
-20°
170°
180°
ikini Atoll
Rongelap Atoll
Utirik Atoll
Ailuk Atoll
Ratak Chain
Ralik Chain
MARSHALL ISLANDS
Kwajalein Atoll
Wotje Atoll
Maloelap Atoll
Ninglapalap Atoll
Majuro
Jaluit Atoll
Arno Atoll
Namorik Atoll
Kili I.
Mili Atoll
Ebon Atoll
PACIFIC OCEAN
170°
-10°
Palmyra Atoll U.S.
160°
Teraina (Washington I.)
Butaritari
Abaiang
Marakei
Tabuaeran (Fanning I.) Kiribati
South Tarawa Lagoon
Tarawa (Bairiki)
GILBERT ISLANDS
Abemama
Howland Island U.S.
Baker Island
Kiritimati (Christmas I.) Kiribati
EQUATOR
0°
AURU
Yaren
Nonouti
K I R I B A T I
Jarvis Island U.S.
LINE ISLANDS
Banaba (Ocean I.)
Tabiteuea
Beru
Tamana
Arorae
Kanton
Enderbury I.
Malden Island
McKean Island
Birnie I.
Rawaki
Nikumaroro
Orona
Manra
PHOENIX ISLANDS
Starbuck Island
170°
180°
170°
160°

AUSTRALIA & OCEANIA

DIGITAL TRAVELER!
People happily swim in Jellyfish Lake in Palau. Do some online research to find out why the jellyfish in this lake do not sting.

5 COOL THINGS TO DO HERE

1 DANCE AT A FATALE
Funafuti

Move to the beat of the drums as you celebrate a *fatale*. Grass skirts, flowers, and joyful music are all part of the festivities.

2 PLUNGE FROM THE SLIDING ROCKS
Papseea

Cool off in a waterfall. Sit on the slippery rocks and glide down into the refreshing natural pool of water. There is one 16-foot (5-m) drop and three smaller ones closer to the pool.

3 DRINK FROM A COCONUT
Tuvalu

Every beach resort and town will have stalls selling coconut milk to drink, necklaces made of seashells, and brightly colored headresses, shirts, and skirts. Buy samples of their goods for a flavor of Polynesian life.

5 SEE AN ANCIENT STONE CALENDAR
Tongatapu Island

In A.D. 1200, the Tu'i Tu'itatui people erected these three huge coral slabs. Recent research tells us that the people used the structure to track the sun and the seasons.

4 LEARN HOW TO MAKE BARK CLOTH
Nuku'alofa

Use a wooden mallet to pound the peeled bark of a mulberry tree. When the bark is thin, several of these tapas are glued together to make a big piece of cloth that is ready for painting.

TUVALU
Vaitupu
Nukufetau
Funafuti
Nukulaelae
Niulakita

TOKELAU N.Z.
Atafu
Nukunonu
Fakaofo
Swains I.

AMERICAN SAMOA U.S.

SAMOA
Savai'i
Apia
Alofaaga Blowholes
Papseea
Upolu
Pago Pago
Manua Is.
Tutuila
Rose Atoll

SAMOA ISLANDS

Îles Wallis
France Uvea
Îles de Horne

FIJI

Niuafo'ou
Tafahi
Niuatoputapu

Vava'u Group
Ha'apai Group

TONGA
Nuku'alofa
Tongatapu Group

Niue N.Z.

(Tongareva) Penrhyn Atoll
Rakahanga Atoll
Manihiki Atoll
Caroline Island (Millennium Island)
Vostok Island

Pukapuka Atoll (Danger Is.)
Nassau
Flint Island

Suwarrow Atoll

SOUTH PACIFIC OCEAN

New Zealand

Palmerston Atoll

COOK ISLANDS

Aitutaki Atoll
Hervey Is.
Mitiaro
Atiu Mauke

Rarotonga
Mangaia

Maria

Rurutu

Motu One
Manuae
Bora-Bora
Maupihaa
Raiatea Huahine
Papeete
Moorea
Ta...

SOCIETY ISLA...

Rimatara
Tubuai

AUSTRAL IS. (TUBUA...

0 — 200 — 400 MILES
0 — 200 — 400 KILOMETERS

POLYNESIA
Heart of the South PACIFIC

More than 1,000 islands make up Polynesia, in the heart of the Pacific, among them Samoa, Tonga, Tuvalu, French Polynesia (Tahiti), and Hawai'i. Beautiful Hawai'i, a U.S. state, is famous for beaches and surf, and Honolulu is one of the Pacific's largest cities. Many Polynesian islands are small, such as Pitcairn and Tokelau, or remote, for example Easter Island. No wonder Polynesians were traditionally skilled seafarers.

ID CARD COUNTRY FACTS

FRENCH POLYNESIA
Population: 278,000
Capital: Papeete

SAMOA
Population: 190,000
Capital: Apia

TONGA
Population: 103,000
Capital: Nuku'alofa

TUVALU
Population: 11,000
Capital: Funafuti

DIGITAL TRAVELER!
The famous artist Paul Gauguin lived on Tahiti in French Polynesia for many years. Search online to find his painting called "The Black Pigs." What does the painting tell you about Tahiti?

MARQUESAS ISLANDS
France

Eiao · Hatutu · Ua Huka · Nuku Hiva · Hiva Oa · Ua Pu · Tahuata · Fatu Hiva

TUAMOTU ARCHIPELAGO

Manihi · Takaroa · Tikei · Mataiva · Rangiroa · Makatea · Makemo · Napuka · Pukapuka · Anaa · Hikueru · Hao · Tatakoto

FRENCH POLYNESIA
France

Hereheretue · Îles du Duc de Gloucester · Tureia · Tematagi · Moruroa · Marutea · Morane · Mangareva · Temoe · Îles Gambier

TROPIC OF CAPRICORN

Raivavae (Vavitu) · Rapa · Marotiri

Globetrotter Attractions

ROBERT LOUIS STEVENSON MUSEUM
In the late 1800s, the author of *Treasure Island* and *Strange Case of Dr. Jekyll and Mr. Hyde* lived here, in Samoa.

STONE MONUMENTS OF MU'A
The tombs, vaults, and mounds were burial sites for Tonga kings between A.D. 1200 and 1600.

ALOFAAGA BLOWHOLES
Ocean waves shoot high into the air through holes in lava rock in Samoa. Locals throw in coconuts and watch them fly out.

ANTARCTICA

An Immense ICE CAP

Centered on the South Pole, Antarctica is the coldest, windiest, and iciest continent. There are mountains, valleys, and lakes but 98 percent of the land is permanently covered in ice. In many places, the ice is more than 1 mile (1.6 km) thick. In winter (May to July), it is always dark and the surrounding sea freezes to form a belt of ice more than 300 miles (483 km) wide. In summer, the ice belt breaks up to form icebergs, some of which are the size of small U.S. states.

With such a harsh climate. no people live permanently on Antarctica. Tourists regularly visit to see the stunning sights on this vast continent.

ANTARCTICA

A Continent WITHOUT COUNTRIES

The immense ice cap of Antarctica holds 70 percent of the world's fresh water. The icy Antarctic waters are ideal for fish and shellfish, which attract seabirds and marine mammals that feed on them. More than 40 countries, including the U.S.A., Australia, New Zealand, Norway, Chile, Argentina, France, Russia, and the United Kingdom, have signed the Antarctic Treaty, which protects the continent's environment. Conservation groups have urged that limits be placed on fishing in these waters to prevent overexploitation of marine life found there.

Globetrotter Attractions

AUNT BERTHA'S
TRAVEL TIPS

FREEZING COLD
Wear weatherproof clothing here. Near the South Pole, temperatures rarely get above 32°F (0°C). Fierce, bitter cold winds can reach speeds of 180 mph (288 kph).

WHALE WATCHING
If you are sailing the Southern Ocean, watch out for blue, sperm, pygmy, and southern right whales. They migrate to the ocean at various times of the year for food.

COMPASS READINGS
If you are using a standard compass to find your way across the ice, be aware that as you approach the south magnetic pole, the compass needle will try to point downward.

ANTARCTIC PENINSULA

This continental arm of the main body of Antarctica is bordered by many islands along the deepwater channels. It lies about 1,000 miles (1,609 km) from the tip of South America.

WEST ANTARCTICA

Some of the massive ice sheet covering this part of the continent has melted away in recent years. This is due to climate change.

TRANSANTARCTIC MOUNTAINS

A mountain range about 2,200 miles (3,541 km) long runs across the continent. Mount Erebus, the world's southernmost volcano, is part of this range.

Map labels: South Orkney Islands, South Shetland Islands, Bransfield Strait, Palmer Archipelago, Anvers I., Palmer Research Station, GRAHAM LAND, ANTARCTIC CIRCLE, ANTARCTIC PENINSULA, PALMER LAND, Larsen Ice Shelf, Alexander Island, 2987, Latady Mts., Sweeney Mts., Merrick Mts., BELLINGSHAUSEN SEA, Fletcher Pen., Abbot Ice Shelf, Thurston Island, Burke I., AMUNDSEN SEA, Carney Island, Getz Ice Shelf, Siple Island, Pine Island Glacier, ELLSWORTH LAND, Vinson Massif 4897, Ellsworth Mts., WEST ANTARCTICA, MARIE BYRD LAND, 1208, Edward VII Peninsula, Cape Norvegia, Riiser-Larsen Ice Shelf, Krau Mts, Lyddan I., WEDDELL SEA, COATS LAND, 86, 1642, Berkner Island, RONNE ICE SHELF, 158, Pensacola Mountain, 1730

236

QUEEN MAUD LAND

Here, a mountainous coastal area has rocky peaks up to 11,000 feet (3,353 m) high that pierce the ice cap.

RESEARCH STATIONS
Anvers Island

A few thousand scientists spend several months at a time at research stations, studying astronomy, wildlife, climate change, and other areas of science.

EAST ANTARCTICA

A few areas of this region are free from ice for part of the year. Plant life here includes mosses, lichens, and algae.

FREE AS A BIRD
Amery Ice Shelf

Penguins leap out of the water onto the ice. They feed on fish, krill, and squid in the ocean.

WILKES LAND

This coastal area features massive ice cliffs and a series of ice shelfs.

ROSS ICE SHELF

This huge floating platform of ice—about the size of France—is several hundred feet thick. It has formed where glaciers and the main ice sheet reach the Ross Sea.

### Map labels

Fimbul Ice Shelf
501
Riiser-Larsen Peninsula
MERIDIAN OF GREENWICH (LONDON)
QUEEN
3212
MAUD
3498
Valkyrie Dome
LAND
ENDERBY LAND
Napier Mts.
1781
ANTARCTIC CIRCLE
SOUTHERN OCEAN
MAC. ROBERTSON LAND
1770
Cape Darnley
Lambert Glacier
Amery Ice Shelf
AMERICAN HIGHLAND
Vestfold Hills
West Ice Shelf
2688
POLAR PLATEAU
Dome Argus
3990
EAST ANTARCTICA
South Pole
DAVIS SEA
TRANSANTARCTIC MOUNTAINS
Grosvenor Mts.
4069
Shackleton Coast
4351
2593
3387
2992
DOME C
3174
ROSS ICE SHELF
Roosevelt Island
Mt. Erebus 3794
Ross I.
Prince Albert Mountains
VICTORIA LAND
2541
2435
WILKES LAND
Masson Island
Shackleton Ice Shelf
Bowman Island
Vincennes Bay
Cape Poinsett
Moscow University Ice Shelf
ROSS SEA
Admiralty Mts.
4165
Cape Adare
Mertz Glacier Tongue
SOUTHERN OCEAN

0 200 400 MILES
0 200 400 KILOMETERS

What in the World?

UATSET FO REIYLBT

TNENEHGESO

DELGON ATEG EIBDRG

ATGER LALW FO AICNH

IGB ENB

LFEEIF WRTOE

ACMUH IPCUCH

JAT AALHM

NIXHPS

240

LOOK OUT, BELOW!

These photographs show aerial views of Earth's surface.
Unscramble the letters to identify each picture.

AMONNITU EGRNA

RFTOSE

LRTAAFLEW

NAONYC

ALCOVON

RSEEDT

DTWSAELN

CGALRIE

PORC LDEISF

What in the World?

NREEBOGAO

OAAKL

RTEGA ARERIBR FREE

ORNGAAKO

LAFG

DRSRBFUOSA

SREAY CKOR

AWSCYSAOR

DENYYS EORAP OESUH

RAIN FOREST ROUNDUP

These photographs show close-up views of animals that live in the rain forest. Unscramble the letters to identify what's in each picture.

GRFO

ABT

OTSHL

RGAAUJ

PREVI

ARPHNIA

SPAGSREHROP

IRAPT

OATNCU

ANSWERS

238-239: Answer A-maze-ing Paris

240: Answers
What in the World Places
- Statue of Liberty
- Stonehenge
- Golden Gate Bridge
- Great Wall of China
- Big Ben
- Eiffel Tower
- Machu Picchu
- Taj Mahal
- Sphinx

241: Answers
What in the World Earth
- Mountain Range
- Forest
- Waterfall
- Canyon
- Volcano
- Desert
- Wetlands
- Glacier
- Crop Fields

242: Answers
What in the World Australia
- Boomerang
- Koala
- Great Barrier Reef
- Kangaroo
- Flag
- Surfboards
- Ayers Rock
- Cassowary
- Sydney Opera House

243: Answers
What in the World Rain Forest
- Frog
- Bat
- Sloth
- Jaguar
- Viper
- Piranha
- Grasshopper
- Tapir
- Toucan

GLOSSARY

archipelago a group or chain of islands

bay a body of water, usually smaller than a gulf, that is partially surrounded by land

border the area on either side of a boundary

boundary most commonly, a line that has been established by people to mark the limit of one political unit, such as a country or state, and the beginning of another; geographical features such as mountains sometimes act as boundaries

breakwater a structure, such as a wall, that protects a harbor or beach from pounding waves

bush in Australia, any area with little or no human settlement. It may have very little plant growth or be wooded and forested

canal a human-made waterway that is used by ships or to carry water for irrigation

canyon a deep, narrow valley that has steep sides

cape a point of land that extends into an ocean, a lake, or a river

capital in a country, the city where the government headquarters are. The capital is usually the largest and most important city

cliff a very steep rock face, usually along a coast but also on the side of a mountain

climate the average weather conditions over many years

continent one of the seven main landmasses on Earth's surface

country a territory whose government is the highest legal authority over the land and people within its boundaries

delta lowland formed by silt, sand, and gravel deposited by a river at its mouth

desert a hot or cold region that receives 10 inches (25 cm) or less of rain or other kinds of precipitation a year

divide an elevated area drained by different river systems flowing in different directions

dune a mound or ridge of wind-blown sand

Eastern Hemisphere the half of the globe that lies east of the prime meridian. It includes most of Africa, most of Europe, all of Asia, all of Australia/Oceania, and about half of Antarctica

elevation distance above sea level, usually measured in feet or meters

environment the conditions surrounding and affecting any living thing including the climate and landscape

Equator an imaginary line circling the broadest part of Earth and representing 0° latitude. It divides the globe into the Northern and Southern hemispheres

exports goods or services produced in one country and sold to another country or countries

fault a break in Earth's crust along which movement up, down, or sideways occurs

fiord a narrow sea inlet enclosed by high cliffs. Fiords are found in Norway, New Zealand, and in Scotland in the United Kingdom

fork in a river, the place where two streams come together

geographic pole 90°N, 90°S latitude; location of the ends of Earth's axis

geomagnetic pole point where the axis of Earth's magnetic field intersects Earth's surface; compass needles align with Earth's magnetic field so that one end points to the magnetic north pole, the other to the magnetic south pole

glacier a large, slow-moving mass of ice. As a glacier moves, it scours the land and, near its end, dumps rock debris

globe a scale model of Earth with accurate relative sizes and locations of continents

gulf a portion of the ocean that cuts into the land; usually larger than a bay

harbor a body of water, sheltered by natural or artificial barriers, that is deep enough for ships

hemisphere literally half a sphere; Earth has four hemispheres: Northern, Southern, Eastern, and Western

highlands an elevated area or the more mountainous region of a country

iceberg a large, floating mass of ice

inlet a narrow opening in the land that is filled with water flowing from an ocean, a lake, or a river

island a landmass, smaller than a continent, that is completely surrounded by water

isthmus a narrow strip of land that connects two larger landmasses and has water on two sides

lagoon a shallow body of water that is open to the sea but also protected from it by a reef or sandbar

lake a body of water that is surrounded by land; large lakes are sometimes called seas

landform a physical feature that is shaped by tectonic activity and weathering and erosion; the four major kinds on earth are plains, mountains, plateaus, and hills

landmass a large area of Earth's crust that lies above sea level, such as a continent

large-scale map a map, such as a street map, that shows a small area in great detail

Latin America cultural region generally considered to include Mexico, Central America, South America, and the West Indies; Portuguese and Spanish are the principal languages

latitude distance north and south of the Equator, which is 0° latitude

leeward the side away from or sheltered from the wind

longitude distance east and west of the prime meridian, which is 0° longitude

lowland an area of land lower than the surrounding countryside that is usually flat and without hills and mountains

mangrove swamp a muddy area along tropical coasts thick with mangrove trees that have special breathing roots leading down from branches

Middle East term commonly used for the countries of Southwest Asia but can also include northern Africa from Morocco to Somalia

molten liquefied by heat; melted

mountain a landform, higher than a hill, that rises at least 1,000 feet (302 m) above the surrounding land and is wider at its base than at its top, or peak; a series of mountains is called a range

nation people who share a common culture; often used as another word for "country," although people within a country may be of many cultures

national park an area of a country set aside to protect the landscape or wildlife from human interference

navigable a body of water deep or wide enough to allow boats, ships, barges, and other vessels to pass; any water vessel that can be steered

Northern Hemisphere the half of the globe that lies north of the Equator. It includes all of North America, a small part of South America, all of Europe, about 65 percent of Africa, and almost all of Asia

oasis a part of a desert or other dry region where water is near the surface and plants grow well

ocean the large body of saltwater that surrounds the continents and covers more than two-thirds of Earth's surface

Pampas a flat, treeless part of South America between the Atlantic Coast and the Andes Mountains.

peninsula a piece of land that is almost completely surrounded by water

permafrost a permanently frozen sub-surface soil in frigid regions

plain a large area of relatively flat land that is often covered with grasses

plateau a relatively flat area, larger than a mesa, that rises above the surrounding landscape

point a narrow piece of land smaller than a cape that extends into a body of water

population density The number of people living on each square mile or square kilometer of land (calculated by dividing population by land area)

prime meridian an imaginary line that runs through Greenwich, England, and is accepted as the line of 0° longitude

primeval belonging to the first or oldest period of era of living things

projection the process of representing the round Earth on a flat surface, such as a map

rain forest dense forest found on or near the Equator where the climate is hot and wet

reef an offshore ridge made of coral, rocks, or sand

renewable resources resources such as water that are replenished naturally, but can run out by overuse and pollution.

Sahel a semiarid grassland in Africa along the Sahara's southern border where rainfall is unreliable

savannah a tropical grassland with scattered trees

scale on a map, a means of explaining the relationship between distances on the map and actual distances on Earth's surface

sea a partially enclosed body of saltwater that is connected to the ocean; completely enclosed bodies of saltwater, such as the Dead Sea, are really lakes

small-scale map a map, such as a country map, that shows a large area without much detail

sound a long, broad inlet of the ocean that lies parallel to the coast and often separates an island and the mainland

Southern Hemisphere the half of the globe that lies south of the Equator. It includes most of South America, a third of Africa, all of Australia/Oceania, all of Antarctica, and a small part of Asia

Soviet Union shortened name for the Union of Soviet Socialist Republics (U.S.S.R.), a former Communist republic (1920–1991) in eastern Europe and northern and central Asia that was made up of 15 republics of which Russia was the largest

spit a long, narrow strip of land, often of sand or silt, extending into a body of water from the land

staple a chief ingredient of a people's diet

steppe a Slavic word referring to relatively flat, mostly treeless temperate grasslands that stretch across much of central Europe and central Asia

strait a narrow passage of water that connects two larger bodies of water

territory land that is under the jurisdiction of a country but that is not a state or a province

tributary a stream that flows into a larger river

tropics region lying within 23½° north and south of the Equator that experiences warm temperatures year-round

upwelling process by which nutrient-rich water rises from ocean depths to the surface

valley a long depression, usually created by a river, that is bordered by higher land

volcano an opening in Earth's crust through which molten rock erupts

weather the day-to-day variation in sunshine, rainfall, wind, cloud cover, and other effects of Earth's atmosphere

Western Hemisphere the half of the globe that lies west of the prime meridian. It includes North America, South America, a part of Europe and Africa, and about half of Antarctica

windward the unsheltered side toward which the wind blows

ADDITIONAL COUNTRY DATA

THIS LIST OF COUNTRIES IS IN ALPHABETICAL ORDER.

COUNTRY	SIZE	OFFICIAL LANGUAGE	CURRENCY	HIGHEST POINT	LIFE EXPECTANCY
Albania	11,100 sq mi (28,748 sq km)	Albanian	Albanian lek	Maja e Korabit (Golem Korab), 9068 ft (2764 m)	77
Algeria	919,595 sq mi (2,381,741 sq km)	Arabic	Algerian dinar	Tahat, 9852 ft (3003 m)	76
Andorra	181 sq mi (468 sq km)	Catalan	Euro	Pic de Coma Pedrosa, 9665 ft (2946 m)	N/A
Antigua and Barbuda	171 sq mi (442 sq km)	English	East Caribbean dollar	Boggy Peak, 1319 ft (402 m)	76
Armenia	11,484 sq mi (29,742 sq km)	Armenian	Armenian dram	Aragats Lerrnagagat', 13419 ft (4090 m)	74
Azerbaijan	33,436 sq mi (86,600 sq km)	Azerbaijani (Azeri)	Azerbaijan manat	Bazarduzu Dagi, 14715 ft (4485 m)	74
Bahrain	277 sq mi (717 sq km)	Arabic, English, Farsi	Bahraini dinar	Jabal ad Dukhan, 400 ft (122 m)	76
Bangladesh	56,977 sq mi (147,570 sq km)	Bangla (Bengali)	Bangladeshi taka	Keokradong, 4035 ft (1230 m)	70
Barbados	166 sq mi (430 sq km)	English	Barbadian dollar	Mount Hillaby, 1102 ft (336 m)	75
Belarus	80,153 sq mi (207,595 sq km)	Belarusian, Russian	Belarusian ruble	Dzyarzhynskaya Hara, 1135 ft (346 m)	72
Belgium	11,787 sq mi (30,528 sq km)	Flemish (Dutch), French, German	Euro	Botrange, 2277 ft (694 m)	80
Belize	8,867 sq mi (22,965 sq km)	Spanish, Creole, Mayan dialects, English	Belize dollar	Doyle's Delight, 3806 ft (1160 m)	73
Benin	43,484 sq mi (112,622 sq km)	French	West African CFA franc	Mont Sokbaro, 2159 ft (658 m)	59
Bhutan	17,954 sq mi (46,500 sq km)	Dzongkha	Bhutanese ngultrum/Indian rupee	Gangkar Puensum, 24836 ft (7570 m)	67
Bosnia and Herzegovina	19,741 sq mi (51,129 sq km)	Croatian, Serbian, Bosnian	Bosnia and Herzegovina convertible mark	Maglic, 7828 ft (2386 m)	76
Botswana	224,607 sq mi (581,730 sq km)	English	Botswana pula	Tsodilo Hills, 4885 ft (1489 m)	47
Brunei	2,226 sq mi (5,765 sq km)	Malay	Brunei dollar	Bukit Pagon, 6070 ft (1850 m)	78
Bulgaria	42,855 sq mi (110,994 sq km)	Bulgarian, Turkish, Roma	Bulgarian lev	Musala, 9597 ft (2925 m)	74
Burkina Faso	105,869 sq mi (274,200 sq km)	French	West African CFA franc	Tena Kourou, 2457 ft (749 m)	56
Burundi	10,747 sq mi (27,834 sq km)	Kirundi, French	Burundian franc	Heha, 8760 ft (2670 m)	53
Cambodia	69,898 sq mi (181,035 sq km)	Khmer	Cambodian riel	Phnum Aoral, 5938 ft (1810 m)	62
Cameroon	183,569 sq mi (475,442 sq km)	French, English	Central African CFA franc	Fako, 13435 ft (4095 m)	54
Cape Verde	1,558 sq mi (4,036 sq km)	Portuguese, Crioulo	Cape Verdean escudo	Mt. Fogo, 9282 ft (2829 m)	74
Central African Republic	240,535 sq mi (622,984 sq km)	French	Central African CFA franc	Mont Ngaoui, 4659 ft (1420 m)	49
Colombia	440,831 sq mi (1,141,748 sq km)	Spanish	Colombian peso	Pico Cristobal Colon, 18947 ft (5775 m)	74
Comoros	719 sq mi (1,862 sq km)	Arabic, French	Comorian franc	Karthala, 7743 ft (2360 m)	60
Congo	132,047 sq mi (342,000 sq km)	French	Central African CFA franc	Mount Berongou, 2963 ft (903 m)	58
Cote D'Ivoire	124,503 sq mi (322,462 sq km)	French	West African CFA franc	Monts Nimba, 5748 ft (1752 m)	50
Croatia	21,831 sq mi (56,542 sq km)	Croatian	Croatian kuna	Dinara, 6007 ft (1831 m)	77
Cuba	42,803 sq mi (110,860 sq km)	Spanish	Cuban peso	Pico Turquino, 6578 ft (2005 m)	78
Cyprus	3,572 sq mi (9,251 sq km)	Greek, Turkish, English	Euro	Mount Olympus, 6401 ft (1951 m)	78
Czech Republic	30,450 sq mi (78,866 sq km)	Czech	Czech koruna	Snezka , 5256 ft (1602 m)	78
Democratic Republic of Congo	905,365 sq mi (2,344,885 sq km)	French	Congolese franc	Margherita Peak on Mount Stanley, 16765 ft (5110 m)	49
Djibouti	8,958 sq mi (23,300 sq km)	French, Arabic	Djiboutian franc	Moussa Ali, 6654 ft (2028 m)	61
Dominica	290 sq mi (751 sq km)	English	East Caribbean dollar	Morne Diablotins, 4747 ft (1447 m)	74
Dominican Republic	18,704 sq mi (48,442 sq km)	Spanish	Dominican peso	Pico Duarte, 10417 ft (3175 m)	73
Ecuador	109,483 sq mi (283,560 sq km)	Spanish	U.S. dollar	Chimborazo, 20561 ft (6267 m)	75
El Salvador	8,124 sq mi (21,041 sq km)	Spanish, Nahua	U.S. dollar	Cerro El Pital, 8957 ft (2730 m)	72
Equatorial Guinea	10,831 sq mi (1,002,000 sq km)	Spanish, French	Central African CFA franc	Pico Basile, 9869 ft (3008 m)	52
Eritrea	46,774 sq mi (121,144 sq km)	Afar, Arabic, Tigre	Eritrean nakfa	Soira, 9902 ft (3018 m)	62
Estonia	17,462 sq mi (45,227 sq km)	Estonian	Euro	Suur Munamagi, 1043 ft (318 m)	76
Ethiopia	437,600 sq mi (1,133,380 sw km)	Amharic, Tigrinya	Ethiopian birr	Ras Dejen, 14872 ft (4533 m)	62

COUNTRY	SIZE	OFFICIAL LANGUAGE	CURRENCY	HIGHEST POINT	LIFE EXPECTANCY
Federated States of Micronesia	271 sq mi (702 sq km)	English	U.S. dollar	Dolohmwar (Totolom), 2595 ft (791 m)	68
Fiji	7,095 sq mi (18,376 sq km)	English	Fijian dollar	Tomanivi, 4344 ft (1324 m)	69
France	210,026 sq mi (543,965 sq km)	French	Euro	Mont Blanc, 15771 ft (4807 m)	82
French Polynesia	1,609 sq mi (4,167 sq km)	French	CFP franc	Mont Orohena, 7352 ft (2241 m)	76
Gabon	103,347 sq mi (267,667 sq km)	French	Central African CFA franc	Mont Iboundji, 5167 ft (1575 m)	63
Gambia	4,361 sq mi (11,295 sq km)	English	Gambian dalasi	unnamed elevation, 174 ft (53 m)	58
Georgia	26,911 sq mi (69,700 sq km)	Georgian	Georgian lari	Mt'a Shkhara, 17064 ft (5201 m)	75
Ghana	92,100 sq mi (238,537 sq km)	English	Ghana cedi	Mount Afadjato, 2904 ft (885 m)	61
Greece	50,949 sq mi (131,957 sw km)	Greek, English, french	Euro	Mount Olympus, 9570 ft (2917 m)	81
Grenada	133 sq mi (344 sq km)	English	East Caribbean dollar	Mount Saint Catherine, 2756 ft (840 m)	73
Guatemala	42,042 sq mi (108,889 sq km)	Spanish, 23 Amerindian Languages	Guatemalan quetzal	Volcan Tajumulco, 13,816 ft (4,211 m)	71
Guinea	94,926 sq mi (245,857 sq km)	French	Guinean franc	Monts Nimba, 5748 ft (1752 m)	56
Guinea-Bissau	13,948 sq mi (36,125 sq km)	Portuguese	West African CFA franc	unnamed elevation, 984 ft (300 m)	54
Guyana	83,000 sq mi (214,969 sq km)	English, Amerindian dialects, Creole	Guyanese dollar	Mount Roraima, 9301 ft (2835 m)	66
Haiti	10,714 sq mi (27,750 sq km)	French, Creole	Haitian gourde	Chaine de la Selle, 8793 ft (2680 m)	62
Honduras	43,433 sq mi (112,492 sq km)	Spanish, Amerindian dialects	Honduran Iempira	Cerro Las Minas, 9416 ft (2870 m)	73
Hungary	35,919 sq mi (93,030 sq km)	Hungarian	Hungarian forint	Kekes, 3327 ft (1014 m)	75
India	1,269,222 sq mi (3,287,270 sq km)	Hindi, English	Indian rupee	Kanchenjunga, 28209 ft (8598 m)	66
Indonesia	742,308 sq mi (1,922,570 sq km)	Bahasa Indonesian	Indonesian rupiah	Puncak Jaya, 16024 ft (4884 m)	70
Italy	116,345 sq mi (301,333 sq km)	Italian	Euro	Mont Blanc (Monte Bianco) de Courmayeur, 15577 ft (4748 m)	82
Jamaica	4.244 sq mi (10,991 sq km)	English, Patois English	Jamaican dollar	Blue Mountain Peak, 7402 ft (2256 m)	73
Jordan	34,495 sq mi (89,342 sq km)	Arabic	Jordanian dinar	Jabal Umm ad Dami, 6083 ft (1854 m)	73
Kazakhstan	1,049,155 sq mi (2,717,300 sq km)	Kazakh (Qazaq), Russian	Kazakhstani tenge	Khan Tangiri Shyngy (Pik Khan-Tengri), 22949 ft (6995 m)	69
Kiribati	313 sq mi (811 sq km)	English	Kiribati dollar/Australian dollar	unnamed elevation on Banaba, 266 ft (81 m)	65
Kosovo	4,203 sq mi (10,887 sq km)	Albanian, Serbian, Bosnian	Euro	Gjeravica/Deravica, 8714 ft (2656 m)	69
Kuwait	6,880 sq mi (17,818 sq km)	Arabic	Kuwaiti dinar	unnamed elevation, 1004 ft (306 m)	75
Kyrgyzstan	77,182 sq mi (199,900 sq km)	Kyrgyz, Russian	Kyrgyzstani som	Jengish Chokusu (Pik Pobedy), 24406 ft (7439 m)	70
Laos	91,429 sq mi (236,800 sq km)	Lao	Lao kip	Phu Bia, 9242 ft (2817 m)	67
Latvia	24,938 sq mi (64,589 sq km)	Latvian	Latvian lats	Gaizina Kalns, 1024 ft (312 m)	74
Lebanon	4,036 sq mi (10,452 sq km)	Arabic	Lebanese pound	Qornet es Saouda, 10131 ft (3088 m)	79
Lesotho	11,720 sq mi (30,355 sq km)	Sesotho, English	Lesotho loti	Thabana Ntlenyana, 11424 ft (3482 m)	48
Liberia	43,000 sq mi (111,370 sq km)	English	Liberian dollar	Mount Wuteve, 4528 ft (1380 m)	60
Liechtenstein	62 sq mi (160 sq km)	German	Swiss franc	Vorder-Grauspitz, 8527 ft (2599 m)	82
Lithuania	25,212 sq mi (65,300 sq km)	Lithuanian	Lithuanian litas	Aukstojas, 965 ft (294 m)	74
Luxembourg	998 sq mi (2,586 sq km)	Luxembourgish	Euro	Buurgplaatz, 1834 ft (559 m)	80
Macedonia	9,928 sq mi (25,713 sq km)	Macedonian, Albanian, Turkish	Macedonian denar	Golem Korab (Maja e Korabit), 9068 ft (2764 m)	75
Madagascar	226,658 sq mi (587,041 sq km)	French, Malagasy	Malagasy ariary	Maromokotro, 9436 ft (2876 m)	64
Malawi	45,747 sq mi (118,484 sq km)	Chichewa	Malawian kwacha	Sapitwa (Mount Mlanje), 9849 ft (3002 m)	54
Malaysia	127,355 sq mi (329,847 sq km)	Bahasa Melayu	Malaysian ringgit	Gunung Kinabalu, 13451 ft (4100 m)	75
Maldives	115 sq mi (298 sq km)	Maldivian Dhivehi, English	Maldivian rufiyaa	Addu Atholhu, 8 ft (2 m)	74
Malta	122 sq mi (316 sq km)	Maltese, English	Euro	Ta'Dmejrek, 830 ft (253 m)	81
Marshall Islands	70 sq mi (181 sq km)	Marshallese	U.S. dollar	unnamed location on Likiep, 33 ft (10 m)	72
Mauritania	397,955 sq mi (1,030,700 sq km)	Arabic	Mauritanian ouguiya	Kediet Ijill, 3002 ft (915 m)	61
Mauritius	788 sq mi (2,040 sq km)	French, Creole, Bhojpuri	Mauritian rupee	Mont Piton, 2717 ft (828 m)	73
Moldova	13,050 sq mi (33,800 sq km)	Moldovan	Moldovan leu	Dealul Balanesti, 1411 ft (430 m)	71
Monaco	.8 sq mi (2 sq km)	French	Euro	Mont Agel, 459 ft (140 m)	N/A
Montenegro	5,415 sq mi (14,026 sq km)	Serbian	Euro	Bobotov Kuk, 8274 ft (2522 m)	74
Myanmar	261,218 sq mi (676,552 sq km)	Burmese	Burmese kyat	Hkakabo Razi, 19295 ft (5881 m)	65
Namibia	318,261 sq mi (824,292 sq km)	English	Namibian dollar	Konigstein, 8550 ft (2606 m)	63
Nauru	8 sq mi (21 sq km)	Nauruan	Australian dollar	unnamed elevation along plateau rim, 200 ft (61 m)	60
Nepal	56,827 sq mi (147,181 sq km)	Nepali	Nepalese rupee	Mount Everest, 29035 ft (8850 m)	68
Netherlands	16,034 sq mi (41,528 sq km)	Dutch, Frisian	Euro	Mount Scenery, 2828 ft (862 m)	81
North Korea	46,540 sq mi (120,538 sq km)	Korean	North Korean won	Paektu-san, 9003 ft (2744 m)	69

COUNTRY	SIZE	OFFICIAL LANGUAGE	CURRENCY	HIGHEST POINT	LIFE EXPECTAN
Oman	119,500 sq mi (309,500 sq km)	Arabic	Omani rial	Jabal Shams, 9778 ft (2980 m)	76
Palau	189 sq mi (489 sq km)	Palauan, Filipino, English, Chinese	U.S. dollar	Mount Ngerchelchuus, 794 ft (242 m)	69
Qatar	4,448 sq mi (11,521 sq km)	Arabic	Qatari riyal	Tuwayyir al Hamir, 338 ft (103 m)	78
Romania	92,043 sq mi (238,391 sq km)	Romanian	Romanian leu	Moldoveanu, 8347 ft (2544 m)	74
Rwanda	10,169 sq mi (26,338 sq km)	Kinyarwanda, French, English	Rwandan franc	Volcan Karisimbi, 14826 ft (4519 m)	63
Samoa	1,093 sq mi (2,831 sq km)	Samoan (Polynesian), English	Samoan tala	Mount Silisili, 6093ft (1857 m)	73
San Marino	24 sq mi (61 sq km)	Itaian	Euro	Monte Titano, 2477 ft (755 m)	84
Sao Tome & Principe	386 sq mi (1,001 sq km)	Portuguese	Sao Tome & Principe dobra	Pico de Sao Tome, 6640 ft (2024 m)	66
Saudi Arabia	756,985 sq mi (1,960,582 sq km)	Arabic	Saudi riyal	Jabal Sawda', 10279 ft (3133 m)	74
Senegal	75,955 sq mi (196,722 sq km)	French	West African CFA franc	unnamed elevation southwest of Kedougou, 1906 ft (581 m)	63
Serbia	29,913 sq mi (77,474 sq km)	Serbian	Euro	Midzor, 7116 ft (2169 m)	74
Seychelles	176 sq mi (455 sq km)	English	Seychellois rupee	Morne Seychellois, 2969 ft (905 m)	73
Sierra Leone	27,699 sq mi (71,740 sq km)	English	Sierra Leone leone	Loma Mansa (Bintimani), 6391 ft (1948 m)	45
Singapore	255 sq mi (660 sq km)	Mandarin, English, Malay	Singapore dollar	Bukit Timah, 545 ft (166 m)	82
Slovakia	18,932 sq mi (49,035 sq km)	Slovak	Euro	Gerlachovsky Stit, 8711 ft (2655 m)	76
Slovenia	7,827 sq mi (20,273 sq km)	Slovene, Serbo-Croatian	Euro	Triglav, 9396 ft (2864 m)	80
Solomon Islands	10,954 sq mi (28,370 sq km)	Melanesian pidgin	Solomon Islands dollar	Mount Popomanaseu, 7579 ft (2310 m)	67
Somalia	246,201 sq mi (637,657 sq km)	Somali	Somali shilling	Shimbiris, 7927ft (2416 m)	54
South Africa	470,693 sq mi (1,219,090 sq km)	Afrikaans, English	South African rand	Njesuthi, 11181 ft (3408 m)	58
South Korea	38,321 sq mi (99,250 sq km)	Korean	South Korean won	Halla-san, 6398 ft (1950 m)	81
South Sudan	248,777 sq mi (644,329 sq km)	English	South Sudanese pound	Kinyeti, 10456 ft (3187 m)	54
Spain	195,363 sq mi (505,988 sq km)	Castilian Spanish	Euro	Pico de Teide (Tenerife) on Canary Islands, 12198 ft (3718 m)	82
Sri Lanka	25,299 sq mi (65,525 sq km)	Sinhala	Sri Lankan rupee	Pidurutalagala, 8281 ft (2524 m)	74
St. Kitts & Nevis	104 sq mi (269 sq km)	English	East Caribbean dollar	Mount Liamuiga, 3793 ft (1156 m)	75
St. Lucia	238 sq mi (616 sq km)	English	East Caribbean dollar	Mount Gimie, 3117 ft (950 m)	75
St. Vincent and the Grenadines	150 sq mi (389 sq km)	English, French Patois	East Caribbean dollar	La Soufriere, 4049 ft (1234 m)	72
Sudan	967,500 sq mi (2,505,813 sq km)	Arabic	Sudanese pound	Jabal Marrah, 10076 ft (3071 m)	62
Suriname	63,037 sq mi (163,265 sq km)	Dutch	Surinamese dollar	Juliana Top, 4035 ft (1230 m)	71
Swaziland	6,704 sq mi (17,363 sq km)	English, siSwati	Swazi lilangeni	Emlembe, 6109 ft (1862 m)	49
Switzerland	15,940 sq mi (41,284 sq km)	German, French, italian	Swiss franc	Dufourspitze, 15203 ft (4634 m)	83
Syria	71,488 sq mi (185,180 sq km)	Arabic	Syrian pound	Mount Hermon, 9232 ft (2814 m)	75
Tajikistan	55,251 sq mi (143,100 sq km)	Tajik	Tajikistani somoni	Qullai Ismoili Somoni, 24590 ft (7495 m)	67
Thailand	198,115 sq mi (513,115 sq km)	Thai, English	Thai baht	Doi Inthanon, 8451 ft (2576 m)	75
Timor-Leste	5,640 sq mi (14,609 sq km)	Tetum, Portuguese	U.S. dollar	Foho Tatamailau, 9721 ft (2963 m)	66
Togo	21,925 sq mi (56,785 sq km)	French	West African CFA franc	Mont Agou, 3235 ft (986 m)	56
Tonga	289 sq mi (748 sq km)	Tongan, English	Tongan pa'anga	unnamed elevation on Kao Island, 3389 ft (1033 m)	72
Trinidad and Tobago	1,980 sq mi (5,128 sq km)	English	Trinidad and Tobago dollar	El Cerro del Aripo, 3084 ft (940 m)	71
Tunisia	63,170 sq mi (163,610 sq km)	Arabic	Tunisian dinar	Jebel ech Chambi, 5066 ft (1544 m)	75
Turkmenistan	188,300 sq mi (488,100 sq km)	Turkmen, Russian, Uzbek	Turkmenistan manat	Gora Ayribaba, 10299 ft (3139 m)	65
Tuvalu	10 sq mi (26 sq km)	Tuvaluan, English	Tuvaluan dollar/Australian dollar	unnamed location, 16 ft (5 m)	65
Uganda	93,104 sq mi (241,139 sq km)	English	Ugandan shilling	Margherita Peak on Mount Stanley, 16765 ft (5110 m)	58
Ukraine	233,090 sq mi (603,700 sq km)	Ukrainian	Ukrainian hryvnia	Hora Hoverla, 6762 ft (2061 m)	71
United Arab Emirates	30,000 sq mi (77,700 sq km)	Arabic	United Arab Emirates dirham	Jabal Yibir, 5010 ft (1527 m)	76
Uzbekistan	172,742 sq mi (447,400 sq km)	Uzbek, Russian	Uzbekistani som	Adelunga Toghi, 14111 ft (4301 m)	68
Vanuatu	4,707 sq mi (12,190 sq km)	pidgin (Bislama or Bichelama)	Vanuatu vatu	Tabwemasana, 6158 ft (1877 m)	71
Vatican City	.2 sq mi (.4 sq km)	Italian, Latin, french	Euro	unnamed elevation, 246 ft (75 m)	N/A
Vietnam	127,844 sq mi (331,114 sq km)	Vietnamese	Vietnamese dong	Fan Si Pan, 10315 ft (3144 m)	73
Yemen	207,286 sq mi (536,286 sq km)	Arabic	Yemeni rial	Jabal an Nabi Shu'ayb, 12336 ft (3760 m)	62
Zambia	290,586 sq mi (752,614 sq km)	English	Zambian kwacha	Mafinga Hills, 7549 ft (2301 m)	56

COUNTRY ABBREVIATIONS

Afghanistan, Afghan.
Albania, Alban.
Algeria, Alg.
Argentina, Arg.
Armenia, Arm.
Austria, Aust.
Australia, Austral.
Azerbaijan, Azerb.
Belgium, Belg.
Bolivia, Bol.
Bosnia and Herzegovina, Bosn. & Herzg.
Brazil, Braz.
Bulgaria, Bulg.
Costa Rica, C.R.
Canada, Can.
Central African Republic, Cen. Af. Rep.
Colombia, Col.
Denmark, Den.
Dominican Republic, Dom. Rep.
Ecuador, Ecua.
El Salvador, El Salv.
Estonia, Est.
Ethiopia, Eth.
Federated States of Micronesia, F.S.M.
Falkland Islands, Falk. Is.
Finland, Fin.
France, French, Fr.
Georgia, Ga.

Germany, Ger.
Greece, Gr.
Honduras, Hond.
Hungary, Hung.
Iceland, Ice.
Ireland, Ire.
Italy, It.
Jamaica, Jam.
Kazakhstan, Kaz.
Kosovo, Kos.
Kyrgyzstan, Kyrg.
Latvia, Latv.
Lebanon, Leb.
Libya, Lib.
Liechtenstein, Liech.
Lithuania, Lith.
Luxembourg, Lux.
Macedonia, Maced.
Mexico, Mex.
Moldova, Mold.
Morocco, Mor.
Northern Ireland, N. Ire.
New Zealand, N.Z.
Netherlands, Neth.
Nicaragua, Nicar.
Norway, Nor.
Papua New Guinea, P.N.G.
Pakistan, Pak.

Panama, Pan.
Paraguay, Parag.
Poland, Pol.
Portugal, Port.
Romania, Rom.
Russia, Russ.
Serbia, Serb.
Slovenia, Slov.
Spain, Spanish, Sp.
Sweden, Sw.
Switzerland, Switz.
Syria, Syr.
Tajikistan, Taj.
Thailand, Thai.
Tunisia, Tun.
Turkey, Turk.
Turkmenistan, Turkm.
United Arab Emirates, U.A.E.
United Kingdom, U.K.
United States, U.S.
Ukraine, Ukr.
Uruguay, Uru.
Uzbekistan, Uzb.
Venezuela, Venez.
Zimbabwe, Zimb.

INDEX

A

Ābhē Bid Hāyk', Djibouti 192
Abidjan, Côte d'Ivoire (Ivory Coast) 177
Abkhazia, Ga. 119
Abomey, Benin 179
Abuja, Nigeria 184
Abuja National Mosque, Abuja, Nigeria 185
Acapulco, Mex. 18
Acre, Israel 124
Acropolis Museum, Athens, Gr. 109
Adhari Park, Adhari, Bahrain 127
Adi Ugri, Eritrea 191
Africaine Market, Algiers, Alg. 169
Agadez, Niger 183
Agra, India 141
Aït Ben Haddou, Mor. 167
Akloa Falls, Badou, Togo 179
Al Hajjarah, Yemen 128
Al Jabal Al Akhadar, Oman 128
Åland Islands, Fin. 75
Alay Valley, Kyrg. 139
Alele Museum and Library, Marshall Islands 231
Alentejo, Port. 89
Aletsch Glacier, Switz. 101
Alexandria, Egypt 172

Algiers, Alg. 169
Alhambra, Granada, Sp. 91
Ali-Sadr, Iran 132
Al-Mogran, Sudan 189
Alonfaaga Blowholes, Samoa 233
Altay Mountains, Asia 149
Altyn-Emel State National Park, Kaz. 138
Amador Causeway, Pan. 29
Amalienborg Palace, Copenhagen, Den. 68
Amazon Rain Forest, Braz. 41, 49
Amery Ice Shelf, Antarctica 237
Amsterdam, Neth. 98
Anatolia Plateau, Turk. 120
Andorra la Vella, Andorra 91
Angel Falls, Canaima National Park, Venez. 45
Angkor Wat Temple, Angkor, Cambodia 155
Ankara, Turk. 120, 121
Annamese Cordillera Mountains, Laos & Vietnam 155
Anne Frank's house, Amsterdam, Neth. 98
Antarctic Peninsula, Antarctica 235, 236
Antigua, Guatemala 20
Anvers Island research stations, Antarctica 237
Arabian Oryx Sanctuary, Oman 129
Aral Sea, Asia 138

Arch, Baja, Mex. 19
Archaeological Museum-Reserve, Tyumen, Russ. 116
Archbishop's Palace, Vigan, Philippines 160
Archipiélago de las Perlas, Pan. 29
Arenal Volcano, C.R. 26, 27
Arghandab River, Afghan. 134
Armenian Plateau, Arm. 119
Ar-Rusayris Dam, Ed Damazin, Sudan 189
Arusha, Tanzania 197
Asan, South Korea 151
Asir National Park, Saudi Arabia 126
Astana, Kaz. 139
Astronomical Clock, Prague, Czech Republic 82
Asunción, Parag. 58, 59
Aswan Botanic Gardens, Aswan, Egypt 173
Atacama Desert, Chile 54
Atakule, Ankara, Turk. 121
Atauro Island, Timor-Leste (East Timor) 158
Athens, Gr. 109
Ati, Chad 187
Atitlán Nature Reserve, Guatemala 21
Atlantis Paradise Hotel, Paradise Island, Bahamas 34
Auckland, N.Z. 224

Australia Zoo, Austral. 223
Autobahns, Würzburg, Ger. 79
Auyantepui Mountain, Canaima National Park,
    Venez. 45
Ayers Rock (Uluru), Austral. 219, 223
Ayutthaya, Thai. 153
Azandi Tower, TehrÐn, Iran 132

B
Baba Wali Shrine, Kandahar, Afghan. 134
Badaling, China 144
Badou, Togo 179
Baghdad, Iraq 131
Baku, Azerb. 119
Bali, Indonesia 158
Bamako, Mali 181
Bamian caves, Bamian, Afghan. 134
Banaue Rice Terraces, Philippines 160
Banc d'Arguin National Park, Mauritania 175
Bandar Seri Begawan, Brunei 157
Band-e Amir National Park, Afghan. 135
Bandiagara Cliffs, Bandiagara, Mali 181
Banff National Park, Can. 10, 14
Bangkok Snake Farm, Bangkok, Thai. 152
Bangladesh Tea Research Institute, Sylhet,
    Bangladesh 143
Barcelona, Sp. 91
Bastimentos, Pan. 28
Batié, Cameroon 202
Batu Caves, Selangor, Malaysia 156
Bavarian Alps, Europe 79
Bay of Bengal, Bangladesh 143
Bayamo, Cuba 31
Beijing, China 145
Beira, Mozambique 209
Belem Tower, Lisbon, Port. 89
Belize Zoo, Belmopan, Belize 21
Bellamar Caves, Cuba 30
Belmopan, Belize 21
Belogradchik Rocks, Bulg. 107
Beppu, Japan 146
Bequia Island, St. Vincent & the Grenadines 37
Berbera, Somalia 192
Bergen, Nor. 71
Bermudian Landing, Belize 21
Bern, Switz. 101
Białowieża Forest, Pol. 85
Billund, Den. 68
Bilwi, Nicar. 25
Biocentro Guembe, Bol. 53
Bismarck Sea, P.N.G. 226
Black Forest, Ger. 79
Black Rocks, Angola 205
Black Sea, Europe 86
Blackcomb Mountain, Can. 15
Blantyre, Malawi 207
Blarney Stone, Blarney, Ire. 95
Blue Grotto, Malta 103
Blue Hole National Monument, Belize 21
Blue Lagoon, Ice. 66
Blue Lagoon Island, Bahamas 35
Blue Nile, Wad Medani, Sudan 189
Bluefields, Nicar. 25
Bluestack Mountains, Donegal Bay, Ire. 94
Bock Casemates, Lux. 99
Bogotá, Col. 43
Bohol, Philippines 160
Bolshoi Theater, Moscow, Russ. 111
Boomerang Beach, Austral. 223
Boquete, Pan. 28
Boracy Island, Philippines 161
B.O.S. Nyaru Menteng Reintroduction Center,
    Palangkaraya, Indonesia 158

Bosawás Biosphere Reserve, Nicar. 24
Bossou Forest, Guinea 177
Botanical Gardens, Victoria, Seychelles 217
Boulders Beach, South Africa 214
Brandenburg Gate, Berlin, Ger. 79
Brankovina, Serb. 104
Brasília, Braz. 48
Braslau Lakes National Park, Belarus 86
Brazzaville, Congo 201
Bridgetown, Barbados 37
Brimstone Hill Fortress National Park, St. Kitts
    & Nevis 36
Broadway theater district, New York City, U.S. 16
Brownsberg Nature Park, Suriname 47
Brussels, Belg. 99
Buchanan, Liberia 177
Bucharest, Rom. 107
Bucovina, Rom. 106
Budapest, Hung. 83
Buenos Aires, Arg. 57
Bujumbura, Burundi 199
Bulawayo, Zimb. 210

C
Cabarete Beach, Dom. Rep. 32
Cahora Bassa Dam, Zambezi River, Mozambique
    209
Cairngorms, Scotland, U.K. 96
Cairo Museum, Cairo, Egypt 172
Calabar, Nigeria 185
Calandula Falls, Angola 205
Callao Cave, Peñablanca, Philippines 161
Camembert Village, Fr. 93
Cameroon Benedictine Monastery, Yaounde,
    Cameroon 203
Canaima National Park, Venez. 45
Canoe and Kundu Drum Festival, P.N.G. 227
Cape Coast, Ghana 179
Cape of Good Hope, South Africa 214
Cape Verde, Africa 174
Cap-Haïtien, Haiti 32, 33
Cappadocia, Turk. 121
Caracas, Venez. 44, 45
Cardiff, Wales, U.K. 97
Carmel, Israel 124
Carnaval, Oruro, Bol. 53
Carnival, Braz. & Pan. 29, 48, 49
Carpathian Mountains, Ukr. 86
Casa de la Vall, Andorra La Vella, Andorra 91
Castillo de la Real Fuerza, Havana, Cuba 30
Castle Lucen, Lucen, Czech Republic 82
Catedral de León, Nicar. 24
Central Kalahari Game Reserve, Botswana 212
Central Market, Djibouti, Djibouti 193
Central Market, Paramaribo, Suriname 47
Cerro Altamirano, Mex. 18
Chã Das Caldeiras, Fogo Island, Cape Verde 175
Chamonix-Mont Blanc, Fr. 93
Chateau Frontenac, Québec City, Can. 14
Chateau Villadry, Fr. 93
Chefchaouen, Mor. 167
Chengdu Research Base of Giant Panda
    Breeding, Chengdu, China 145
Chiang Mai, Thai. 113, 152
Chiang Mai Zoo, Chiang Mai, Thai. 152
Chichén Itzá, Mex. 19
Chichicastenango, Guatemala 20
Chihuahua, Mex. 18
Chinatown Heritage Center, Singapore 156
Chitwan National Park, Nepal 141
Chocolate Hills, Bohol, Philippines 160
Chocolate Museum, Antigua, Guatemala 20

Citadelle, Haiti 33
City of Arts and Sciences, Valencia, Sp. 91
Cliffs of Moher, Ire. 95
Cloudbreak, Fiji 229
CN Tower, Toronto, Can. 15
Cobblers' Bridge, Ljubljana, Slov. 104
Cochabamba, Bol. 52
Coiba National Park, Pan. 29
Colonia del Sacramento, Uru. 61
Colosseum, Rome, It. 103
Colossus of Rhodes, Gr. 108
Community Baboon Sanctuary, Bermudian
    Landing, Belize 21
Community Hippo Sanctuary, Wechiau, Ghana
    179
Conakry, Guinea 176
Congo River, Africa 200, 201
Conimbriga, Ruínas de, Port. 89
Conkouati-Douli National Park, Congo 200
Constantine, Alg. 169
Coober Pedy, Austral. 223
Cooper Canyon Railroad, Copper Canyon, Mex. 19
Copán, Ruinas de, Hond. 22
Copenhagen, Den. 68, 69
Corcovado Mountain, Rio de Janeiro, Braz. 49
Corfu, Gr. 108
Cornwall, England, U.K. 97
Cotton Castle, Pamukkale, Turk. 121
Courland Spit, Lith. 77
Cousin Island, Seychelles 216
Cox's Bazar, Bangladesh 143
Cracow, Pol. 84, 85
Crimea, Ukr. 86
Crocodile Festival, P.N.G. 227
Crocodile Park, Davao, Philippines 161
Cu Chi, Vietnam 155
Cueva de las Maravillas, Dom. Rep. 33
Cuidad Vieja, Montevideo, Uru. 60
Cupnoodle Museum, Yokohama, Japan 147
Cusuco National Park, Hond. 23
Czarny Dunajec, Pol. 85

D
Dahab, Red Sea, Egypt 172
Dahlak Archipelago, Eritrea 190
Dakar, Senegal 174
Dalmatian, Croatia 105
Damascus, Syr. 123
Damnoen Saduak, Thai. 153
Dasht-e Kavîr, Iran 133
Davao, Philippines 161
Day Forest National Park, Djibouti 193
Dead Sea 124
Debre Berhan Selassie, Gondor, Eth. 190
Decebalus statue, Orşova, Rom. 107
Defensores del Chaco National Park, Parag. 58
Dhaka, Bangladesh 143
Dhofar Springs, Oman 128
Dieng Plateau, Java, Indonesia 159
Dili, Timor-Leste (East Timor) 159
Dinder National Park, Sudan 189
Dinosaur Plateau, Kugitang Nature Reserve,
    Turkm. 139
Discoveries Monument, Lisbon, Port. 89
Disneyland, Hong Kong, China 145
Djénné, Mali 181
Djibouti, Djibouti 193
Dominica, Caribbean 36
Donegal Bay, Ire. 94
Donostia-San Sebastián, Sp. 90
Doolin Cave, Doolin, Ire. 94
Dosso Reserve, Dosso, Niger 182
Douro Valley, Port. 88

Drill Monkey Rehab Center, Calabar, Nigeria 185
Dubai, U.A.E. 127
Dublin, Ire. 95
Dunajec River, Pieniny National Park, Pol. 85
Dunn's River Falls, Jam. 30
Dzanga-Sangha Special Reserve, Cen. Af. Rep.
    200

E
Easter Island, Chile 55
Ed Damazin, Sudan 189
Edinburgh, Scotland, U.K. 97
Eiffel Tower, Paris, Fr. 93
Eisriesenwelt Ice Caves, Aust. 81
Ekasup Village, Efate, Vanuatu 229
El Ávila National Park, Venez. 44
El Jemm, Tun. 168
Elephant World, Seoul, South Korea 150
Eleuthera Island, Bahamas 35
Ellis Park Stadium, Johannesburg, South Africa
    214
Emi Koussi, Chad 186
Ephesus, Turk. 120
Erdenet, Mongolia 148
Ericsson Globe, Stockholm, Sw. 73
Estadio Centenario, Montevideo, Uru. 61
Estadio Cuscatlan, San Salvador, El Salv. 22
Etchmiadzin Cathedral, Etchmiadzin, Arm. 118
Ethnological Museum, Timbuktu, Mali 181
Eureka Tower, Melbourne, Austral. 223
Eyjafjallajökull Volcano, Ice. 66

F
Falls of Baleine, Bequia Island, St. Vincent & the
    Grenadines 37
Faroe Islands, Den. 69
Fasil Ghebbi, Eth. 190
Fes, Mor. 166
Festival of Chocolate, San Carlos de Bariloche,
    Arg. 57
Festival of the Sun, Peru 40
Fiesa festival, Pera, Port. 89
Fiesta De La Patria Gaucha, Tacuarembó, Uru. 60
Filadelfia, Parag. 58
Flåm Railway, Bergen, Nor. 71
Fogo Island, Cape Verde 175
Formula One Grand Prix Race, Monte Carlo,
    Monaco 93
Fortaleza de São Miguel, Luanda, Angola 205
Fortress of Suomenlinna, Helsinki, Fin. 75
Foteviken Viking Reserve, Sw. 73
Fountain, Jeddah, Saudi Arabia 126
Frankfurt am Main, Ger. 78
Funafuti, Tuvalu 232

G
Galápagos Islands, Ecua. 42
Gambia River, Gambia 175
Gäncä, Azerb. 118
Ganges River, Asia 141
Ganges River Delta, Bangladesh 143
Garden of the Sleeping Giant, Fiji 228
Gate of the Sun ruins, Tiahuanaco, Bol. 52
Gateway to Abuja, Nigeria 184
Gathering, Minneriya National Park, Sri Lanka
    141
Gdańsk, Pol. 84
Gedi Ruins, Kenya 195
Geiranger, Nor. 71
Geirangerfjord, Nor. 70
Genghis Khan statue, Tsonjin Boldog, Mongolia
    149
Georgetown, Guyana 46

Ghazni towers, Ghazni, Afghan. 135
Giant's Causeway, N. Ire., U.K. 97
Gîza, El, Egypt 173
Gobi desert, China & Mongolia 145, 148, 149
Gobustan, Azerb. 118
Gold Museum, Bogotá, Col. 43
Gold Museum, Lima, Peru 51
Golden Falls, Gullfoss, Ice. 66
Golestan National Park, Iran 133
Gonder, Eth. 190
Goroka, P.N.G. 226
Grand Bahama Island, Bahamas 34
Grand Canal, Venice, It. 102
Grand Canyon, U.S. 16
Grand Place, Brussels, Belg. 99
Grand Square, Kraców, Pol. 84, 85
Great Barrier Island, N.Z. 224
Great Barrier Reef, Austral. 220, 223
Great Mosque, Djénné, Mali 165, 181
Great Mosque, Hama, Syr. 122
Great Mosque, Sâmarrâ, Iraq 131
Great Rift Valley, Africa 162
Great Wall of China, China 115, 144
Great Zimbabwe, Zimb. 211
Green Mountain, Oman 128
Grootfontein, Namibia 212
Gruyères, Switz. 100
Guadalajara, Mex. 19
Guadalcanal American Memorial, Solomon
    Islands 228
Guaraní Museum, Hernandarias, Parag. 59
Guayaquil, Ecua. 43
Guelta D'Archei, Chad 186
Gulf of Aqaba, Jordan 123
Gulf of Tadjoura, Djibouti 192
Gullfoss, Ice. 66
Gurgi Mosque, Tripoli, Lib. 171

H
Ha Long Bay, Vietnam 154
Hadera, Israel 124
Hagia Sophia, Istanbul, Turk. 120
Hal Saflieni Hypogeum, Paola, It. 103
Hallgrimskirkja Church, Reykjavík, Ice. 67
Hallstatt, Aust. 80
Hamburg, Ger. 79
Hanging Gardens of Babylon, Iraq 130
Harare, Zimb. 211
Harbor of Rhodes, Gr. 108
Hassan II Mosque, Casablanca, Mor. 167
Hato El Cedral, Venez. 44
Havana, Cuba 30
Helsinki, Fin. 75
Herat, Afghan. 134
Hermitage Museum, St. Petersburg, Russ. 111
Hernandarias, Parag. 59
Himeji Castle, Himeji, Japan 147
Hindu Kush, Asia 135
Hiroshima Peace Memorial Park, Hiroshima,
    Japan 146
Ho Chi Minh City, Vietnam 155
Hoba meteorite, Grootfontein, Namibia 212
Hohe Tauern National Park, Aust. 81
Holi holiday, Georgetown, Guyana 46
Hong Kong, China 145
House of Crafts, Ventspils, Latv. 76
House of Slaves, Senegal 175
Huambo, Angola 205
Húsavík, Ice. 67
Hustai National Park, Mongolia 149
Hwange National Park, Zimb. 211
Hyderabad, India 140

I
Ibo Island, Quirimbas Archipelago, Mozambique
    208
Iguazú Falls, Arg. 57
Inca Ruins, Ingapirca, Ecua. 42
Indian Pacific train, Perth, Austral. 222
Inle Lake, Myanmar 153
Innsbruck, Aust. 80
Inti Raymi, Peru 40
Iquitos, Peru 50
Irkutsk, Russ. 117
Isla del Ometepe, Lake Nicaragua, Nicar. 24
Isla del Sol, Bol. 52
Islamabad, Pak. 136
Istanbul, Turk. 120, 121
Itaipú Dam, Parag. 58, 59
Ivindo National Park, Gabon 202
Iwokrama Rain Forest, Guyana 47

J
Jacmel, Haiti 32
Jebel Acacus Mountains, Lib. 170
Jeddah, Saudi Arabia 126
Jeju, South Korea 151
Jellyfish Lake, Palau, F.S.M. 231
Jeongbang Waterfall, Jeju, South Korea 151
Jerusalem, Israel 125
Jesus Christ statue, Cochabamba, Bol. 52
Jesus Christ statue, Rio de Janeiro, Braz. 49
Jigme Dorjl National Park, Bhutan 143
Johannesburg, South Africa 214
Jostedalsbreen Glacier, Nor. 70
Jukkasjärvi, Sw. 72
Jungfrau peak, Switz. 101

K
Kabul, Afghan. 135
Kachikally Crocodile Pool, Serekunda, Gambia 174
Kafue National Park, Zambia 206
Kaieteur Falls, Guyana 47
Kaitoke Hot Springs, Great Barrier Island, N.Z.
    224
Kakum National Park, Cape Coast, Ghana 179
Kamarãn Island, Yemen 129
Kamloops, Can. 14
Kandahar, Afghan. 134
Karachi, Pak. 137
Karakoram Highway, Pak. 136
Karathala, Comoros 216
Karst Caves, Slovakia 82
Kasanka National Park, Zambia 206
Kasbah, Aït Ben Haddou, Mor. 167
Kathmandu, Nepal 141
Kavîr Desert, Iran 133
Keetmanshoop, Namibia 213
Kennedy Island, Solomon Islands 228
Kennedy Space Center, U.S. 16
Keti Koti holiday, Suriname 47
Keukenhof Flower Garden, Lisse, Neth. 99
Khan Shatyr tent, Astana, Kaz. 139
Khartoum, Sudan 189
Khyber Pass, Afghan. 135
Kidepo Valley National Park, Uganda 198
Kiev, Ukr. 87
Kigoma, Tanzania 197
Kimbe Bay, P.N.G. 226
King John's castle, Limerick, Ire. 94
Kingdom Center, Riyadh, Saudi Arabia 127
Kingdom of Crystal, Småland, Sw. 73
Kingston, Jam. 31
Kinshasa, Democratic Republic of Congo 201
Kiribati Battle Sites, Kiribati 231
Klagenfurt, Aust. 81

Koh Adang, Thai. 153
Kokkola, Fin. 74
Korhogo, Côte d'Ivoire (Ivory Coast) 177
Koror, Palau, F.S.M. 230
Kracóv. *See* Cracow
Krakatau, Indonesia 159
Kremlin, Moscow, Russ. 111
Kremnica Mint, Kremnica, Slovakia 83
Krkonoše Mountains, Czech Republic & Pol. 82
Kruger National Park, South Africa 214
Krujë, Alban. 104
Kuala Lumpur, Malaysia 156
Kugitang Nature Reserve, Turkm. 139
Kuremäe, Est. 76
Kursk, Russ. 110
Kushiro-Shitsugen National Park, Japan 147
Kuwait City, Kuwait 127
Kyrenia, Cyprus 109

L

La Asunción, Venez. 45
La Ceiba, Hond. 22
La Fortuna, C.R. 26
La Paz, Bol. 52, 53
La Sagrada Familia Church, Barcelona, Sp. 91
La Vuelta Ciclista, Mendoza, Arg. 56
Laas Geel, Somalia 193
Lac 'Assal, Djibouti 193
Lac Ruhondo, Rwanda 199
Lae, P.N.G. 227
Lago de. *See* Lake
Lagos, Nigeria 184
Lagos, Port. 89
Lahore, Pak. 137
Lake Andreyevskoye, Tyumen, Russ. 116
Lake Angara, Irkutsk, Russ. 117
Lake Assal, Djibouti 193
Lake Baikal, Russ. 117
Lake Balaton, Hung. 82
Lake Biwa, Japan 147
Lake Chad, Chad 186
Lake Geneva, Switz. 100
Lake Malawi (Nyasa), Malawi 206
Lake Manyara National Park, Tanzania 196
Lake Maracaibo, Venez. 45
Lake Nakuru, Kenya 194
Lake Nicaragua, Nicar. 24
Lake Ritsa, Abkhazia, Ga. 119
Lake Titicaca, Bol. & Peru 50, 51, 52, 53
Lake Turkana, Kenya 195
Lake Victoria, Africa 199
Lake Volta, Ghana 178
Lake Windsor, Bahamas 34
Lake Yojoa, Hond. 22
Lalibela, Eth. 191
Laongo, Burkina Faso 178
Lapland, Fin. 74
Latvian School Youth Song and Dance Festival,
    Riga, Latv. 77
Le Felicia stadium, Abidjan, Côte d'Ivoire (Ivory
    Coast) 177
Leaning Tower, Pisa, It. 103
Leggett, U.S. 16
Legoland, Billund, Den. 68
Leptis Magna, Lib. 171
Likoma Island, Malawi 207
Lilongwe, Malawi 207
Lima, Peru 51
Limerick, Ire. 94
Lindwurm statue, Klagenfurt, Aust. 81
Lisbon, Port. 89
Lisse, Neth. 99
Little Mermaid statue, Copenhagen, Den. 69

Ljubljanica River, Ljubljana, Slov. 104
Loango National Park, Gabon 203
London, England, U.K. 97
Los Glaciares National Park, Arg. 57
Louangphrabang, Laos 154
Louvre Museum, Fr. 93
Luanda, Angola 205
Lublin, Pol. 85
Lucayan National Park, Bahamas 34
Lucen, Czech Republic 82
Lund, Sw. 73
Lundey Island, Ice. 67
Luzon, Philippines 160

M

Macaw Mountain Bird Park and Nature Reserve,
    Copán Ruinas, Hond. 22
Machu Picchu, Peru 51
Madagascar, Africa 217
Madain, Iraq 130
Madrid, Sp. 90
Madurodam, The Hague, Neth. 99
Magha as-Sa'a, Tripoli, Lib. 171
Maiden's Tower, Baku, Azerb. 119
Majdanek concentration camp, Lublin, Pol. 85
Makgadikgadi Pans Game Reserve, Botswana 213
Malakal Island, Palau, F.S.M. 230
Malalcahuello-Nalcas National Reserve, Andes
    Mountains, Chile 55
Malbork Castle, Malbork, Pol. 84
Malbun, Liech. 101
Maldives, Asia 141
Malealea, Lesotho 215
Malecon, Cuba 30
Malmö, Sw. 73
Mamba Village, Mombassa, Kenya 195
Manaus, Braz. 48
Mangyongdae Children's Palace, Pyongyang,
    North Korea 150
Manila, Philippines 160
Manuel Antonio, C.R. 26
Mao, Chad 187
Maputo, Mozambique 209
Mar del Plata, Arg. 57
Maradi, Niger 182
Mariculture Demonstration Center, Makal Island,
    Palau, F.S.M. 230
Marienburg, Suriname 46
Marinarium, Punta Cana, Dom. Rep. 33
Marrakech, Mor. 167
Masada, Israel 124
Masai Mara National Reserve, Kenya 195
Masaya, Nicar. 25
Masaya Volcano, Nicar. 24
Mashhad, Iran 133
Massawa War Memorial, Taulud Island, Eritrea
    190
Massif de la Hotte, Haiti 33
Matopos Hills, Zimb. 211
Maṭraḥ, Oman 129
Matterhorn, Switz. 101
Matusadona National Park, Zimb. 211
Maya Ruins at Copán, Hond. 23
Maypole Festival, Bluefields, Nicar. 25
Mbabane, Swaziland 215
Mbare flea market, Harare, Zimb. 211
Medellín, Col. 42
Melbourne, Austral. 223
Mendoza, Arg. 56
Meroë, Sudan 188
Merzouga, Mor. 167
Mesopotamia, Asia 130
Metropolitan Park, Pan. 29

Middle of the World Monument, San Antonio de
    Pichincha, Ecua. 43
Milad Tower, Tehrān, Iran 132
Milford Sound, N.Z. 224
Milford Track, N.Z. 225
Millennium Stadium, Cardiff, Wales, U.K. 97
Miniatur Wunderland, Hamburg, Ger. 79
Minneriya National Park, Sri Lanka 141
Minsk, Belarus 86
Mir Castle, Mir, Belarus 86
Miraflores Palace, Caracas, Venez. 44
Mirnny Diamond Pit, Mirnyy, Russ. 117
Mochima National Park, Venez. 45
Mohéli, Comoros 216
Mohenjo-Daro, Pak. 136
Mombasa, Kenya 195
Monte Carlo, Monaco 93
Monteverde Forest Reserve, C.R. 26
Montevideo, Uru. 60, 61
Monument Des Martyrs, Algiers, Alg. 168
Mopti, Mali 180
Moraine Lake, Banff National Park, Can. 10
Morne Trois Pitons National Park, Dominica 36
Morumbi Stadium, São Paulo, Braz. 49
Moscow, Russ. 110, 111
Mosi oa Tunya (Victoria Falls), Zambia & Zimb.
    206, 210, 211
Mosul, Iraq 130, 131
Mother of the Fatherland statue, Kiev, Ukr. 87
Motherland Statue, Russ. 111
Mount Ararat, Turk. 121
Mount Carmel, Israel 124
Mount Chirropó, C.R. 27
Mount Damavand, Iran 133
Mount Erebus, Antarctica 236
Mount Etna, It. 103
Mount Everest, Nepal 141
Mount Fuji, Japan 147
Mount Kenya, Kenya 195
Mount Kilimanjaro, Tanzania 163, 196
Mount Kinabalu, Malaysia 156
Mount Mayon, Luzon, Philippines 160
Mount Rushmore National Monument, U.S. 17
Mount Sinai, Egypt 173
Mount Snezka, Czech Republic 82
Mount Vesuvius, It. 103
Mountains of the Moon, Uganda 199
Mozart festival, Salzburg, Aust. 80
Mtatsminda Mountain, Ga. 118
Multan Cricket Stadium, Multan, Pak. 137
Munich, Ger. 79
Museo del Barro, Parag. 58
Museo Pambata, Manila, Philippines 160
Museum of Clay, Parag. 58
Museum of Smuggling and Fishing, Polperro,
    England, U.K. 97
Museum of the Armed Forces, Luanda, Angola
    205
Musical Ride, Ottawa, Can. 15
M'Zab Valley, Alg. 168
Mzilikazi Art and Crafts Center, Bulawayo, Zimb.
    210

N

Naantali, Fin. 74
Nairobi, Kenya 164
Nairobi National Park, Nairobi, Kenya 194
Namibe, Angola 204
Nampula, Mozambique 208
Nan Madol, Pohnpei, F.S.M. 231
Napo River, Ecua. 42
Nasca Lines, Peru 50
Nassau, Bahamas 35

National Museum, Niamey, Niger 183
National Museum of Art, Maputo, Mozambique 209
National Park of the Marshland, Iraq 130
National Parliament House, P.N.G. 226
National Theater, San José, C.R. 26
N'dalatando, Angola 204
N'Djamena, Chad 186
Negril, Jam. 31
Nemegt Basin, Mongolia 148
Neuschwanstein Castle, Fussen, Ger. 62, 78
New Orleans, U.S. 17
New York City, U.S. 16
Newgrange, Ire. 95
Ngardmau Waterfall, Palau, F.S.M. 231
Ngorongoro Conservation Area, Serengeti National Park, Tanzania 197
Ngorongoro Crater, Tanzania 196
Ngwenya Valley, Swaziland 214
Niagara Falls, Can. & U.S. 15, 17
Niamey, Niger 182
Nimba Mountains, Africa 176
Nineveh, Iraq 130
Nino Konis Santana National Park, Timor-Leste (East Timor) 159
Nizwá, Oman 129
Norse Folk Museum, Oslo, Nor. 71
Nouabalé-Ndoki National Park, Congo 201
Nouakchott, Mauritania 174
Novosibirsk, Russ. 117
Nuku'alofa, Tonga 232
Nyanza, Rwanda 199
Nyati Beach, Mozambique 209

O
Odense Zoo, Odense, Den. 68
Oedu Island, South Korea 151
Oía, Gr. 109
Okavango Delta, Botswana 213
Olavinlinna Castle, Savonlinna, Fin. 74
Old Bridge of Mostar, Bosn. & Herzg. 105
Olumo Rock, Nigeria 185
Olympic Winter Games, Sochi, Russ. 110
Omdurman, Sudan 189
Orango Islands National Park, Guinea-Bissau 176
Øresund Bridge, Den. & Sw. 73
Orhei, Mold. 87
Orşova, Rom. 107
Oruro, Bol. 53
Oslo, Nor. 71
Osogbo, Nigeria 184
Ottawa, Can. 15
Ouagadougou, Burkina Faso 179
Ouidah Museum of History, Benin 178
Oulanka National Park, Fin. 75

P
Paektu-san, North Korea 151
Palace of Parliament, Bucharest, Rom. 107
Palangkaraya, Indonesia 158
Palm Islands, U.A.E. 126
Palmyra, Syr. 123
Pamir Mountains, Asia 138
Pampas, Arg. 56
Pamplemousses, Mauritius 217
Pamukkale, Turk. 121
Panama Canal, Pan. 28, 29
Panama City, Pan. 29
Pantanal, Braz. 49
Paola, It. 103
Papseea, Samoa 232
Paradise Island, Bahamas 34
Paramaribo, Suriname 46

Parc National des Volcans, Rwanda 199
Paris, Fr. 65, 93
Paro Taktsang, Paro, Bhutan 142
Parque del Este, Caracas, Venez. 45
Parthenon, Athens, Gr. 108
Patagonia, Arg. & Chile 55
Patara Beach, Turk. 121
Peñablanca, Philippines 161
Peneda-Gerês National Park, Port. 89
Penshurst, C.R. 27
Pêra, Port. 89
Persepolis, Iran 133
Perth, Austral. 222
Petra, Jordan 123
Petronas Twin Towers, Kuala Lumpur, Malaysia 156
Phagwah holiday, Georgetown, Guyana 46
Phong Nga Bay, Thai. 153
Pico de São Tomé, Sao Tome & Principe 202
Pieniny National Park, Pol. 85
Pilpintuwasi Butterfly Farm, Iquitos, Peru 50
Piura, Peru 50
Place de la République, Niamey, Niger 182
Plain of Jars, Laos 155
Playa Brava, Uru. 61
Pohnpei, F.S.M. 231
Pointe-Noir, Congo 200
Pokaiņi Forest, Latv. 77
Pompeii, It. 103
Port Moresby Nature Park, Port Moresby, P.N.G. 227
Port of Spain, Trinidad & Tobago 37
Prague, Czech Republic 82
Praslin, Seychelles 217
Prince's Palace, Monaco 93
Puerto Cabezas (Bilwi), Nicar. 25
Puerto Natales, Chile 55
Puffin Island, Ice. 67
Pulpit Rock, Nor. 70
Puncak Mandala, Papua, Indonesia 159
Punjab Province, Pak. 136
Puno, Peru 51
Punta Cana, Dom. Rep. 33
Punta del Este, Uru. 60
Punta Roca, El Salv. 23
Pyongyang, North Korea 150
Pyramids, Giza, Egypt 172
Pyrenees Mountains, Andorra 91

Q
Qadisha Valley, Leb. 123
Québec, Can. 14
Queenstown, N.Z. 225
Quiçama National Park, Angola 204
Quirimbas Archipelago, Mozambique 208
Quisqueya Stadium, Santo Domingo, Dom. Rep. 32
Quthing, Lesotho 215

R
Rabaul, P.N.G. 227
Railroad Museum, Asunción, Parag. 58
Rain Forest Habitat, Lae, P.N.G. 227
Ramoji Film City, Hyderabad, India 140
Ramparts, Québec, Can. 14
Raut River, Orhei, Mold. 87
Recife, Braz. 48
Red Square, Moscow, Russ. 110
Restaurants, Fiji 229
Retalhuleu, Guatemala 20
Reykjavík, Ice. 67
Rhodes, Gr. 108
Rhoko Forest, Nigeria 184
Rhumel River, Constantine, Alg. 169

Riga, Latv. 77
Rila National Park, Bulg. 107
Rio de Janeiro, Braz. 48, 49
Riyadh, Saudi Arabia 127
Riyam Park, Maţraḥ, Oman 129
Robert Louis Stevenson Museum, Samoa 233
Robinson Crusoe Island, Chile 55
Rock of Cashel, Tipperary, Ire. 95
Rome, It. 103
Rosenborg Castle, Copenhagen, Den. 69
Roskilde Fjord, Roskilde, Den. 69
Ross Ice Shelf, Antarctica 237
Rotorua, N.Z. 224
Rub' Al Khali Desert 126, 128
Rubavu, Rwanda 198
Ruins at Butrint, Alban. 105
Ruwenzori Mountains, Uganda 199

S
Salar de Uyuni, Bol. 53
Salou resort, Sp. 65
Salto Grande Dam, Salto, Uru. 60
Salzburg, Aust. 81
Samariá Gorge, Crete, Gr. 109
Sāmarrā, Iraq 131
Samburu National Reserve, Kenya 195
San Antonio, Ecua. 43
San Carlos de Bariloche, Arg. 57
San José, C.R. 27
San Juan del Sur, Nicar. 25
San Miguel, El Salv. 22
San Rafael Waterfall, Ecuador Park, Ecua. 38
San Salvador, El Salv. 22
Sandy Point Town, St. Kitts & Nevis 36
Sanganeb Lighthouse, Sudan 189
Santa Catalina, Col. 43
Santa Rosa castle, La Ascunción, Venez. 45
Santiago de Compostela, Sp. 91
Santo Domingo, Dom. Rep. 32
São Paulo, Braz. 49
São Tomé, Sao Tome & Principe 203
Sarajevo, Bosn. & Herzg. 104
Savo Island, Solomon Islands 228
Savonlinna, Fin. 74
Schönbrunn Palace, Aust. 81
Sea of Galilee, Israel 125
Seal Island, Donegal Bay, Ire. 94
Seaside Open-Air Museum, Ventspils, Latv. 76
Ségou, Mali 181
Selangor, Malaysia 156
Selfoss, Ice. 66
Selimiye, Turk. 120
Selous Game Reserve, Tanzania 196
Sentinel Ranch, Zimb. 210
Sentosa, Singapore 156
Seoul, South Korea 150
Serekunda, Gambia 174
Serengeti National Park, Tanzania 197
Serpent's Mouth, Venez. 45
Sevastopol', Ukr. 87
al-Shaheed Monument, Baghdād, Iraq 131
Shahhat, Lib. 171
Shahristan, Taj. 138
Shell Beach, Guyana 47
Shinkansen train, Tokyo, Japan 147
Shipwreck Beach, Baía do Bengo, Angola 205
Shott el Jerid, Tun. 169
Shwedagon Pagoda, Yangon, Myanmar 153
Šiauliai, Lith. 76
Siberia, Russ. 117
Sidon, Leb. 122
Sighişoara, Rom. 106
Silk Road, Asia 139

Simien Mountains National Park, Eth. 190
Sinbusi Beach, Somalia 193
Singapore, Asia 156, 157
Sistine Chapel, Vatican City 103
Skagen, Den. 68
Skeleton Coast Park, Namibia 212
Skogafoss waterfall, Skogafoss, Ice. 67
Skopje, Maced. 105
Skrokkur geyser, Selfoss, Ice. 66
Sloth Sanctuary, Penshurst, C.R. 27
Slovak Karst, Slovakia 82
Słowinski Sand Dunes, Pol. 85
Småland, Sw. 73
SnowDays Festival, Banff National Park, Can. 14
Soap Museum, Sidon, Leb. 122
Sochi, Russ. 110
Socotra Islands, Yemen 128
Sofia, Bulg. 107
Songnisan National Park, South Korea 151
S.O.S. Rescate de Fauna, Uru. 60
Sossusvlei, Namibia 212
South Tarawa Lagoon, Kiribati 231
Spanish Riding School, Vienna, Aust. 81
Sphinx, Giza, Egypt 173
Spis Castle, Slovakia 83
Spišské Podhradie, Slovakia 83
Sri Siva Subramaniya Temple, Nadi, Fiji 228
St. Basil's Cathedral, Moscow, Russ. 110
St. Mary's Basilica, Kracòw, Pol. 84
St. Mary's Church, GdaÐsk, Pol. 84
St. Petersburg, Russ. 110, 111
Statue of Liberty, U.S. 16
Stingray City, Blue Lagoon Island, Bahamas 35
Stockholm Archipelago, Sw. 73
Stone Forest, Tsingy de Bemeraha National Park,
    Madagascar 216
Stone Monuments of Mu'a, Tonga 233
Stone Sculptures, Loango, Burkina Faso 178
Stone Town harbor race, Zanzibar, Tanzania 197
Stonehenge, England, U.K. 96
Strawberry Carnival, Suonenjoki, Fin. 74
Sudan National Museum, Khartoum, Sudan 189
Suez Canal, Egypt 172
Sugarloaf Mountain, Braz. 49
Sultan's Palace, Zinder, Niger 183
Sundarbans, Bangladesh 143
Suoi Tien Cultural Theme Park, Ho Chi Minh City,
    Vietnam 155
Suonenjoki, Fin. 74
Suva, Fiji 229
Suwon, South Korea 151
Svaneti, Ga. 119
Swarovski Crystal Worlds, Innsbruck, Aust. 80
Sydney Opera House, Austral. 223
Sylhet, Bangladesh 143

T

Tabacon Hot Springs, La Fortuna, C.R. 26
Tabarqa, Tun. 169
Tabrīz Historic Bazaar, Tabrīz, Iran 133
Tacuarembó, Uru. 60
Taj Mahal, Agra, India 141
Tallinn Old Town, Est. 77
Tamaki Maori Village, Rotorua, N.Z. 224
Taman Negara National Park, Malaysia 156
Tangier, Mor. 166
Tankar Lighthouse, Kokkola, Fin. 74
Taq Kisra, Madain, Iraq 130
Tarkwa Beach, Lagos, Nigeria 184
Tarutao National Marine Park, Koh Adang, Thai.
    153
Tasek Merimbun, Brunei 156
Tashigang, Bhutan 142

Tashkent, Uzb. 139
Tassili-n-Ajjer, Alg. 168
Taulud Island, Eritrea 190
Tavarua, Fiji 229
Tbilisi, Ga. 118
Tehran, Iran 132
Temple of the Sun ruins, Ingapirca, Ecua. 42
Temple of the Sun ruins, Isla del Sol, Bol. 52
Temple of Zeus, Shahhat, Lib. 171
Teotihuacan, Mex. 19
Terelj, Mongolia 148
Terra-cotta Army, Xi'an, China 144
Thar Desert, India & Pak. 141
The Hague, Neth. 99
Three Gorges Dam, China 145
Tibesti Massif, Chad 187
Tierra del Fuego, Arg. & Chile 54, 57
Tiger's Nest Monastery, Paro, Bhutan 142
Tikal National Park, Guatemala 12, 21
Timbuktu, Mali 180
Timna Park, Israel 125
Tivoli Gardens, Copenhagen, Den. 69
Tiwanacu, Bol. 52
Todra Gorge (Gorges du Todrha), Mor. 167
Tofo Beach, Mozambique 209
Tokyo, Japan 147
Tombs of the Kings, Cyprus 108
Tombs of the Nobles, Aswan, Egypt 173
Tongatapu Island, Tonga 232
Tonle Sap, Cambodia 155
Torre de Belem, Lisbon, Port. 89
Torres del Paine National Park, Andes Mountains,
    Chile 55
Tortuguero National Park, C.R. 27
Tortumo Volcano, Santa Catalina, Col. 43
Tourou, Cameroon 203
Tree of Tenere, National Museum, Niamey, Niger
    183
Trevi Fountain, Rome, It. 103
Trinidad, Parag. 59
Tripoli, Lib. 170, 171
Tromsø, Nor. 70
Tsarevets Palace complex, Veliko Tŭrnovo, Bulg.
    107
Tsingy de Bemaraha National Park, Madagascar
    216
Tsonjin Boldog, Mongolia 149
Tuli Block Farms, Botswana 212
Tuvalu, Polynesia 232
Two Moons Island, Yemen 129
Tyumen, Russ. 116

U

Ubari Sand Sea, Lib. 170
Uluru (Ayers Rock), Austral. 219, 223
Underwater World and Dolphin Lagoon, Sentosa,
    Singapore 156
Ur, Iraq 131
Ureca, Equatorial Guinea 203
Ustaoset, Nor. 71
Uyuni Salt Flat, Bol. 53

V

Vaduz Castle, Liech. 101
Valencia, Venez. 44
Valle de los Ingenios, Cuba 31
Valley of the Kings, Egypt 172
Valparaíso, Chile 55
Varirata National Park, P.N.G. 226
Vatican Palace, Vatican City 103
Veliko Tŭrnovo, Bulg. 107
Venice, It. 102
Ventspils, Latv. 76

Versailles Palace, Versailles, Fr. 92
Vianden, Lux. 99
Victoria, Seychelles 217
Victoria Falls, Zambia & Zimb. 206, 210, 211
Vienna, Aust. 80, 81
Vigan, Philippines 160
Viña del Mar, Chile 55
Vlad Dracula's home, Sighişoara, Rom. 106
Vladivostok, Russ. 117
Volcán Misti, Andes Mountains, Peru 50
Volcan Nyirogongo, Goma, Democratic Republic
    of Congo 200
Volcano Observatory, Rabaul, P.N.G. 227

W

"W" National Park, Niger 183
Wad Medani, Sudan 189
Wadi Rum, Jordan 123
Waitomo Caves, N.Z. 225
Walled City, Baku, Azerb. 119
Washington D.C., U.S. 16
Wāw-an-Nāmūs Crater, Lib. 171
The Way of St. James, Santiago de Compostela,
    Sp. 91
Waza National Park, Cameroon 202
Wechiau, Ghana 179
Wellington, N.Z. 225
Westerkerk Church, Amsterdam, Neth. 98
Wewak, P.N.G. 226
Whistler Mountain, Can. 15
White Beach, Boracay Island, Philippines 161
White Cliffs of Dover, England, U.K. 96
White House, Washington D.C., U.S. 16
Winter Palace, St. Petersburg, Russ. 111
Witchcraft Museum, Boscastle, England, U.K. 97
World Hockey Championships, Minsk, Belarus 86
World of the Ice Giants, Aust. 81
Würzburg, Ger. 79

X

Xcaret, Mex. 19
Xetulul amusement park, Retalhuleu, Guatemala
    20
Xi'an, China 144

Y

Yaama Mosque, Niger 183
Yakutia, Russ. 117
Yamoussoukro Basilica, Yamoussoukro, Côte
    d'Ivoire (Ivory Coast) 176
Yangiabad Rocks, Tashkent, Uzb. 139
Yangon, Myanmar 153
Yankari National Park, Nigeria 185
Yaoundé, Cameroon 203
Yap, F.S.M. 230
Ybycui National Park, Parag. 58
Yellowknife Dog Derby, Yellowknife, Can. 14
Yergaki National Park, Russ. 117
Yogyakarta, Indonesia 158
Yokohama, Japan 147
Yol Valley, Gobi Desert, Mongolia 148
Yusuf Karamanli house, Tripoli, Lib. 170

Z

Zaanstad, Neth. 98
Zakouma National Park, Chad 187
Zambezi River, Zambezi National Park, Zambia
    207
Zanzibar, Tanzania 197
Zinder, Niger 183
Zoological Museum, St. Petersburg, Russ. 110
Zugspitze, Ger. 79
Zytglogge zodiacal clock, Bern, Switz. 101

Published by the National Geographic Society

John M. Fahey, *Chairman of the Board and Chief Executive Officer*

Declan Moore, *Executive Vice President; President, Publishing and Travel*

Melina Gerosa Bellows, *Publisher; Chief Creative Officer, Books, Kids, and Family*

Prepared by the Book Division

Hector Sierra, *Senior Vice President and General Manager*

Nancy Laties Feresten, *Senior Vice President, Kids Publishing and Media*

Jennifer Emmett, *Vice President, Editorial Director, Kids Books*

Eva Absher-Schantz, *Design Director, Kids Publishing and Media*

Jay Sumner, *Director of Photography, Kids Publishing*

R. Gary Colbert, *Production Director*

Jennifer A. Thornton, *Director of Managing Editorial*

Staff for This Book

Priyanka Lamichhane, *Project Editor*

Kathryn Robbins, *Associate Designer*

Lori Epstein, *Senior Photo Editor*

Bender Richardson White, *Designer*

Martha Sharma, *Geography Consultant*

Ariane Szu-Tu, *Editorial Assistant*

Angela Modany, *Executive Assistant*

Paige Towler, *Editorial Intern*

Callie Broaddus, *Design Production Assistant*

Margaret Leist, *Photo Assistant*

Carl Mehler, *Director of Maps*

Sven Dolling, *Map Editor*

Michael McNey, *Map Production Manager*

Mapping Specialists, Martin S. Walz, and XNR Productions, *Map Research and Production*

Grace Hill, *Associate Managing Editor*

Joan Gossett, *Production Editor*

Lewis R. Bassford, *Production Manager*

Susan Borke, *Legal and Business Affairs*

Production Services

Phillip L. Schlosser, *Senior Vice President*

Chris Brown, *Vice President, NG Book Manufacturing*

George Bounelis, *Senior Production Manager*

Nicole Elliott, *Director of Production*

Rachel Faulise, *Manager*

Robert L. Barr, *Manager*

The National Geographic Society is one of the world's largest nonprofit scientific and educational organizations. Founded in 1888 to "increase and diffuse geographic knowledge," the Society's mission is to inspire people to care about the planet. It reaches more than 400 million people worldwide each month through its official journal, *National Geographic*, and other magazines; National Geographic Channel; television documentaries; music; radio; films; books; DVDs; maps; exhibitions; live events; school publishing programs; interactive media; and merchandise. National Geographic has funded more than 10,000 scientific research, conservation, and exploration projects and supports an education program promoting geographic literacy.

For more information, please visit nationalgeographic.com, call 1-800-NGS LINE (647-5463), or write to the following address:

National Geographic Society
1145 17th Street N.W.
Washington, D.C. 20036-4688 U.S.A.

Visit us online at nationalgeographic.com/books

For librarians and teachers: ngchildrensbooks.org

More for kids from National Geographic: kids.nationalgeographic.com

For information about special discounts for bulk purchases, please contact National Geographic Books Special Sales: ngspecsales@ngs.org

For rights or permissions inquiries, please contact National Geographic Books Subsidiary Rights: ngbookrights@ngs.org

Trade paperback ISBN: 978-1-4263-1488-9
Reinforced library edition ISBN: 978-1-4263-1489-6

Printed in the United States of America

14/CK-CML/1